Fossils and Faith

Understanding Torah and Science

Fossils and Faith

Understanding Torah and Science

Nathan Aviezer

Professor of Physics
Bar-Ilan University
Ramat-Gan, Israel

KTAV PUBLISHING HOUSE

FOSSILS AND FAITH

Understanding Torah and Science

KTAV PUBLISHING HOUSE

527 Empire Blvd

Brooklyn, NY 11225

www.ktav.com

orders@ktav.com

Ph: (718) 972-5449 / Fax: (718) 972-6307

Typeset in Arno Pro by Raphaël Freeman, Renana Typesetting

ISBN 978-0-88125-607-9

Printed and bound in the United States of America

To My Wife Dvora

Companion and Friend for Forty Years

Contents

Preface   ix
Acknowledgments   xv

FAITH

Chapter 1:   Faith and the Era of Science   3
Chapter 2:   The Age of the Universe   13
Chapter 3:   The Anthropic Principle   23
Chapter 4:   The Creation of Man   39
Chapter 5:   Proofs for the Existence of God   53
Chapter 6:   Evolution: Is There a Problem Here?   67
Chapter 7:   Free Will, God, and Science   85
Chapter 8:   Miracles: Natural and Supernatural   99
Chapter 9:   Prayer and Divine Providence   107

ON SCIENCE AND THE BIBLE

Chapter 10:   Chaos, Rain, and the Bible   119
Chapter 11:   The Extreme Longevity of the
              Early Generations in Genesis   133
Chapter 12:   May You Live to 120!   145
Chapter 13:   The Spread of Languages and the
              Tower of Babel   151

FOSSILS

Chapter 14:   Misreading the Fossils   165
Chapter 15:   The Scientific Quest for the Origins of Man   179
Chapter 16:   Darwin's Theory of Evolution   187

Chapter 17:   Non-Darwinian Theories of Evolution   199
Chapter 18:   Darwinian Fundamentalism   215
Chapter 19:   Life on Mars?   231

Biblical Commentators   237
Index of Scientists   241
Subject Index   243

Preface

Science and Religion

The subject of science and the Bible has undergone a surge of popularity in recent years. Institutions of higher education in the United States now offer over a thousand courses for credit on science and religion, whereas a student of the 1960s would have been hard put to find even one.[1] The cover of a recent issue of *Newsweek* was emblazoned with the words "Science Finds God,"[2] and other leading newsmagazines have picked up the theme. This newfound interest in science and religion is not limited to the popular press. An article entitled "Scientists and Religion in America" appeared in the September 1999 issue of the prestigious *Scientific American*. This was not the only instance of the subject of religion being reported by *Scientific American*. Just the previous year, this widely-read journal published a full-page report, entitled "Renowned Scientists Contemplate the Evidence for God," about a Science and Religion Conference held at the University of California at Berkeley, once famous as a institutional center of radical atheistic thought.[3]

What has happened? What has generated this sudden interest in the interactions between science and religion? Why are we suddenly hearing that some of the world's most respected scientists are also deeply religious people?

Perhaps the answer can be found in the fact that the latest scientific findings have revealed the universe to be a far richer and more subtle place than previously imagined. Quite naturally, the relationship between science and religion is being re-examined in the light of the new scientific findings.

Although I am a scientist by profession, a theoretical physicist who has published more than a hundred scientific articles in the standard professional journals, I have also spent much time exploring the subject of science and the Bible, and have written a book on this topic, *In the Beginning: Biblical Creation and Science*. My book has been well received, having been translated into nine languages and reprinted dozens of times.

In addition, I have often lectured on science and the Bible to audiences comprising a remarkably wide range of diverse groups, both religious and secular. In the course of these lectures, I have met many thoughtful and intelligent people, from all walks of life and with every point of view, who are deeply interested in the topic of science and religion, and are thirsty for additional knowledge. This is what motivated me to write *In the Beginning*. However, the subject is so vast and so important that I have come to realize that there is need for another book

There is, of course, no lack of books nowadays on the subject of science and religion. The names Ian Barbour, Arthur Peacocke, and John Polkinghorne immediately come to mind. But these important books were all written in the Christian tradition, as is natural given their authors. However, the traditional Jew seeks a book on science and religion in the spirit of traditional Judaism, written by an author who is a committed practicing Jew. Another important point is that an active research scientist is best able to write about science with authority, accuracy and clarity. Such qualities are often lacking in the books on science and religion by non-scientists – rabbis, journalists, lawyers.

A comment should be made about the few books that are available on science and religion in the Jewish tradition. They are quite fundamentalist, almost creationist, both in tone and in content. The result is generally bad science, as well as bad theology.

A creationist approach is not the Jewish point of view to understanding Genesis, as was firmly established by Maimonides back in the twelfth century.[4] The writings of Maimonides have served as a beacon for me and are often quoted in this book.

There is an additional pressing reason for a book on science and religion addressed to a popular audience. The non-fiction best-seller lists include books by militant atheists, three of whom have made the following statements: (1) "The kindly God who loves us, is, like Santa Claus, a myth of childhood, that no sane undeluded adult could believe in." (2) "Religion is a dreadful disease of society and I think that science liberates people from the world's religions." (3) "Human vanity cherishes the absurd notion that our species is special." Such pronouncements, made in the name of science, must not go unchallenged.

SCIENTIFIC KNOWLEDGE AND RELIGIOUS BELIEF

The proliferation of knowledge in the last few decades has revolution-ized many branches of science. Completely new disciplines that did not even exist half a century ago now occupy a central place in the modern scientific enterprise. These new or revolutionized disciplines include big bang cosmology, evolutionary biology (punctuated equi-librium, impact theory), quantum theory (nature of physical reality), molecular biology, chaos, nanotechnology, space exploration, com-plexity theory, fractals, artificial intelligence, cloning, human genome, mass extinctions, stem cells, black holes, extra-solar planets, neural networks, genetic engineering, compacted dimensions. The list goes on and on. The simple clockwork universe of Newton, Galileo, and Laplace has been replaced by a universe so complex and so wonderful that it almost defies comprehension.

It is time to ask whether this scientific knowledge has any impli-cations for a person who believes in God. The goal of this book is to demonstrate the implications are profound. We will see that maintaining one's belief in God and accepting the truth of the Bible do not require one to abandon rational thinking. Quite the contrary. Modern science has become an important tool for understanding many biblical passages as well as for deepening and strengthening one's faith in God.

We shall deal with the very essence of religion – faith, prayer, belief, miracles, free will, life on other planets, the interaction between God and the world – showing how recent advances in science touch on each of these subjects in important ways.

THE PHYSICAL UNIVERSE AND THE ALMIGHTY

Throughout the generations, people have wondered about the relationship between the physical universe and the Almighty. What can one learn about God by observing His world? To scientists of earlier centuries, the physical world seemed self-contained. They tried to explain all physical phenomena without the need for a deity, comparing the world to a clock whose springs, gears, and cogs work in perfect harmony. Although exponents of this view sometimes spoke of the Divine Watchmaker who had created the universe, God seemed to have retired from the scene once His task of creation was completed, letting the laws of nature carry on. Human beings were described as simply aggregations of atoms, subject to the same laws of nature as stones and planets. It is not surprising that Laplace had cynically questioned the need for the hypothesis of God.

The problem became even more acute in 1859, when Charles Darwin proposed that the vast panorama of animals and plants that we observe today had developed inevitably from the simplest bacteria according to the principles of evolution. This seemed to imply that human beings not only shared similar origins with the crocodile and the cockroach, but that we were equally devoid of any spirituality. In short, religion was on the defensive.

All of this changed beyond recognition during the twentieth century. Today, cosmologists regularly use the word "creation" to describe the origin of the universe.[5] Secular scientists in all fields point to numerous examples of apparent design in the laws of nature, design with human beings in mind.[6] Quantum theory and chaos theory have established the impossibility of predicting the future. Archaeologists write of the abrupt appearance of civilization, "with no premonitory signs,"[7] and speak of a sudden "revolution" in human cultural behavior.[8]

The far-reaching theological implications of these scientific findings can hardly be overemphasized. Many seemingly intractable
theological dilemmas of previous generations have melted away with
our increasing awareness of the laws that govern the physical universe.
Its complexity and subtlety, as revealed within the last few decades,
provides the framework for understanding the modes of interaction
between God and His world.

NOTES

1. E.J. Larson and L. Witham, September 1999, *Scientific American*, p. 79.

2. Cover story, 20 July 1998, *Newsweek Magazine*.

3. "Science and Religion", August 1998, *Scientific American*, pp. 10–11.

4. Maimonides, *Guide for the Perplexed*, Part II, Chap. 25.

5. See, for example, J. Silk, 1989, *The Big Bang* (Freeman: New York), p. 113.

6. G. Gale, December 1981, *Scientific American*, pp. 114–122.

7. N. Eldredge, 1986, *Time Frames* (Simon and Schuster: New York), p. 87.

8. G.H. Pelto and P.J. Pelto, 1979, *The Cultural Dimensions of the Human Adventure* (Macmillian: New York), p. 93.

Acknowledgments

I now come to the pleasant obligation of thanking those who have helped me in writing this book. Appreciation goes to my son Hillel and to my long-time friend and scientific colleague, Professor Avraham Greenfield. I am grateful to them both for their many perceptive comments and insightful criticisms, which have greatly improved the final version. Rabbi Moshe Litoff was also kind enough to comment on a number of points.

The title of this book is that of a seminar on Torah and Science, held in 1997 in the Westwood Jewish Community of Los Angeles. The organizers of that seminar, Greg and Andy Smith, graciously permitted me the use of their felicitous title.

My wife, Dvora, read and re-read every page of the manuscript. Her myriad suggestions helped guide the text through constantly improved drafts and produced a vastly enriched book.

Finally, I would like to thank my publisher, Bernard Scharfstein of Ktav Publishing House, who has been a constant source of encouragement to me in all my writings.

Faith

1

Faith and the Era of Science

Plausibility Arguments

The word "faith" is defined as "belief in religious doctrines for which there is no proof." Although religious belief is based on *faith*, rather than on *proof*, our faith has recently been buttressed by important plausibility arguments. Today, there is widespread harmony between the Genesis account of creation and the findings of science. That is, one finds *consistency* between recent scientific discoveries and the worldview of a person of faith. This is what is meant by plausibility arguments for religious belief and faith.

Before describing some of these plausibility arguments for faith, it should be emphasized that not only religion, but also science, relies heavily on plausibility arguments. The naive picture of the white-coated scientist in his laboratory watching the pointer move across a scale to the predicted reading and thereby establishing a scientific theory beyond doubt, bears little relation to reality. Indeed, the empirical nature of science precludes the absolute proof of any theory. Science advances by postulating concepts and making assumptions, and then investigating to see whether these assumptions and concepts are successful in explaining phenomena observed in nature or in the laboratory. As successful explanations multiply, it becomes more and more plausible that the assumed concepts and ideas are basically correct, although experience has shown that some alterations and adjustments in the original concepts will be almost inevitable.

An instructive example is the quarks, the tiny particles that constitute the basic building blocks of the universe. The quark is *not* an exotic particle, unrelated to the everyday world. Quite the contrary. Quarks form 99.9% of all the materials with which we are familiar, including stars, planets, rocks, water, air, the book you are reading, and the tissues of your body. (The remaining 0.1% are the electrons.)

Despite the fact that quarks have never been seen, scientists are convinced of their existence. Professor David Bailin of the University of Sussex explains: "Even though no particle detector has ever "seen" a quark, everyone agrees that they actually *do* exist."[1] Moreover, quarks will *never* be seen, because according to the standard theory of elementary particles, they are forever "locked up" in the protons and neutrons (each of which consists of a triplet of quarks). Professor David Callaway of CERN (European Research Center for Nuclear Physics) explains, "The fundamental particles of matter – the quarks – are permanently confined inside protons and neutrons."[2]

If no one has ever seen a quark, why are scientists absolutely convinced not only that quarks exist, but that they rank among the most important building blocks of the entire universe? The answer is that if one assumes that quarks exist, then a great many observed features of the universe can be explained. "Theorists developed the quark model as a neat, compact description of the myriad of new particles detected in the 1950s and 1960s, as well as the familiar proton and neutron. The properties and interactions of all these particles fell into patterns that could be completely explained if all these particles are made up of three species of quarks."[3]

The findings described above, as well as many others discovered subsequently, have led scientists to believe in the existence of quarks, even though they have never been detected. This is an example of a plausibility argument in science.

One should be aware that the use of plausibility arguments constitutes an important similarity between the methods of science and those of religion,[4] and both disciplines rely on them. In both religion and science, as plausibility arguments accumulate, faith in fundamental tenets becomes increasingly reasonable. Let us examine some of the important plausibility arguments for religious belief.

Creation and Science

Where did the universe come from? A person of faith would probably answer that the universe was created out of nothing, as stated in the first verse of Genesis. Such an answer was long considered a scientific impossibility, because it contradicted the law of the conservation of matter and energy. According to this law of science, which was established in the middle of the 19th century, matter and energy can be changed from one form to another, but something cannot come out of nothing. Therefore, scientists viewed the universe as eternal, thus neatly avoiding questions regarding its origin. The Genesis assertion that the universe was created, presumably from nothing, became an area of conflict between science and the Bible. That is how matters stood for many years.

But this situation has now changed. The twentieth century witnessed an unprecedented explosion of scientific knowledge, which is nowhere more dramatic than in cosmology, the discipline that deals with the origin and development of the universe. Astronomers had been studying the heavenly bodies for thousands of years, but their studies dealt almost exclusively with charting the paths of the stars, planets, and comets, and determining their composition, spectrum, and other properties. The *origin* of the heavenly bodies remained a complete mystery. As one Nobel laureate wrote, "in the 1950s, the study of the early universe was widely regarded as a subject to which a respectable scientist would not devote his time . . . there simply did not exist an adequate observational and theoretical foundation on which to build a history of the universe."[5]

Important advances in cosmology during the past few decades have, for the first time, permitted scientists to construct a coherent history of the origin of the universe.[6] Today, an overwhelming body of scientific evidence supports the "big bang" theory of cosmology.[7]

There are four major pieces of evidence: (1) the discovery in 1965 of the remnant of the initial ball of light, (2) the hydrogen-to-helium ratio in the universe, (3) the Hubble expansion of the galaxies, and (4) the perfect black-body spectrum of the microwave background radiation measured by the COBE space satellite in 1990. Only the big bang theory can account for all these observations, and therefore, this theory is now accepted by all mainstream cosmologists.

The most surprising assertion of the big bang theory is that *the universe was literally created from nothing*. It is instructive to quote leading authorities.

Professor Paul Dirac, Nobel laureate from the University of Cambridge, writes:

> *"It seems certain that there was a definite time of creation."*[8]

Professor Alan Guth, of the Massachusetts Institute of Technology, writes:

> *"The instant of creation remains unexplained."*[9]

Professor Stephen Hawking, of the University of Cambridge, writes:

> *"The creation lies outside the scope of the known laws of physics."*[10]

Professor Joseph Silk, of the University of California, begins his book on modern cosmology with the words:

> *"The big bang is the modern version of creation."*[11]

Today, it is hardly possible to carry on a meaningful discussion of cosmology without the creation of the universe assuming a central role. Professor Brian Greene, theoretical physicist at Columbia University, wrote: "The modern theory of cosmic origins [asserts] that the universe erupted from an enormously energetic event, which spewed forth all space and all matter... The currently accepted scientific theory of creation is often referred to as the *standard model of cosmology*."[12]

When cosmologists use the term "creation," to what are they

referring? Precisely what object was created? Scientists have discovered that the universe began with the sudden appearance from nothing of an enormous *ball of light*, commonly called the "primeval light-ball." This "explosion of light" was dubbed the "big bang" by the British astrophysicist Professor Fred Hoyle. The remnant of the initial ball of light was detected in 1965 by two American physicists, Arno Penzias and Robert Wilson, who were awarded the Nobel Prize for their important discovery.

People sometimes ask what existed before the big bang, the event that marked the creation of the universe. Professor John Wheeler of Princeton University explains that the very concept of time did not exist before the creation. "There was no 'before' prior to the Big Bang. The laws of nature came into existence together with the Big Bang, as surely as did space and time."[13] Wheeler emphasizes that scientists view space and time as the "stage" upon which the events of the physical world take place. If there is no physical world – if the universe does not exist – then neither time nor space can exist. "Time" and "space" are not independent entities; these concepts have meaning only *after* the creation of the physical universe.

This property of time and space can be illustrated by analogy to the concept of color. "Red" or "black" are not free-standing characteristics, independent of any physical object. Only if macroscopic objects exist, such as grass, rocks or houses, can one speak of these objects as being red or black. If nothing but atoms and molecules existed, then there would be no meaning to "red" or "black," or to the entire concept of color. There is no such thing as a red molecule. In the same way, there were no such concepts as time and space before the universe came into being.

Creation and Genesis

In addition to confirming the creation of the universe, the discovery of the initial primeval light by Penzias and Wilson also answers another long-standing puzzle regarding the Genesis account of creation. On the First Day of Creation, Genesis explicitly asserts: *And there was light*

(1:3). But at that time, there existed neither stars, nor sun, nor moon, nor people, nor any other known source of light. Therefore, how can one understand the "light" mentioned in Genesis?

Scientists have now discovered that *there was light at the very beginning of time*: the primeval light-ball whose appearance heralded the origin of the universe. The creation of light did not occur *within* the existing universe. Rather, the creation of light *was* the creation of the universe. Thus, Genesis does not record *two* separate creations on the first day – the creation of the universe *and* the creation of the light – but *only one*.

We now turn to the question of the time scale. How much time was required for the cosmological events that took place at the creation of the universe? How many millions of years had to elapse before the universe was complete and assumed its present form? The remarkable answer is that all the cosmological events involved in the creation of the universe occurred within *a very few minutes*. This fact was emphasized by the dramatic title that Nobel laureate Steven Weinberg chose for his famous book on modern cosmology: *The First Three Minutes*.

Nowadays, cosmological events – events that alter the structure of the universe – require many millions of years to occur. How could such events have taken place within just a few moments? The answer is that during the period of creation, the temperature of the universe was extremely high. Just as food cooks much more rapidly in a pressure cooker than over a low flame, in the same way, events occurred with amazing rapidity in the blazing universe at the origins of time. Professor Greene explains: "The newborn universe evolved with phenomenal haste. Tiny fractions of a second formed cosmic epochs during which long-lasting features of the universe were first imprinted … During the first three minutes after the big bang, as the simmering universe cooled, the predominant nuclei emerged."[14]

Thus, the formation of the first atomic nuclei – the basic building blocks of every material – was completed within three minutes after the instant of creation.

Faith

It should be emphasized that the comprehensive agreement between science and Genesis described above *does not prove* that the Book of Genesis is of divine origin, and it certainly *does not prove* that God exists. These matters remain articles of *faith*. However, as we enter the twenty-first century, the person of faith is not forced to *choose* between accepting the latest scientific discoveries *or* accepting the Genesis account of creation. All leading cosmologists now discuss the creation of the universe, while the text of Genesis discusses the Creator of the universe. It is, therefore, not unreasonable to assume that science and the Bible are both referring to one and the same subject. It is a pleasure for a person of faith to be living in this day and age!

It is important to realize that the current confluence between science and faith was not always the case. Only a few decades ago, the outstanding Torah scholar Rabbi Joseph B. Soloveitchik expressed the then-existing dichotomy between science and faith in a classic essay entitled "The Lonely Man of Faith."[15] Using the word "lonely" to describe the feelings of the man of faith who lives in a scientific world, Rabbi Soloveitchik wrote: "Being people of faith in our contemporary world is a lonely experience. We are loyal to visionary expectations which find little support in present-day reality ... Religious faith is condescendingly regarded as a subjective palliative, but is given little credence as a repository of truth."[16]

Now, half a century later, in one scientific discipline after another, the words of the scientist can hardly be distinguished from the words of "the man of faith." Professor Stephen Jay Gould of Harvard University writes: "human intelligence is the result of a staggeringly improbable series of events, utterly unpredictable and quite unrepeatable."[17] The term "luck" is now commonly used by evolutionary biologists like Professor David Raup, past president of the American Paleontological Union, to "explain" the existence of human beings.[18] Archaeologists express their amazement at the "radical and sudden changes ... with no premonitory signs"[19] that mark the appearance of civilization, and they speak of a sudden "quantum leap in mental abilities"[20] that appears in the archaeological record of human cultural behavior. Scientists in a wide variety of disciplines discuss the "anthropic principle," which states that the universe looks as if it were specifically designed to permit the existence and promote the welfare of human beings.[21] Finally, *The Cambridge Encyclopedia of Astronomy* expresses this idea in the following poetic words: "In truth, we are the children of the Universe."[22]

The scientific discoveries and statements listed above – and many more – are exactly what one would expect if the Genesis account of the origin and development of the universe were, in fact, correct. Therefore, the existence of such harmony between science and Genesis constitutes an important plausibility argument for our religious belief. Science is no longer the antagonist of the believing person. Indeed, modern science has become a significant element in the strengthening of ancient faith.

NOTES

1. D. Bailin, 1987, *Contemporary Physics*, vol. 28, p. 179.
2. D.J.E. Callaway, 1985, *Contemporary Physics*, vol. 26, p. 95.
3. K. Rith and A. Schafer, July 1999, *Scientific American*, p. 42.
4. Of course, there are also important differences between scientific claims and those of religion. For example, a characteristic feature of a scientific theory is that it is subject to disproof (what Karl Popper calls "falsification"). By contrast, statements about religion are usually not subject to disproof.
5. S. Weinberg, 1977, *The First Three Minutes* (Andre Deutsch: London), pp. 13–14.
6. The important discoveries, instrumentation, and techniques in modern cosmology include X-ray astronomy, the Hubble space telescope, radio galaxies and radio emissions, pulsars and quasars, the COBE satellite, and gravitational lensing.
7. For a layman's account of the big bang theory, see N. Aviezer, 1990, *In the Beginning* (Ktav Publishing House: New York), Chapter I.
8. P.A.M. Dirac, 1972, *Commentarii*, vol. 2, no. 11, p. 15.
9. A.H. Guth, May 1984, *Scientific American*, p. 102.
10. S.W. Hawking, 1973, *The Large Scale Structure of Space-Time* (Cambridge University Press), p. 364
11. J. Silk, 1989, *The Big Bang* (W.H. Freeman: New York), p. xi.
12. B. Greene, 1999, *The Elegant Universe* (Jonathan Cape: London), pp. 345–346.
13. J.A. Wheeler, 1998, *Geons, Black Holes, and Quantum Foam* (W.W. Norton: New York), p. 350.
14. Greene, pp. 347, 350.
15. J.B. Soloveitchik, Spring 1965, *Tradition*, pp. 5–67.
16. See the adaptation of the 1965 Soloveitchik essay (especially p. 8) by A.R. Besdin, 1989, *Man of Faith in the Modern World* (Ktav: New York), pp. 36–37.
17. S.J. Gould, 1989, *Wonderful Life* (W.W. Norton: New York), p. 14.
18. D.M. Raup, 1991, *Extinctions: Bad Genes or Bad Luck?* (Oxford University Press).
19. N. Eldredge, 1985, *Time Frames* (Simon and Schuster: New York), p. 87.
20. N. Eldredge and I. Tattersall, 1982, *The Myths of Human Evolution* (Columbia University Press: New York), p. 154.
21. J.D. Barrow and F.J. Tipler, *The Cosmological Anthropic Principle*, 1986 (Oxford University Press); G. Gale, December 1981, "The Anthropic Principle", in *Scientific American*, pp. 114–122.
22. S. Mitton, editor-in-chief, 1987, *The Cambridge Encyclopedia of Astronomy* (Jonathan Cape: London), p. 125.

2

The Age of the Universe

Questions

How old is the universe? This question immediately confronts anyone who studies fossils, those remnants of an ancient animal kingdom – relics of a by-gone era.

Fossils of prehistoric animals and plants are generally found embedded in rocks containing radioactive particles whose age of formation can be determined by means of radioactive dating. If, for example, radioactive dating shows that a fossil-bearing rock was formed 280 million years ago, then it is reasonable to assume that the prehistoric animal whose bones are embedded in that rock also lived about 280 million years ago.

Such vast geologic time scales seem to present a serious problem to the believer in the Bible, because the Book of Genesis speaks of Six Days of Creation followed by about six thousand years of human history until the present day. How can hundreds of millions of years of fossil history be crammed into the biblical time scale of only a few thousand years from the Creation until today? Moreover, nothing is gained by trying to find fault with the scientific technique used for dating fossils, because hundred-million-year time scales are not restricted to fossils. Geologists have discovered that the present-day continents and oceans were also formed hundreds of millions of years ago; astronomers have demonstrated that the constituents of the solar system (including the earth and the sun) were formed about five

13

billion years ago; and according to the big bang theory of cosmology,[1] the universe suddenly began more than 10 billion years ago.

It is important to realize that each of these scientific disciplines uses a *different method* for arriving at its time-scale. Therefore, attempting to maintain the biblical tradition of a 6000-year-old universe by denying these diverse scientific results, claiming that *each* of them may be in error by a factor of a million, is tantamount to denying almost the entire enterprise of modern science.

Recently, there has been an attempt to reconcile the biblical time-scale with modern science by invoking Einstein's theory of relativity.[2] According to relativity theory, time is not absolute (as Isaac Newton had assumed some three centuries ago). Rather, the rate at which time passes varies from place to place in the universe according to the local strength of the force of gravity – an effect called "time dilation." For example, the gravitational force on the sun is much stronger than on the earth because the sun is so massive. Therefore, time passes more slowly on the sun than on the earth.

In this way, one can perhaps reconcile the biblical Six Days of Creation with the scientific assertion that more than 10 billion years have passed since the universe began. One need only assume that the biblical "clock" was measuring time at a place in the universe where large gravitational forces are present, and thus, biblical time passed much more slowly.

This explanation fails because relativistic time dilation is an extremely small effect. For example, a year measured on the sun is only *one minute* shorter than a year measured on earth, a change of two parts per million. Such a small effect cannot possibly compress 10 billion years into a mere six days. Indeed, this proposal was characterized by Professor Barry Simon, a distinguished physicist at the California Institute of Technology, as "a fundamental misunderstanding of basic physics ... immediately recognized as fallacious by professional physicists."[3] Recently, an attempt was made to reconcile the biblical and the scientific time scales by invoking the expansion of the universe (the red-shift of the spectral lines of distant galaxies).[4] Professor Simon's words apply equally well to this latter attempt.

Another approach to reconciling the biblical and the scientific time scales is quite popular in certain circles. This view asserts that the universe is in fact very young, but *appears old* to the scientists because God created it to appear old. For example, if Adam were created as a 30-year-old man, then the day after his creation, a scientist who examined him would declare that Adam had already lived for thirty years. This approach, while unassailable from the standpoint of abstract logic – for who can prove the contrary? – *does not* constitute a reconciliation between the biblical and the scientific time scales. Correlating science with Genesis implies resolving apparent contradictions *without* invoking miracles.

It is important to recognize that if one understands the Genesis creation *"day"* to mean 24 hours, then there is *no way* to reconcile Genesis with science. However, if one interprets the creation "days" metaphorically, then *all the events* recorded in the first chapter of Genesis are in remarkable agreement with recent discoveries in cosmology, astronomy, geology, climatology, biology, and archaeology. In fact, a detailed analysis[5] of the *events* associated with each of the "Days of Creation" yields complete harmony between modern science and the literal text of Genesis.

Maimonides' Approach

In his major work on Torah thought, the great medieval philosopher Moses Maimonides discusses how to interpret the words in the narrative portions of the Bible.[6] (Interpreting the words in the *legal* portions of the Bible is a different issue that does not concern us here.) Maimonides states that one should first attempt to interpret the biblical text literally. However, if the literal meaning contradicts logic or well-established facts, then one should interpret the biblical words *metaphorically*.

We may apply this Maimonidean principle to the present case. If one interprets the Six Days of Creation as six 24-hour periods of time, then a wealth of well-established scientific knowledge is completely contradicted. Therefore, one must understand the creation "days" metaphorically, as referring to phases in the development of the universe, without any indication of how long each phase lasted. Once one adopts this approach for the time scale, then the *events* recorded in the Genesis account of creation, *every phrase and every word*, are in complete agreement with modern science.[7]

What is particularly relevant to our discussion is the fact that Maimonides used precisely the creation story of Genesis as his example to illustrate how to interpret the words of the Bible. In his time, the twelfth century, the accepted view of cosmology was that of the Greek philosophers who believed that the universe was eternal and that no act of creation had ever occurred – which is, of course, in complete contradiction to the entire first chapter of Genesis. Maimonides writes that he rejects the Greek view, *not* because it disagrees with Genesis, but because it was not convincingly proven. However, Maimonides emphasizes, if the Greek position could be proven, then from the Torah point of view, there would be *no problem* in accepting the idea of an eternal universe, *in spite of the fact* that a denial of creation flatly contradicts the text of Genesis. One would simply interpret the entire first chapter of Genesis as an allegory. (For the reader who recoils at even the *possibility* that the entire first chapter of Genesis might never have happened, we point out that one of the Sages of the Talmud interpreted *the entire book of Job* as an allegory that never happened.[8])

In his discussion, Maimonides gives an extremely interesting example to show why a non-literal interpretation of the biblical text is sometimes *mandatory*.[9] Throughout the Bible, God is described in anthropomorphic terms, as if He had a human body. God is said to have taken the Children of Israel out of Egypt *"with a mighty hand and an outstretched arm"* (Deuteronomy 26:8); He tells Moses, *"I will remove My hand and you will see My back, but My face may not be seen"* (Exodus 33:23); He punishes the sinner, *"I will set My face against that man"* (Leviticus 20:3); Israel sees God's *"mighty hand"* (Exodus 14:30); the Ten Commandments *"were written by the finger of God"* (Deuteronomy 9:10), and so on. Moreover, God is often described as speaking, hearing, seeing, or walking. Maimonides stresses that anyone who interprets these biblical words literally is a heretic, because it is a central pillar of Jewish belief that God has no physical manifestation. And if the Bible seems to say otherwise, then these biblical words *must be interpreted metaphorically.*

Maimonides goes on to say that in the same way, *any* biblical word, phrase, or verse that contradicts well-established knowledge or common sense is also to be understood *metaphorically*, and not literally.

This idea was not new with Maimonides. The Sages of the Talmud had previously commented that at least for the first three days of creation, when the sun was not yet in the sky, one cannot speak of a "day" or of "evening and morning" in the usual sense, because these are astronomical events associated with the sun.[10,11] If the sun does not exist, then there cannot be an evening, a morning, or a day.

What is the implication of this? The implication is that the biblical calendar starts from the *end* of the Six Days of Creation, and does *not* include the six phases of creation. The usual meaning of days and years in the Bible applies only *after* the creation of man on the Sixth Day. We defer (until Chapter 4) a discussion of the biblical approach to prehistoric man and the remarkable events that occurred about six thousand years ago that explain the biblical verse, *"God created Man in His image ... male and female He created them"* (Genesis 1:27).

Starting the calendar after the appearance of Adam and Eve is also consistent with the only talmudic source that deals with the Jewish calendar year, Sanhedrin 97a. This talmudic passage gives the age of the universe until the teaching of the Torah and until the coming of the Messiah. The concepts of Torah and Messiah are meaningful only *after* human beings exist. These concepts have no relevance in earlier times, when only stars, planets, rocks, plants, and cattle existed. Therefore, this talmudic statement refers to *human history* – the number of years that have elapsed *after* the creation of Man.

Biblical Chronology

The chronology of the Genesis creation story has generated an extensive literature by traditional Jewish commentators. A selection of commentaries regarding biblical chronology can be found in the important books, *Challenge*[10] and *The Seven Days of the Beginning*.[11] In the latter book, Rabbi Eli Munk presents a comprehensive etymological study of the first chapter of Genesis. Rabbi Munk italicizes the Genesis word *day* throughout his book to prevent its being *misunderstood* as a time interval of 24 hours.

The question still remains: Why is the term "day" (*yom*) used in the Genesis creation narrative if a 24-hour period of time is not intended? The answer is given in Genesis 2:1–3, which discusses the seventh day – the Sabbath:[12]

> *"The Heaven and the Earth were completed with all their hosts. By the seventh day, God had completed His work, and He ceased on the seventh day from all His work. God blessed the seventh day and sanctified it, because on that day He ceased from all His creative work"*

God designated the seventh day as holy because it marked the completion of the creation of the universe. This connection between the Sabbath and the creation is reinforced in the Ten Commandments (Exodus 20:8–11), where it states that the Sabbath serves as a weekly reminder that God created the universe. Since the Sabbath *is* an actual 24-hour day, the six phases of creation are *also* referred to as days to strengthen the connection between the Sabbath and the creation of the universe.

The "Six Days"

The six phases of the development of the universe, the "Six Days," are divided into two cycles. The first cycle of creation, comprising four phases, deals with the formation of the infrastructure of the universe that is necessary for the existence and welfare of humankind. The second cycle of creation, comprising two phases, deals with the animal kingdom and culminates with the appearance of human beings.

FIRST CYCLE OF CREATION

The building of the infrastructure of the universe, the first cycle, is divided into the following four phases:[13]

First Day/Phase:	Creation of the universe
Second Day/Phase:	Formation of the solar system
Third Day/Phase:	Formation of the continents and oceans; appearance of seed-bearing plants
Fourth Day/Phase:	Fixing the present-day seasons

SECOND CYCLE OF CREATION

The formation of the animal kingdom, the second cycle, is divided into the following two phases:

Fifth Day/Phase:	Marine and winged animals
Sixth Day/Phase:	Mammals and other large terrestrial animals; human beings

The order recorded in Genesis for the four phases of the first cycle corresponds to the actual sequence in which these events occurred. In particular, the two events associated with the Third Day/Phase, the formation of the continents and the appearance of seed-bearing plants, occurred *simultaneously*, during the geological period known as the Permian Period.

These two cycles of creation ran *concurrently*. That is, the second cycle did *not* follow the first cycle, but the two ran in parallel. This idea of two independent cycles of creation is consistent with the Genesis text. The verb "create" occurs at the beginning of the First Day/Phase (Genesis 1:1, beginning of first cycle) and then again on the Fifth Day/Phase (Genesis 1:21, beginning of second cycle), but does *not* appear in any verse in-between.

Interestingly, Genesis places the formation of plants on a totally different footing from the formation of animals. From the biological point of view, there is no essential difference between plants and animals. However, Genesis is not a biology text. The Bible views plants as objects whose purpose is to serve human beings by providing food, clothing (linen, cotton), shelter (wood), medicines, rope, and so forth. Therefore, the plants appear in the *first cycle* of creation, which deals with the infrastructure of the universe. By contrast, the Bible views the animals as sharing with human beings the characteristic features of living creatures. Therefore, the animals appear in the *second cycle* of creation dealing with human beings.

There is also another reason why plants appear in the first cycle of creation. Plants played a key role in the development of our planet. The oxygen gas in the atmosphere, vital for respiration, was generated by the primitive plants via the process of photosynthesis. In this process, green plants produce food from water and carbon dioxide, using the energy of sunlight. A by-product of photosynthesis is oxygen. Scientists now recognize that the green plants were the source of *all* the oxygen that exists in the atmosphere today. As noted by Professor Claude Allegre of the University of Paris: "It is now agreed that the present-day 20% oxygen content of the atmosphere was the result of photosynthetic activity."[14] Oxygen gas plays yet another vital role. "It filters the deadly ultraviolet radiation impinging from the sun ... It was not until oxygen was abundant in the atmosphere that life had a chance to survive on land."[15]

Summary

The Six Days of Creation were not six 24-hour periods of time, but six phases in the development of the universe: from the initial creation of the physical universe to the appearance of human beings. This approach is consistent with the writings of many biblical commentators, ranging from the Sages of the Talmud down to the present time.

NOTES

1. For a non-technical account of the big bang theory of cosmology, see N. Aviezer, 1990, *In the Beginning* (Ktav Publishing: New York), Chapter 1.
2. C. Friedland and M. Greenblatt, editors, 1996, *Jewish Action Reader* (Menorah Publications: New York), pp. 298–301.
3. B. Simon, Spring 1992, *Jewish Action*, p. 10.
4. *Your Jerusalem*, January 1998, p. 9; *ibid.*, February 1998, p. 9; 1997, *The Science of God* (Free Press: New York), pp. 57–59.
5. N. Aviezer, 1990, *In the Beginning* (Ktav Publishing: New York).
6. Maimonides, *Guide for the Perplexed*, Part II, Chapter 25.
7. Aviezer.
8. Talmud, Bava Bathra 15a.
9. Maimonides.
10. A. Carmell and C. Domb, 1978, *Challenge* (Feldheim: Jerusalem), pp. 124–140.
11. E. Munk, 1974, *The Seven Days of the Beginning* (Feldheim: Jerusalem).
12. One may wonder why the three verses dealing with the seventh day, the Sabbath, were placed in the second chapter of Genesis. Since the Sabbath marks the completion of the biblical account of creation, one would expect these verses to be placed as the finale to the creation story, at the end of the first chapter of Genesis. The interesting explanation is that these verses *were* placed at the end of the first chapter, exactly where they belong, in the Jewish division of Genesis into chapters (see, for example, the *Koren* edition of the Torah). However, the Catholic Vulgate shifted these verses to the second chapter of Genesis, separating them from the creation story, because in the Catholic view, the significance of the Sabbath is not related to the creation of the universe. For historical reasons, most Hebrew Bibles use the Vulgate division into chapters.
13. For a description of the events that occurred during each of the six phases of creation, see N. Aviezer, 1990, *In the Beginning* (Ktav Publishing: New York).
14. C.J. Allegre, October 1994, *Scientific American*, p. 49.
15. Allegre, pp. 49–50.

3

The Anthropic Principle

Introduction

In recent years, it has become clear to many scientists that the universe seems to have been specifically designed for the existence and well-being of Man. This phenomenon, which has attracted considerable scientific attention, has become known as the anthropic principle,[1,2] from the Greek word *anthropos*, meaning "man." The anthropic principle expresses itself in two ways: (1) very slight changes in the laws of nature would have made it impossible for life to exist, and (2) human life would not have been possible if not for the occurrence in the past of a large number of highly improbable events. Whereas the secular scientist sees these occurrences as mere lucky accidents, the believing person sees in them the guiding hand of the Creator.

Our subject consists of two parts: an explanation of exactly what is meant by the anthropic principle, and a discussion of its importance for the believing person. The first topic is purely scientific, whereas the second topic deals with religion. This distinction must be kept clear because the words commonly used by secular scientists in discussing the anthropic principle often sound remarkably similar to those used by rabbis!

The thesis to be developed here is that the anthropic principle – the idea that the universe seems to have been designed for the existence and well-being of man – may be taken as evidence that the universe *really was* so designed by the Almighty. This statement requires a detailed explanation and justification, because secular scientists view the anthropic principle as merely a curious property of nature, having no significance whatsoever. Therefore, it is important to understand why the believing person is justified in seeing in the anthropic principle a confirmation of his belief in the Almighty.

The Laws of Nature and the Existence of Life

The anthropic principle refers to the discovery of a remarkable connection between the laws of nature and the existence of life. A relationship between the principles of biology and the existence of life is not surprising, but one would not expect to find such a relationship when it comes to the physical sciences. However, new discoveries have shown that the existence of living creatures is intimately dependent on the details of the laws of physics, astronomy and cosmology.

SOLAR ENERGY

It is not necessary to elaborate on the fact that life on earth is crucially dependent on the sun, whose heat and light are the primary source of all terrestrial energy (aside from radioactivity, which is not relevant to our discussion). Without solar energy, our planet would be incapable of supporting life. Therefore, we begin our discussion of the anthropic principle by examining the mechanism that produces the sun's energy.

The sun contains only two kinds of atoms: hydrogen and helium. Helium is inert, unconnected with solar energy, and therefore need not concern us further. Our discussion centers on hydrogen, the simplest atom, whose nucleus consists of only one proton. Thus, the sun is basically a vast assemblage of protons. How protons produce solar energy was first explained in the late 1930s by Professor Hans Bethe, who was awarded the Nobel Prize for his discovery. Bethe was a German Jew, and like all other Jews, he was dismissed from his university post by the Nazis in 1933. He settled in the United States and joined the physics faculty of Cornell University, where he made his Nobel Prize-winning discovery.

Because of the extreme conditions present in the interior of the sun, a proton may occasionally transform spontaneously into a neutron, another fundamental particle of nature. The resulting neutron can combine with another proton to form a composite particle known as a deuteron. Deuterons "burn" via a thermonuclear reaction, and this reaction provides the intense heat and brilliant light of the sun. Thus, deuterons are the solar fuel that generates the energy of the sun which enables life to exist on earth.

A very important feature of solar "burning" is that it occurs very gradually. Since neutrons are only rarely formed from protons, a relatively small number of deuterons are produced at any one time, and thus solar fuel (deuterons) constitutes but a tiny fraction of the total material in the sun. This ensures that the sun burns slowly, generating solar energy only gradually.

Another possible nuclear reaction that could, in principle, occur is the combination of one proton with another proton. Fortunately for us, however, such proton-proton combination does not occur. If one proton were able to combine with another proton, then all the protons in the sun would immediately combine with each other, leading to a gigantic explosion of the entire sun.

The possibility of proton-neutron combination and the impossibility of proton-proton combination both depend on the strength of the nuclear force, one of the fundamental forces in nature. The other fundamental forces include the familiar force of gravity and the electromagnetic force. Detailed calculations[3] of the nuclear force lead to the following results:

1. If the nuclear force were only a *few percent* weaker, then a proton could not combine with a neutron to form a deuteron. If this were the case, no deuterons would be formed in the sun, and hence, there would be no solar fuel. As a result, the sun would not shine, but would merely be a cold ball of inert protons, precluding the possibility of life on earth.

2. If the nuclear force were only a *few percent* stronger, then each proton would rapidly combine with another proton, with explosive results. If this were the case, the sun would explode, once again precluding the possibility of life on earth.

It is an extraordinary fact that the strength of the nuclear force *just happens* to lie within the narrow range in which neither of these two catastrophes occurs. The proton-proton explosion of the sun *does not* occur, but the gradual burning of deuterons *does* take place in the sun, providing the warmth and light that are vital for life to exist on earth. This is our first example of the anthropic principle.

WATER AND AIR ON OUR PLANET

It is not necessary to elaborate on the necessity of water and air for the existence of life. The Earth is blessed with an abundant supply of both, permitting life to flourish here, whereas our two neighboring planets, Venus and Mars, are both devoid of water and air, and hence devoid of life, as the space program has established. These facts may not seem particularly noteworthy, but we shall show just how remarkable they really are.

It was recently discovered that, shortly after they were formed, all three planets (Earth, Venus and Mars) had large amounts of surface water. The deep channels that are observed today on the surface of Mars were carved out long ago by the copious fast-flowing Martian primordial surface waters.[4] Similarly, Venus was once covered by deep oceans that contained the equivalent of a layer of water three kilometers deep over its entire surface.[5] However, in the course of time, all surface waters on Mars and Venus disappeared. How did our planet escape this catastrophe?

The surprising answer is that the Earth escaped this catastrophe by *sheer accident*! Earth *just happens* to be sufficiently distant from the sun that our surface water neither evaporated nor decomposed, as happened on Venus. Moreover, Earth *just happens* to be sufficiently near the sun that the temperature remains high enough to prevent all the oceans from freezing permanently, as happened on Mars. Therefore, Earth *alone*, among the planets of the solar system, is capable of supporting life.

Similar remarks apply to the atmosphere. Studies have shown that the planetary atmosphere is controlled by a very delicate balance, involving the subtle interplay of many factors.[6] This balance is so delicate that if the Earth were only slightly closer to the sun, the surface temperature would be much higher than the boiling point of water, precluding all possibility of life. Similarly, if the Earth were only slightly farther from the sun, the concentration of carbon dioxide in the atmosphere would become so high that "the atmosphere would not be breathable by human beings."[7] Fortunately, the Earth's orbit *just happens* to be at the crucial distance from the sun that permits the formation of a life-sustaining atmosphere ("life could appear in this extremely narrow zone"[8]).

This remarkably fortunate coincidence is known as the "Goldilocks problem of climatology." Recall the children's story of Goldilocks and the Three Bears, in which the various items of Baby Bear were "not too hot and not too cold; not too hard and not too soft; not too long and not too short; but *just right*." In the same vein, scientists view the existence of water and air on Earth as another example of the anthropic principle.

PHYSICS AND ASTRONOMY

The two examples of the anthropic principle presented above are taken from the many that could be brought from the physical sciences. Indeed, the examples are so numerous and so dramatic that many scientists have commented on the severe restraints that the existence of life places on the laws of nature. Particularly perceptive are the impressions of Professor Freeman Dyson of the Institute for Advanced Study in Princeton, whose words capture the essence of the anthropic principle[9]:

> *"As we look out into the universe and identify the many peculiarities of physics and astronomy that have worked together for our benefit, it almost seems as if the universe knew that we were coming."*

THE ORIGIN OF LIFE

The branch of science that deals with the origin of life is called molecular biology. There has been enormous progress in the past few decades. Scientists have unraveled the structure of DNA (the long, thread-like molecules that form the genetic material found in each cell of every living creature) – the famous double helix. The genetic code has been deciphered. Hundreds of complex chemical reactions that occur within the cell are now understood. From all this scientific progress, one could easily form the impression that the "riddle of life" has been solved; in other words, that scientists have succeeded in explaining all the steps by which inanimate material became transformed into the complex biological systems that we call life. However, such a conclusion would be completely erroneous.

After half a century of intensive research into molecular biology, scientists have come to appreciate the extreme improbability and incredibility of the transformation of inanimate material into living cells. This was the central theme of a recent *Scientific American* article, appropriately entitled, "In the Beginning."[10] This article describes the enormous difficulties encountered by current proposals to explain the origin of life ("points out the inadequacy of all proposed explanations of a terrestrial genesis of life"), quoting leading experts in the field.

Professor Harold Klein, chairman of the U.S. National Academy of Sciences committee that reviewed origin-of-life research, is quoted as follows: *"The simplest bacterium is so complicated that it is almost impossible to imagine how it happened."*[11] Professor Francis Crick, who shared the Nobel Prize for discovering the structure of DNA, is also quoted: *"The origin of life appears to be almost a miracle, so many are the conditions which would have had to be satisfied to get it going."*[12]

If this Nobel laureate, known as a man completely devoid of any religious feeling, sees fit to use the words *"almost a miracle"* to describe the origin of life, it is clear that quite an incredible series of unlikely events must have occurred to transform inanimate material into living cells.

Highly Improbable Events and Human Beings

THE DESTRUCTION OF THE DINOSAURS

Thus far, we have been discussing the many unlikely events that were necessary to make possible the existence of life itself. But our main concern is, of course, with human life. Therefore, we ask: Did any extremely unusual events have to occur to permit the existence of human beings? As we shall see, scientists answer with a resounding "Yes!" This is the very heart of the anthropic principle.

We begin our analysis of the highly improbable events that culminated in human life with a discussion of the dinosaurs, those terrible monsters of the past. The dinosaurs were one of the most successful groups of animals that ever lived – the largest, strongest, fastest, and fiercest animals of their time. Dinosaurs (and their close relatives) inhabited every continent, the air (flying dinosaurs) and the oceans (marine dinosaurs). All other animals lived in constant fear of being devoured or destroyed by these gigantic reptiles. Because the dinosaurs dominated the earth, this era is referred to as the Age of Reptiles.

After being the undisputed masters of our planet for over 150 million years, the dinosaurs suddenly became extinct. The sudden destruction of all the world's dinosaurs, together with most other animal species, is the most famous of the mass extinctions that have occurred periodically in the history of our planet, each time abruptly wiping out the majority of animal species. The cause of this mass extinction had baffled scientists for many years. What could have caused the abrupt demise of these extremely successfully animals after they had enjoyed such a long period of dominance? What happened that suddenly wiped out all the dinosaurs?

After years of debate, the riddle of the sudden and total destruction of the dinosaurs was solved in 1980 by Nobel laureate Luis Alvarez and his son Walter. These scientists showed that a giant meteor from outer space collided with the earth to cause this worldwide catastrophe.[13] The explanation for the mass extinctions – the impact of meteors or comets colliding with the earth – is known as the impact theory. Evidence in favor of the impact theory accumulated rapidly, and by 1987, Professor Alvarez could point to *fifteen* different pieces of scientific data that support this theory.[14]

The point of central importance to our discussion is that the collision of the meteor with the earth was a matter of *sheer luck*. This has been repeatedly stressed by the leading paleontologists (scientists who study fossils). Professor David Raup, past president of the American Paleontological Society, took precisely this point as the central theme of his famous article (later expanded into a book with same title), entitled *Extinctions: Bad Genes or Bad Luck?* Raup emphasizes the importance of luck in mass extinctions: "The extinction of a given species is more bad luck than bad genes... Pure chance would favor some biologic groups over others."[15]

The important role played by luck in mass extinctions has also been emphasized by Professor Stephen J. Gould of Harvard University: "*If extinctions can demolish more than 90% of all species, then we must be losing groups forever by pure bad luck.*"[16]

Professor George Yule of the University of Oxford puts it in the following way: "*The species exterminated were not killed because of any inherent defects, but simply because they had the ill-luck to stand in the way of the cataclysm.*"[17]

Finally, we quote Professor David Jablonski of the University of Chicago, a renowned authority on the subject of mass extinctions: "*When a mass extinction strikes, it is not the "most fit" species that survive; it is the most fortunate. Species that had been barely hanging on, suddenly inherit the earth.*"[18]

These leading paleontologists are emphasizing that if a giant meteor suddenly falls from the sky, wiping out some species while permitting other species to survive and ultimately to flourish, then the Darwinian principle of the survival of the fittest is irrelevant. The species that survived were blessed with *good luck* – the occurrence of an extremely improbable and totally unexpected event.

THE DINOSAURS AND MAN

What is the relationship between the dinosaurs and human beings? Why does the sudden destruction of all the dinosaurs worldwide constitute a dramatic example of the anthropic principle? The explanation is straightforward. As long as dinosaurs dominated the earth, there was no possibility for large mammals to exist. Only after the dinosaurs were wiped out could the mammals flourish and become the dominant fauna.

This intimate connection between human beings and the dinosaurs was emphasized by Professor Alvarez, who ends his article about the meteoric impact that destroyed all the dinosaurs, with the following words[19]:

> *"From our human point of view, that impact was one of the most important events in the history of our planet. Had it not taken place, the largest mammals alive today might still resemble the rat-like creatures that were then scurrying around trying to avoid being devoured by dinosaurs."*

But there is more to the story. For human beings to exist today, it was not sufficient that our planet was struck by a meteor. The impact had to occur with *just the right strength*. Alvarez writes[20]:

> *"If the impact had been weaker, no species would have become extinct; the mammals would still be subordinate to the dinosaurs, and I [Alvarez] wouldn't be writing this article. If the impact had been stronger, all life on this planet would have ceased, and again, I wouldn't be writing this article. The impact was just the right strength to ensure that the mammals survived, while the dinosaurs didn't."*

"WONDERFUL LIFE" BY STEPHEN JAY GOULD

It has become clear to scientists that the sudden destruction of the world's dinosaurs was just one of a long series of completely unexpected, highly improbable events whose occurrence was necessary for human beings to exist – and that *all these events just happened to occur in precisely the required sequence*. This is a major theme of the book entitled *Wonderful Life* by Professor Stephen Jay Gould of Harvard University. Again and again, Gould emphasizes how amazing it is that human beings exist at all, because *"we are an improbable and fragile entity … the result of a staggeringly improbable series of events, utterly unpredictable and quite unrepeatable.*"[21] His 320-page book abounds with examples of the anthropic principle:

> "*Consciousness would not have appeared on our planet if a cosmic catastrophe had not claimed the dinosaurs as victims. In a literal sense, we owe our existence, as large reasoning mammals, to our lucky stars.*"[22]

> "*Let the "tape of life" play again from the identical starting point, and the chance is vanishingly small that anything like human intelligence would grace the replay.*"[23]

> "*It fills us with amazement (because of its improbability) that human beings exist at all. Replay the tape a million times from the same beginning, and I doubt that Homo sapiens would ever appear again. It is, indeed, a wonderful life.*"[24]

Calculating Probabilities

Having described in detail the scientific meaning of the anthropic principle, we now turn to the second part of the discussion and ask: What are the implications of the anthropic principle? In particular, what are the implications for the believing person?

I would like to begin the discussion on a personal note. A decade ago, I wrote a book on Genesis and science entitled *In the Beginning*, showing that current scientific evidence is in remarkable agreement with the biblical account of the origin and development of the universe. My book has enjoyed a measure of success, having been reprinted thirty times and translated into nine languages.

However, the book was not to everyone's taste. Professor Raphael Falk, geneticist at the Hebrew University and a militant secularist, was so outraged by my book that he published a ten-page article, devoted *solely* to attacking both my book and me personally ("fundamentalist," "commits scientific rape," "writes pseudo-science," "manipulates facts, etc." [25]). In particular, Falk ridiculed my discussion of the anthropic principle by means of the following counter-argument[26]:

THE ANTHROPIC PRINCIPLE · 33

"Aviezer places particular emphasis on the "remarkable coincidences" which characterize the universe. The point of this claim is that such remarkable events could not have occurred through chance, but rather are the result of a guiding hand. Superficially, this claim appears convincing, but a little thought shows that that it is without foundation. According to Aviezer's logic, the probability that I am writing these lines with a dull yellow pencil, using my left hand, sitting at my kitchen table, on the third floor of a specific Jerusalem address – this probability is completely negligible. Nevertheless, all these events happened and they clearly mean nothing"

It is important to explain what is wrong with Falk's argument, because his error is not immediately obvious and, in fact, has been repeated by other writers. For example, the same error appears in an article on the anthropic principle,[27] by a distinguished philosopher who is also an observant Jew. This author brings the following example:

"I pull a \$1 bill from my wallet and observe its serial number to be G65538608D. The probability for this occurrence was less than one in ten billion. Thus, undeniably, I am faced here with an extremely rare event, but I am not surprised. What is essential is to make the crucial distinction between improbable events that are genuinely surprising and those that are not"

There are two erroneous statements here. The first erroneous statement is that we are *not* faced with a rare event. The second is that *all* improbable events are surprising. Indeed, that is what is normally meant by the word "surprising."

The key to understanding this topic can be found in the words of Nobel laureate Richard Feynman, one of the most brilliant physicists of the twentieth century. In his book on quantum electrodynamics (he explains this most complex of theories simply and without the use of a single equation!), Professor Feynman emphasizes that: *"In order to calculate correctly the probability of an event, one must define the event clearly."*[28]

DEFINING THE EVENT

Following Feynman's advice, we shall clearly define the event described above, which immediately leads to the conclusion that there is a probability of 100% that the dollar bill pulled from the wallet has G65538608D for its serial number! Why? Because this number was chosen *after looking* at the serial number on the bill. In other words, one was asking, "What is the probability that the serial number found on the bill *is* the serial number on the bill?" And the answer to this question, clearly, is 100%. Since the event was not improbable at all, but certain, there is no reason to be surprised by its occurrence.

Let us now apply the same logic to invalidate Falk's argument. What was the probability that Falk wrote his article on his kitchen table, using a dull yellow pencil held in his left hand, on the third floor of a specific Jerusalem address? The answer is: 100%! Why? Because Falk *chose* these unusual conditions on the basis on what he *already knew* to have happened. In other words, Falk simply asked, "What is the probability that what I know to have happened, really did happen?" The answer is clearly 100%.

A rare, extremely improbable event occurs if one defines the conditions *before* knowing what will happen. For example, if one chooses a serial number *before* pulling a dollar bill from his wallet, and then finds that the number chosen is exactly the same as the number on the bill, we would all be absolutely astonished – and with good reason! Similarly, if Falk had guessed correctly all the conditions under which *someone else* had written an article, then we would all be flabbergasted – and rightly so.

EVENTS IN CONTEXT – PLAYING THE LOTTO

We now turn to the second important aspect of Feynman's statement: *events must be defined in context.* An example will illustrate this point.

Among the popular Israeli lotteries is Lotto. Say, for concreteness, that one million people buy a Lotto ticket each week. If I am informed that this week's winner is Haim Cohen from Tiberias, I will certainly not get excited. But why not? The chances that Haim Cohen would be the winner were only one in a million – and it happened! The reason for my lack of excitement is the following. I could not care less if the Lotto winner is Haim Cohen from Tiberias, Sarah Levi from Be'er Sheva or Shmerel Berel from Ramat Gan. In other words, each of the one million Lotto players is completely equivalent in my eyes to Haim Cohen from Tiberias (the technical term in statistics is "equivalent microstates"). Although the chances were only one in a million that the winner would be Haim Cohen from Tiberias, there exist one million "equivalent" Haim Cohens. Therefore, the substance of what I heard is that *someone* won the Lotto this week. And the chances for that event happening – *someone* winning – are 100%. Hence, I have no reason to be surprised.

Now consider the following week. If I were informed that Haim Cohen *again* won the Lotto, I would most certainly be amazed, and so would everyone else. But why? The chances of Haim Cohen winning the Lotto the second week were exactly the same as his chances of winning the first week. The answer is that the *context* is entirely different. In the first week, Haim Cohen was just one of a million equivalent Lotto players. But in the second week, he was a *unique* individual – the fellow who won last week. In other words, in the second week, there exists only *one* Haim Cohen – only *one* previous week's winner – and the chances of this unique individual winning the Lotto again are truly one in a million. When such a rare event occurs, we are all genuinely surprised.

Finally, we turn to the third week. If we were to learn that Haim Cohen had *again* won the Lotto, for the *third* consecutive week, it is clear that *suspicion*, not surprise, would be the natural reaction. Indeed, there is little doubt that the fraud division of the police department would soon be paying a visit to Haim Cohen to discuss with him just how it happened that Haim won the Lotto for three consecutive weeks.

But why? The chances of Haim Cohen winning the Lotto in the third week were *exactly the same* as his chances of winning the first week. The answer lies in the *context* of the event. By the third week, Haim Cohen has become an *extremely* unusual individual – the fellow who has already won the Lotto for *two* weeks running. The chances that this same person will win the Lotto *once again* are easily shown to be only one in a million millions (1000 billion). Such events are so rare that they simply *do not occur.* Therefore, the police department correctly suspects that a guiding hand was behind Haim Cohen's triple win. A guiding hand in the creation of the universe means the intercession of the Almighty, but a guiding hand in the determination of the Lotto winner means five years in Ramla Prison!

EVENTS IN CONTEXT – PLAYING CARDS

We next consider card games, beginning with the game of poker (five-card poker without a draw). In this game, each player is dealt five cards from the deck, and these cards form a combination (pair, three-of-a-kind, flush, etc.). Each combination has a ranking, and the game is won by the player whose cards form the highest-ranking combination.

The highest ranking combination of cards in poker is the straight flush (it is not necessary to know what a straight flush is). A straight flush is so rare that one can play poker all day, every day of his life and never encounter one. And if a poker player should ever get a straight flush, he will never forget it. There is nothing more wondrous in poker: the dream of every poker player!

We now turn to a different card game, bridge. In this game, each player is dealt thirteen cards, but we will consider only the first five cards to make a comparison with poker. If a bridge player's first five cards were to be the combination that constitutes a straight flush in poker, *he would probably not even be aware of it,* because in bridge, a "straight flush" has no value whatever. This combination of cards is not even defined in bridge, and so I put quotation marks around the words "straight flush." Thus, we see that the *same combination of cards* is considered a wondrous combination in poker because of its rarity and value, but is considered a meaningless combination in bridge, *in spite of its rarity,* because it has *no value.*

The Anthropic Principle and the Believing Person

The preceding examples and discussion pave the way for an answer to our central question: What conclusions can one draw from the anthropic principle? The answer depends on one's views about the significance of human beings. In our example about poker and bridge, we explained why the extremely rare straight flush was a wondrous event in a poker game but a meaningless event in a bridge game. In other words, the *same rare event* can be either wondrous or meaningless; it all depends on the importance that one attributes to the event.

Returning to the subject of our essay, human beings, we saw that many extremely unlikely events (*"a staggeringly improbable series of events ... quite unrepeatable"*[29]) had to occur to make possible the appearance of human beings. Thus, the extreme rarity of the events leading to human existence is well established. Indeed, that is the scientific content of the anthropic principle. But before we can decide on the *meaning* of these events, we must first decide on the *meaning* of the end product: human beings.

If human beings are assumed to be just another species in the animal kingdom (as secularists believe), not more important than any other of the approximately two million species discovered so far, then the anthropic principle has no meaning. We have seen that rarity by itself is not significant. It is the straight flush in bridge, rare and interesting, but without meaning. If, however, one believes that human beings are the most important species in the world, and that mankind is the entire reason for the creation of the universe, as the Torah and the Sages of the Talmud repeatedly emphasize, then the anthropic principle is of the utmost significance. It is the straight flush in poker, the most meaningful of occurrences.

In summary, scientists have discovered that in the existence of human beings, the universe has dealt out the extremely rare straight flush. Everyone agrees with this; the anthropic principle has become a scientifically established fact. But the nonbeliever is "playing bridge" and therefore the anthropic principle means nothing to him. By contrast, the believing person is "playing poker," and therefore the anthropic principle is yet another example of the harmony between modern science and words of the Torah.

NOTES

1. J.D. Barrow and F.J. Tipler, 1986, *The Anthropic Cosmological Principle* (Oxford University Press).

2. G. Gale, December 1981, *Scientific American*, pp. 114–122.

3. P.C.W. Davis, 1972, *Journal of Physics*, vol. 5, pp. 1296–1304.

4. J. Audouze *et al.*, eds., 1985, *The Cambridge Atlas of Astronomy* (Cambridge University Press), pp. 124–149.

5. *Ibid.*, pp. 70–81.

6. J.F. Kasting *et al.*, February 1988, *Scientific American*, pp. 46–53.

7. *Ibid.*, p. 53.

8. Audouze, p. 63.

9. F.J. Dyson, September 1971, *Scientific American*, p. 59.

10. J. Horgan, February 1991, *Scientific American*, pp. 100–111.

11. H.P. Klein, February 1991, *Scientific American*, p. 104.

12. F. Crick, February 1991, *Scientific American*, p. 109.

13. W. Alvarez *et al.*, 1984, *Science*, vol. 223, pp. 1135–1140.

14. L.W. Alvarez, July 1987, *Physics Today*, pp. 24–33.

15. D.M. Raup, 1981, *Acta Geologica Hispanica*, vol. 15, pp. 25–33.

16. S.J. Gould, 1981, *The Flamingo's Smile* (W.W. Norton: New York), p. 242.

17. G.U. Yule, 1981, *Philosophical Transactions of the Royal Society*, vol. 213, p. 24.

18. D. Jablonski, June 1989, quoted in *National Geographic*, p. 673.

19. Alvarez, p. 33.

20. *Ibid.*, p. 29

21. S.J. Gould, 1989, *Wonderful Life* (W.W. Norton: New York), pp. 14, 319.

22. *Ibid.*, p. 318.

23. *Ibid.*, p. 14

24. *Ibid.*, p. 289

25. R. Falk, Spring 1994, *Alpai'im*, vol. 9, pp. 133–142.

26. *Ibid.*, p. 136.

27. G.N. Schlesinger, Spring 1988, *Tradition*, vol. 23, pp. 1–8.

28. R.P. Feynman, 1985, *QED* (Princeton University Press), p. 81.

29. Gould, p. 14.

4

The Creation of Man

Questions

Where did human beings come from? One who believes in the Bible would respond that God created human beings a few thousand years ago as a unique species, as recorded in the first chapter of Genesis.

In complete contrast to the biblical account of man's origins, science books tell us that hominids, the "man-like" species, first appeared on our planet about six million years ago. The textbooks state that the first hominids eventually evolved into more advanced hominids, finally culminating in the contemporary species, Modern Man, whose scientific designation is *Homo sapiens*. It follows from this scenario that there is no difference between the evolutionary history of human beings and the evolutionary history of any other species in the animal kingdom.

How is one to resolve this striking contradiction between science and Genesis?

"GOD CREATED MAN IN HIS IMAGE"

The key to understanding the statement that *"God created man in His image"* (Genesis 1:27) is to recognize that the Bible is *not* a biology textbook. Therefore, the word "man" in the biblical creation story need not have the same meaning as the word "man" when used by a scientist.

To the biologist, the species Modern Man (*Homo sapiens*), like any other species, is defined by his *physical* characteristics (skull, jaw, teeth, pelvic structure, limbs, etc.) and, using the more modern techniques, by his DNA sequences. However, in the biblical understanding of the term "man," physical features play no role. The "man" who appears in the culmination of the Genesis creation story and is described as "created by God" is characterized *solely* by his unique intellectual, creative, and spiritual qualities. Standing six feet tall, walking upright, and possessing a hominid skull are of no relevance at all in the Genesis classification scheme. A particularly important feature of "Genesis man" is his ability to speak. Onkeles, the second-century translator of the Bible into Aramaic, designates man as "the speaking being" (Genesis 2:7). In their comments on this verse, the commentators Rashi, Sa'adiah Gaon, Sforno, and Ramban all emphasize that man's uniqueness lies in his powers of speech and reason.

The origin of human beings is described in Genesis by the words "God created" (*vayivra*). However, one need not understand these words as implying creation in the physical sense. "Creation" means the formation of something that is *fundamentally new*, either physically (creation *ex nihilo*) or conceptually (the creation of a totally new kind of entity, such as a living creature). In this vein, Jewish commentators explain the creation of man *"in the image of God"* as referring to the unique intellectual and spiritual faculties with which man was endowed by his Creator.

In his commentary, Sforno points out that the word "man" (*odom* in Hebrew) in the phrase *"and God created man"* is to be understood as a generic term, denoting mankind as a whole, rather than referring to a particular individual (i.e., Adam).[1]

Having explained the meaning of "Genesis man" (a creature who speaks and displays intelligence, creativity and spirituality), we may ask where prehistoric man fits in the Genesis scheme of the creation of man. Does "Genesis man" refer to the first hominids that appeared about six million years ago? Or only to our genus *Homo*, which dates from about two million years ago? Or only to our species *Homo sapiens*, Modern Man, who first appeared about 100,000 years ago? However, even this more recent date presents a problem, because

Genesis speaks of the creation of man as having occurred only a few thousand years ago.

The preceding discussion suggests that the "creation of man" described in Genesis does not refer to a new species at all, but to sudden and radical changes in human behavior. If the changes in human behavior were so dramatic, sudden, and revolutionary that they completely altered all aspects of human society, then one can truly say that contemporary mankind was "created" by these revolutionary changes. This is the meaning of the phrase: "*God created man.*"

Have scientists discovered any evidence for such sudden and radical changes in human society and in human behavior having taken place within the last few thousand years? The remarkable answer to this question is: "Yes."

Archaeological findings show that only a few thousand years ago, human society suddenly changed so comprehensively that scientists speak of a "revolution." Before discussing this revolution, we must first trace the cultural history of prehistoric man.

Prehistoric Man and Modern Man

NEANDERTAL MAN

The Neandertals were the prehistoric people who immediately preceded Modern Man. They lived for over 200,000 years throughout Europe, western Asia, and the Middle East. Then, for unknown reasons, the Neandertals suddenly disappeared from the fossil record. *Only* Modern Man is found in the archaeological sites that date from the last 30,000 years. (Other names given to peoples who lived during this period, such as Cro-Magnon Man, refer to *cultural* groups, and not to physical types of people. Cro-Magnon Men were as much Modern Men as are contemporary Frenchmen or Chinese.)

Scientists agree that Modern Man did *not* evolve from the Neandertals. Professor Ian Tattersall, of the Department of Anthropology of the American Museum of Natural History and a recognized authority on Neandertal Man, writes: "*Homo heidelbergensis quite likely gave rise to the Neandertals, whereas a less specialized population founded the lineage that ultimately produced Modern Man.*"[2] Professor Erik Trinkaus of the University of New Mexico, another authority on the Neandertals, writes: "*The situation... suggests that modern humans did not evolve out of the local Neandertal population.*"[3]

Our principal sources of information regarding the culture of prehistoric man are the tools and other artifacts found in his ancient campsites. It might seem natural to ask about the level of sophistication that characterizes prehistoric tools, and to compare these tools with those of contemporary Modern Man. However, such a comparison would not be meaningful, because the large well-developed brain of Modern Man gives him an obvious advantage over the small-brained earlier hominids. However, there is one exception to the general pattern of the earlier hominids having smaller brains. The striking exception is Neandertal Man. "*Neandertals had brains as large and as complex as our own.*"[4]

An important question concerns the physical capabilities of Neandertal Man. Were these people physically deficient or limited in any way that might have hindered their cultural development? Professor Trinkaus writes[5]:

> "*Neandertals were not less human than Modern Men; they had the same postural abilities, manual dexterity, range and character of movement as Modern Men ... a much stronger grip than Modern Men, but there was nothing gorilla-like about it; their control of movement was the same as ours.*"

The foregoing discussion shows that it is meaningful to compare the cultural achievements of Modern Man and Neandertal Man. Significant cultural differences between the Neandertals and ourselves cannot be explained away in terms of physical limitations of Neandertal Man.

NEANDERTAL CULTURE

What were the tools of Neandertal Man? What were his major artistic achievements? What great cities did he build? What profound writings did he leave for posterity? What important moral teachings did he expound? What marvelous paintings, stirring musical compositions, magnificent sculpture, moving poetry, breathtaking architecture, beautiful gardens, and profound scientific discoveries remain from the Neandertals to mark their 200,000-year-long sojourn on our planet? The answer is that their meager cultural legacy contains not a single one of these items!

Scientists have discovered that Neandertal tools were primarily flints with a sharp edge. Their tools look quite similar to the sharp stones that are strewn along every beach. In fact, Neandertal tools are so primitive that one who is not a professional archaeologist would not even recognize them as man-made objects. Professor Tattersall explains[6]:

> "The stone-working skills of the Neandertals consisted [of using] a stone core, shaped in such a way that a single blow would detach a finished implement. They rarely, if ever, made tools from other materials. Archaeologists question the sophistication of their hunting skills. Despite misleading earlier accounts, no substantial evidence has ever been found for symbolic behavior among the Neandertals, or for the production of symbolic objects. Even the occasional Neandertal practice of burying their dead may have been simply to discourage hyena incursions, or have a similar mundane explanation, for Neandertal burials lack the "grave goods" that would attest to ritual and belief in an afterlife ... Though they were successful in the difficult circumstances of the late Ice Age, the Neandertals lacked the spark of creativity that distinguishes Modern Man"

Regarding artistic accomplishments, it is important to mention that the magnificent cave paintings found in southwestern France, Spain, and elsewhere, were *all* the work of Modern Man.[7] No cave has ever been discovered that was painted by a Neandertal.

What are the reasons for Neandertal Man's lack of culture? Why was Modern Man able to revolutionize all aspects of his environment, while Neandertal Man hardly left a trace of his existence? In fact, archaeologists must search very hard to find *any* remnants of

Neandertal Man. Recall that the Neandertal brain *"does not suggest any differences [from Modern Man] in intellectual or behavioral capabilities."*[8] The fact is that scientists have no explanation for the great disparity in culture and intellectual capabilities between these two hominid species that were physically so similar.

THE CULTURE OF MODERN MAN

In discussing the impressive culture that characterizes Modern Man, we need not limit ourselves to the latest technological developments, such as supercomputers and space satellites. As soon as he appeared, Modern Man demonstrated his *enormous* cultural superiority over Neandertal Man. The archaeological data are so striking that every scientific account emphasizes the far-reaching technological advances introduced by Modern Man many thousands of years ago. [9]

> *"The toolmaking industries of Modern Man are completely different from those of Neandertal Man ... reflecting a quantum leap in mental abilities ... Modern Men who followed the Neandertals were their intellectual superiors in every way."*

We repeat that there are *no* significant physical differences between Modern Man and Neandertal Man that can account for these dramatic cultural changes. The average brain size is the same for the two species, and in physical capabilities, the Neandertals were the equal of modern humans. Therefore, the utter primitiveness of Neandertal culture is one of the great mysteries surrounding these physically quite advanced, but culturally so very backward predecessors of Modern Man.

The Development of Modern Human Culture: the Neolithic Revolution

From his initial appearance, Modern Man gradually developed his technological and artistic skills. Then, about 10,000 years ago, there occurred an explosion of cultural innovations of enormous dimensions. In fact, this was the most comprehensive series of cultural advances that has ever taken place, covering all aspects of human behavior. The cumulative effect of all these changes was to completely revolutionize human society. The sudden appearance of so many fundamental technological and artistic advances is referred to by archaeologists as the Neolithic Revolution or the Agricultural Revolution.[10]

The Neolithic Revolution was so all-encompassing that it has become *the major milestone* in prehistoric chronology. Archaeologists denote all earlier times as Paleolithic (Old Stone Age), whereas subsequent times are denoted as Neolithic (New Stone Age).

The many fundamental cultural innovations that occurred during or shortly after the Neolithic Revolution include agriculture, animal husbandry, metalworking, the wheel, the first written language, ceramic pottery, weaving, prepared foods (bread, wine, cheese, butter), musical instruments, and advanced architecture, to name but a few. This vast proliferation of cultural advances permitted the formation of the complex social organization that soon gave rise to the first cities and thus to modern civilization (a term that means "city-making"). The enormous range of these profound cultural and social developments is emphasized in every archaeological account of this period. For example:

> *"A crucial event in human history was the beginning of agriculture 10,000 years ago in the Near East. The accumulation of surplus food supplies enabled large settlements to be established, leading to the emergence of Western civilization."*[11]

> *"Agriculture and animal husbandry appeared at roughly the same time ... Technological progress, the mastery of new materials (such as metals) and new energy sources (such as wind and water power) ... The acceleration of human history cannot be better illustrated than by comparing the changes of the past 10,000 years with those of the previous four million years."*[12]

> *One cannot avoid being impressed at how rapidly the transition occurred from Paleolithic hunting groups to regionally organized communities ... domestication of plants and animals, establishment*

of farming communities, development of pottery ... painted and decorated pots developed quite rapidly ... Bronze tools and weapons were produced. Writing evolved from pictographic notations, while specialized artisans made quantities of diverse goods ... market centers became towns ... The urban revolution was underway, the world of people was radically transformed and the first civilizations were taking shape."[13]

"The development of plant and animal domestication is referred to as the Neolithic Revolution... The changes arising from food production so altered human life that all manner of new developments came into being... village ways of life, population growth, and increasingly complex forms of social organization."[14]

"Major characteristics of agricultural economies began to be evident ... animal domestication and advanced cultivation techniques, such as irrigation, occurred with explosive consequences... populations increased enormously ... the pace of change was so rapid and their effects were so far-reaching."[15]

What were the causes of the Neolithic Revolution? What triggered all these *"explosive," "far-reaching,"* and *"revolutionary"* changes that so altered human society? The fact is that no one really knows.

"What were the factors that caused a shift away from hunting-gathering to food production? The question continues to be debated by archaeologists and anthropologists."[16]

"Why, after many hundreds of millennia of subsistence by hunting and gathering, did man only recently adopt the alternative strategy of cultivating crops and husbanding animals? The reasons for this dramatic shift are still debated."[17]

The Text of Genesis

Let us summarize the archaeological findings and relate them to Genesis. Archaeological studies have shown that Modern Man is a unique creature from a cultural point of view (*"intellectual superiors in every way"*[18]), being vastly more proficient and advanced than his immediate predecessors, the Neandertals. Neandertal Man did not suffer from any obvious physical deficiencies, either in the size of his brain (*"as large and as complex as our own brain"*[19]) or in his manual dexterity (*"not less than modern men"*[20]), that could explain the marked cultural and intellectual superiority of Modern Man.

After a period of gradual technological advance, Modern Man suddenly developed a dramatic and far-reaching surge of cultural innovations that covered all aspects of human activity. This remarkable behavioral revolution was characterized by the cultivation of food, the domestication of animals, and the invention of all manner of technological and artistic implements and processes, all of which *"occurred with explosive consequences."*[21] This cultural explosion – the Neolithic Revolution – occurred only a few thousand years ago and completely transformed human society.

It is this sudden, unexplained, comprehensive revolution in human society that is the true meaning of the Genesis phrase *"God created man."* In other words, man's "creation" refers to the sudden appearance of completely new patterns of human behavior that are so fundamentally different from all previous behavior that this "revolution" is equivalent to a new species of mankind suddenly emerging out of nowhere. These "new humans" were characterized by an enormous surge of creativity, intelligence, and spirituality, which remain to this day the distinguishing features of "Genesis man."

The events that comprised the Neolithic Revolution are consistent with the details given in biblical text. Genesis states that God blessed mankind and told him to *"fill the land and subdue it"* (1:28). Nachmanides explains that the words *"subdue it [the land]"* refer to agriculture and animal husbandry.[22]

Scientific accounts of the Neolithic Revolution describe the vast and sudden changes that took place in every phase of human activity. Archaeologists confirm that mankind subdued the land (*"the beginning of agriculture and animal husbandry was a crucial event in human history [that occurred] 10,000 years ago in the Middle East"*[23]) and that mankind filled the land (*"populations increased enormously"*[24]). The fulfillment of the divine will is thus recorded in every archaeological site.

The Time Scale

A discrepancy still remains between the time scale of science and that of Genesis. The creation of man, described in the first chapter of Genesis, is traditionally viewed as having occurred less than 6000 years ago, whereas the Neolithic Revolution occurred about 11,000 years ago. Therefore, the identification of these two events leads to a discrepancy of about 5000 years.

Before turning to the resolution of this problem, we note that great progress has already been achieved by the approach of identifying the Genesis creation of man with the creation of a revolutionary new human society. Since the appearance of Genesis man refers to the Neolithic Revolution, about 11,000 years ago, we are no longer faced with the great difficulty of explaining the multimillion-year history of prehistoric man. This latter date is now seen to be irrelevant to Genesis man.

The key to resolving the time-scale discrepancy lies in the recognition that there is a clear distinction between the first-chapter Genesis man and the second-chapter person named Adam. The traditional 6000-year calendar refers to Adam.

The commentator Sforno points out that the word "man" in the first chapter of Genesis refers "to the species of living creatures known as man" – what we denote as "Genesis man" – whereas the specific person named Adam is not mentioned until the second chapter.[25] Thus, the meaning of the Hebrew word *odom* in the first chapter of Genesis ("Genesis man") is different from its meaning in the second chapter ("Adam").

The differences between the first-chapter *odom* and the second-chapter *odom* have been discussed by a number of Jewish writers, including Rabbi Joseph B. Soloveitchik.[26]

The time-scale problem is thus resolved. The traditional 6000-year reckoning begins with Adam in the second chapter, whereas the first-chapter Genesis man corresponds to the Neolithic Revolution, which occurred a few thousand years earlier.

The Uniqueness of Man

We have emphasized that the Genesis characterization of man as having been created *"in the image of God"* refers to the unique spiritual and mental qualities of contemporary human beings. We shall here focus on three aspects of man's uniqueness.

LANGUAGE AND COMMUNICATION

The past few thousand years have witnessed the enormous progress made by man in all areas of intellectual endeavor. An essential ingredient of this progress is the unique ability of human beings to speak to each other. This enables human beings to benefit from the accomplishments of their predecessors. The distinguished physicist Isaac Newton once remarked: *"If I have seen further than others, it is by standing on the shoulders of giants."*

The importance of language and communication can hardly be overestimated. The many technological innovations that have revolutionized human society resulted from the cumulative efforts of many talented people. Because man can communicate, a scientist need not "reinvent the wheel" before making new contributions. The fact that one can build upon the work of others has led to the rapid technological progress that is the hallmark of civilization.

Man's ability to speak with his fellows is an aspect of man's having been created *"in the image of God."*

INTELLECTUAL CURIOSITY

Man is the only species that displays intellectual curiosity regarding matters that do not directly enhance his chances for survival. All other species concern themselves exclusively with food, shelter, safety, mating, and so on, for themselves and their family, tribe, or colony. By contrast, human beings express great interest in, and devote much time to, the pursuit of knowledge and art which have no practical consequences.

An excellent illustration of this phenomenon is the book that you are now holding in your hands. Reading this book will *not* increase your salary, will *not* put better food on your table, and will *not* in any way improve your physical situation. Nevertheless, in spite of the complete absence of any tangible benefit, you continue to read in order to satisfy your intellectual curiosity.

Man's intellectual curiosity is another aspect of man's having been created *"in the image of God."*

CONSCIENCE

The most striking feature of man's uniqueness lies in the realm of conscience and morality. Man, and *only* man, is capable of making decisions based on the abstract principles of right and wrong. We humans may sacrifice our personal welfare, and indeed even our lives, in the cause of morality.

The plight of starving people in Africa has generated a worldwide appeal for help. These Africans have nothing at all in common with the average American or European – neither race nor religion nor language nor ideology nor life-style. Yet, the sight of starving children on the TV screen touched the hearts of viewers, and their conscience "demanded" that they contribute money to alleviate the suffering.

Of all the species in the animal kingdom, only man deals with moral problems. And only man possesses the spiritual faculties for making moral judgments. This divine privilege and accompanying responsibility are ours alone, because only mankind was created *"in the image of God."*

> *"I set before you this day, life and good, and death and evil ... choose life."*
>
> (Deuteronomy 30:15, 19)

NOTES

1. Sforno, commentary on Genesis 2:7.
2. I. Tattersall, April 1997, *Scientific American*, p. 52.
3. E. Trinkaus and P. Shipman, 1993, *The Neandertals* (Jonathan Cape: London), p. 414.
4. Trinkaus and Shipman, p. 418.
5. E. Trinkaus and W.W. Howells, December 1979, *Scientific American*, p. 99.
6. I. Tattersall, January 2000, *Scientific American*, p. 43.
7. A. Leroi-Gourhan, June 1982, *Scientific American*, pp. 80–88.
8. Trinkaus and Howells, p. 97.
9. N. Eldredge and I. Tattersall, 1982, *The Myths of Human Evolution* (Columbia University Press: New York), pp. 154, 159.
10. Strictly speaking, there are differences between the Agricultural Revolution and the Neolithic Revolution and these two did not occur at exactly the same time in each locality. However, such subtleties are of more interest to the professional archaeologist than to the layman, and we shall here treat these two revolutionary events as equivalent.
11. S. Lev-Yadun, A. Gopher, and S. Abbo, June 2000, *Science*, Vol. 288, p. 1602.
12. S.L. Washburn, September 1978, *Scientific American*, p. 154.
13. E.A. Hoebel and T. Weaver, 1979, *Anthropology and the Human Experience* (McGraw-Hill: New York), pp. 183, 195, 201.
14. G.H. Pelto and P.J. Pelto, 1979, *The Cultural Dimensions of the Human Adventure* (Macmillan: New York), p. 93.
15. A. Sherratt, ed., 1980, *The Cambridge Encyclopaedia of Archaeology* (Cambridge University Press), p. 407.
16. J. Diamond, 1997, *Guns, Germs, and Steel* (W.W. Norton: New York and London), p. 109.
17. L.G. Straus, G.A. Clark, J. Altuna, and J.A. Ortea, June 1980, *Scientific American*, p. 128.
18. Eldredge and Tattersall, p. 159.
19. Tattersall, p. 52.
20. Trinkaus and Howells, p. 99.
21. Sherratt, p. 407.
22. Nachmanides, commentary on Genesis 1:28.
23. Lev-Yadun, Gopher, and Abbo, p. 1602.
24. Sherratt, p. 407.
25. Sforno, commentary on Genesis 1:26.
26. J.B. Soloveitchik, Spring 1965, *Tradition*, pp. 5–67, especially p. 10.

5

Proofs for the Existence of God

Medieval Philosophy

Seeking proofs for the existence of God may sound quaint to the modern ear, but it was a matter of utmost importance to medieval philosophers, both Jewish (e.g., Maimonides) and non-Jewish (e.g., Thomas Aquinas). Why was it so important to these outstanding thinkers to be able to prove that God exists?

To answer this question, one must return to the period that preceded the rise of modern science. In the ancient world, discovering the laws of nature by experimentation was a foreign idea. The mathematicians had discovered the laws of geometry by pure reason, and it was viewed as self-evident that this was the appropriate method for studying the physical universe as well. Indeed, performing careful experiments and detailed observations seemed unbecoming to the philosopher. His realm of activity was the mind; only a servant or an artisan would "get his hands dirty" with the many menial tasks required to carry out an experiment. An exception was astronomy, where the ancients excelled at observing the motion of the heavenly bodies, the great handiwork of the Creator. Since the heavenly bodies were exalted, observing their motion could not be degrading. However, examining earthly objects was deemed inappropriate for the philosopher – the thinker. Thus, we find in philosophical texts that in contrast to a man, a woman has only twenty teeth (the correct number for both sexes is thirty-two). It would never have occurred to the scholastic philosopher to actually count a woman's teeth. Such a prosaic act was completely unnecessary. Everything worth knowing could be determined by reason, logic, thought.

The above approach was not limited to the study of the universe. Indeed, it was generally believed that *all* fundamental questions could be answered by logical deduction and pure reason. Since the Jewish philosophers viewed as self-evident the fact that God exists, as does every person of faith, they naturally assumed that His existence must be susceptible to rigorous proof. Indeed, in their eyes, the inability to prove that God exists might even cast doubt on His existence.

Because of this reverent attitude towards the power of logic, it is not surprising that many Jewish philosophers devoted considerable effort to arguments intended to prove that God exists. Although this subject is nowhere discussed in the Bible or in the Talmud, proofs for the existence of God are a major topic in the writings of the most prominent medieval Jewish philosophers, including Maimonides, Sa'adia Gaon, Bachya ibn Paquda, and Yehuda Halevi. The two principal proofs given are the prime mover argument and the argument from design (also known as the "watchmaker argument"). In fact, both of these "proofs" are erroneous, each for a different reason. It is instructive to analyze these arguments and discuss their shortcomings.

Prime Mover Argument

Common experience teaches us that no object moves unless there is cause for its motion. Aristotle asserted: "Matter does not move of its own accord." Examples abound of this simple truism. A piece of furniture that is pushed along the floor will cease to move as soon as the pushing stops. No matter how energetically one throws a ball, it eventually comes to rest. Consider now the heavenly bodies. The sun, moon, stars, and planets have always been observed to be in motion. It follows, therefore, that some agency ("mover") must be moving the heavenly bodies along their paths. This agency, called the "prime mover," can only be God, because what other power would be able to move the heavenly bodies around the sky. Thus, the perpetual motion of the heavenly bodies *proves* the existence of God.

REFUTATION

The most important book about science ever written, the *Principia*, was published in 1687 by Isaac Newton. The *Principia* contains the laws of motion. Newton's first law of motion (law of inertia) states, in complete contrast to Aristotle, that a moving object *will continue to move forever* unless some force causes the object to *stop moving*. In the examples given above, the force which causes the furniture or the ball to stop moving is the force of friction. However, if there were no friction present, then the motion would persist *forever*. In the heavens, there is no friction. Therefore, according to Newton's law of inertia, the heavenly bodies will continue to move forever *without any agency being required to keep them moving*.

To complete the picture, Newton's law of inertia predicts straight-line motion, whereas the planets move around the sun in an ellipse. This was explained by Newton as resulting from the gravitational attraction between the sun and the planets. The famous elliptical orbits of the planets, first discovered by Johannes Kepler in 1609, are therefore explained by Newton's laws of nature, without the need to invoke divine intervention. The prime mover argument for the existence of God is thus refuted.

SEQUEL

There is an interesting sequel to this story. As explained above, the refutation of the prime mover argument follows from Newton's scientific discoveries. Isaac Newton was a deeply religious man, for whom belief in God was of paramount importance. When he realized that his scientific findings had refuted one of the primary proofs for the existence of God, he was greatly troubled. After giving the matter considerable thought, Newton "solved" the problem in the following ingenious way.

The path of a planet around the sun is an ellipse because of the gravitational attraction of the sun. However, this is only an approxima-tion. In fact, each planet also feels the gravitational attraction of all the other planets. Although this additional force is very small because the sun is a thousand times more massive than all the planets combined, it may nevertheless have a significant effect on planetary motion. Therefore, Newton set out to calculate the effect on planetary motion due to the gravitational attraction of other planets. This extremely dif-ficult calculation, known as the many-body problem, cannot be solved exactly but only approximately. Newton introduced an approximation that he considered adequate, and calculated the effect on planetary motion. The result was startling! Newton found that the solar system was *unstable*. The small gravitational force exerted by each planet on every other planet disrupted the stability of the entire solar system. According to Newton's calculations, each planet will slowly drift away from the sun. Eventually, the sun will be devoid of planets and the solar system will cease to exist.

However, thousands of years of continuous star-gazing had firmly established that the solar system was, in fact, stable. The planets do not move further apart in the course of time. They move in stable elliptical orbits, with each planet remaining at a fixed maximum distance from the sun. How could the contradiction between Newton's calculations and observations be resolved? The explanation given by Newton was that it must be God who maintains the stability of the solar system! Undoubtedly it is He who pushes the planets back when they tend to drift away from the sun.[1]

Thus, Newton had found that there is a need to invoke God after all to explain the motion of the heavenly bodies. The prime mover argument for the existence of God, suitably modified, had been restored.

A hundred years later, the brilliant French mathematician Pierre-Simon Laplace re-examined the problem of the stability of the solar system. Laplace was able to show that Newton's approximation was inadequate. He introduced a more accurate approximation, solved the resulting equations, and found that the solar system *was* stable after all. In other words, the instability of the solar system claimed by

Newton did not really exist, but was simply an artifact of Newton's inadequate approximation.

The unequivocal conclusion to be drawn from this discussion is that the prime mover argument is erroneous. It is not possible to prove the existence of God from the motion of any object – not the heavenly bodies or the more mundane earthly bodies.

Argument from Design

The argument from design dates back at least a thousand years, but the following convenient formulation, called the "watchmaker argument," was given in 1802 by the English theologian William Paley[2]:

"If one were to walk in the forest and find a rock, one could imagine that the rock had always been there and had not been made by anyone. However, were one to find a watch in the forest, no one would suggest that the watch had always been there and had not been made by a person. The precision with which the cogs, springs, and gears of the watch have been fashioned, and the intricacy with which these parts have been assembled to serve a particular purpose, all demonstrate that the watch could not have been formed by natural processes. Rather, its complexity and specific design prove that the watch must have been made by a watchmaker.

If one now considers the natural world, with its vast panorama of animals and plants, each consisting of many complex patterns of tissues and organs that function together in intricate ways to permit each animal and plant to live and bear young, one sees far more complexity than is found in any watch. Therefore, if the complex design of a watch requires a watchmaker, how much more so must the complex design of the natural world require a 'Maker,' who must be God"

REFUTATION

The error in the watchmaker argument can be demonstrated by means of two counter-examples: snowflakes and the letters of the alphabet. Snowflakes are objects of great complexity that have no maker, whereas the letters, as physical objects, have no complexity and serve no physical purpose, but nevertheless, letters are written *only* by conscious agents.

Snowflakes are crystals of snow in the form of beautifully intricate structures, no two of which are alike, each having a perfect six-fold pattern of amazing fractal symmetry. Nevertheless, as we all know, there is no need for a "snowflake designer." The delicate beauty of the snowflake is *not* consciously designed, for snowflakes form spontaneously under certain weather conditions.

Snowflakes are not the only example of complex items that do not imply the presence of a designer. Any chemist can list unbelievably complex molecules that form spontaneously whenever the required raw materials are present under appropriate conditions of pressure and temperature. Therefore, it is clear that the existence of a complex universe does not provide any evidence that the universe was designed.

It should be emphasized that the argument from design is concerned *only* with the origin of the *physical object* before us, whether snowflake, watch, or rock. An entirely different question relates to the origin of the *laws of nature* themselves – the laws that lead to the beautiful and complex snowflake. The argument from design *does not* deal with the conclusions that one may draw from the harmony of the laws of nature, whose many unusual features permit the presence of thinking beings who are conscious of their own existence. Indeed, the origin of the laws of nature has become the subject of intense scientific inquiry in recent years, under the rubric of the "theory of everything." Scientists are now investigating whether the laws of nature could have been different from those that we observe. For example, could there, in principle, exist a universe whose laws of nature would make it impossible for living creatures to exist? Such highly complex scientific questions lie beyond the scope of this book.

We now turn to our second counter-example to the argument from design. Imagine walking in the forest and finding the letters ABC carved on a tree trunk. You would immediately conclude, and rightly so, that someone had carved these letters into the wood. There is nothing *physically* complex about the shapes of the letters – merely a few lines arranged in a very simple pattern. Moreover, as *physical objects*, the letters do not serve any purpose at all. A visitor from another planet, not familiar with the alphabet, would consider the letters to be mere scratches that disfigure the tree. Nevertheless, it is clear that someone had carved the letters into the wood.

It is our *experience* that tells us that the letters ABC *never* form spontaneously via the processes of nature, but are *invariably* written by a person. Neither complexity nor design, but *experience* tells us whether an object was fashioned by a conscious agent or was formed without any such intervention. The reason we conclude that snowflakes and rocks are not the result of any person's design, is that our *experience* tells us that all snowflakes and rocks are formed spontaneously. Similarly, the reason we conclude that the watch found in the forest was made by a watchmaker is that our *experience* tells us that watches *never* form spontaneously. The complex design of the watch is irrelevant to this conclusion.

What about the universe? Was it fashioned by a conscious being or did it come into existence spontaneously? Here, we have *no experience* to guide us because *only one* universe exists. Therefore, the argument from design does not permit us to conclude *anything* about the origin of the universe, regardless of its extreme complexity and intricate design.

Finally, to avoid a common error, it should be emphasized that the argument from design for the existence of God is fundamentally different from the anthropic principle discussed in Chapter 3. The argument from design is a *theological argument*, dating back at least a thousand years, that attempts to use the *complexity* of the universe to prove the existence of God. The anthropic principle is a *scientific principle*, formulated recently, in the 1970s. It expresses the scientific discovery that the existence of human life depends very sensitively on the laws of nature and the history of the universe. Very slight changes in either one of these would have made it impossible for human beings to exist. The *theological implications* of the anthropic principle, a topic that lies outside the province of science, are treated in Chapter 3.

The Bible Codes

In recent years, a new form of "proof," the so-called Bible codes, has swept the Jewish religious world. What is claimed is not merely a proof for the existence of God, but a proof for the divine origin of the Torah, which of course is much more impressive. After all, the existence of God does not imply that the Jewish faith is correct. Thomas Aquinas used the argument from design to prove the validity of Catholicism.

What is claimed is that there are hidden messages encoded in the Hebrew text of the Torah, messages that are so comprehensive that no human agency could have possibly have inserted them. Only today, with the availability of high-speed electronic computers, can one decipher the Bible codes to reveal these messages. In earlier generations, before the era of computers, no human mind, however brilliant, could have devised such intricate codes. Since these complex codes could not possibly have been inserted in the Torah by human beings, the divinity of the Torah is thereby proven.

The popularity of the Bible codes has been nothing short of phenomenal. Public lectures, conferences, debates, numerous articles, and entire books have been devoted to this subject. The interest in proving the validity of our religious beliefs does not seem to have abated since the Middle Ages. The modern packaging is, of course, very different from that of medieval scholasticism, but the motivation remains unchanged: if the validity of one's faith can be proved, then belief will be enhanced and doubts will be removed.

The most unsettling feature of this new "proof" is the nature of the messages allegedly encoded in the Torah. Bible code proponents claim that the Torah contains *every detail about the life of every human being that ever lived or ever will live.* The enormity of this claim lies in the fact that the words "every detail" mean *every event that ever happened,* including dates of birth and death, residence, name of spouse, telephone number, profession, hobbies, favorite foods, allergies, and so on and so forth.

Before discussing the validity of these claims, one must surely wonder *why* the Torah would contain the information that Nathan

Aviezer loves spaghetti but hates beets. One cannot escape the obvious question of what possible divine purpose could be served by encoding in the Torah detailed information about my personal food preferences, which would not seem to be of relevance to anyone but my wife, who has long since become bored with preparing spaghetti for me night after night. This, in my view, constitutes the most serious (but certainly not the only) objection to the Bible codes.

The explanation by code proponents for believing that detailed information of this kind is indeed contained in the Hebrew text of the Torah is based on a passage in the kabbalah writings of Rabbi Elijah ben Solomon Zalman, the Gaon of Vilna. Since the Gaon is justly famous for his brilliant talmudic and halachic analyses, it is not generally realized that most of his writings deal with the subject of kabbalah. In view of the succinctness and profundity of the Gaon's writings, it is hardly a trivial matter to penetrate the depths of his meaning on matters of kabbalah, and the simple literal translation of his words does not necessarily reflect their true meaning. Nevertheless, a single passage in the Gaon's writings on kabbalah, a passage that could readily be interpreted differently in view of its context, constitutes the sole basis for the claim that the Torah contains *all possible information about the life of every single human being.* In view of its importance, we quote the passage in its entirety[3]:

> "The principle is that everything that was, is, and will be, until the end of time, is included in the Torah, from its first word until its last word – and not just in a general sense, but even the minutest details of every event that ever happened to every individual human being, from his birth until his death. Similarly, [the Torah includes] the minutest details of every event that ever happened to every beast and animal in the world, every grass and plant and inanimate object."

Particularly important is the second sentence, often omitted when quoting this passage,[4] which shows that the Gaon's statement is not limited to human beings, but also includes *all animals, all plants, and even all inanimate objects.* Therefore, the claim of the code proponents is *even more* comprehensive than stated previously, namely, that *the complete details of the history of every object in the entire universe is encoded in the Torah.*

The code proponents have scored two important coups. First, they succeeded in publishing an article in the respected journal *Statistical Science* that describes their analysis and presents their conclusion that the codes they find in the Genesis text could not possibly be the result of pure chance.[5] Second, they obtained a letter, signed by four highly respected mathematicians, stating that their methods and conclusions seem sound and worthy of further study. Armed with these successes, the code proponents have circled the globe, lecturing on the validity of their methods and their conclusion that the codes are a real phenomenon that point to the divine origin of the Torah.

Opponents of the Bible codes have not been lacking, and include most prominently Professor Shlomo Sternberg of Harvard University and Professor Barry Simon of the California Institute of Technology. Both men are world-famous mathematicians and also religious Jews and outstanding Torah scholars. They have vigorously challenged the conclusions of the code proponents, asserting not only that these claims are bad science, but even worse, they are also bad Judaism. For example, Sternberg refers to the Bible codes as "a hoax"[6] and has attacked them in an article[7] bearing the vitriolic title, "Snake Oil for Sale."

Many articles have been written by both sides, and the Internet has been enriched by the debate. It is not our purpose here to engage in an analysis of the pros and cons of this spirited controversy. Rather, we wish to discuss the question of where this debate has led.

MICHAEL DROSNIN'S BOOK

The originators of the Bible codes, Doron Witztum and Professor Eliyahu Rips of the Hebrew University in Jerusalem, have always been careful to use the codes only to examine past events. However, if the past is encoded in the Torah, it follows that the future must also be encoded. Today's past was the future of earlier centuries. Based on this idea, an American journalist named Michael Drosnin published

The Bible Code in 1997. The central dramatic idea of this book is that the assassination of the Israeli Prime Minister Yitzhak Rabin was discovered in the Bible codes in 1994. Moreover, Drosnin claims that this information was passed on to Rabin. The prime minister ignored the warning and was subsequently assassinated in November 1995. This book created a sensation, sold well over a million copies, was translated into many languages, and made a multimillionaire out of Michael Drosnin. If political assassinations can be predicted from the Bible using a computer program, then it is not surprising that Drosnin's book should be so popular!

What do professionals think of Drosnin's book? A review in a journal published by the American Mathematical Society described the book as *"a series of wild, unfounded claims"* and characterized Drosnin as *"deluded by his ignorance."* [8]

The book's reliability can be assessed by examining its dust jacket. As expected, Rabin's assassination figures very prominently on the jacket, which reproduces the Hebrew text of the biblical passage that supposedly predicts it. (The biblical text is rearranged by the standard codes procedure, which need not be described here.) The illustration shows the words "Yitzhak Rabin" crossing some the Hebrew words that are translated into English as "assassin that will assassinate," thus showing a clear correlation between the person ("Rabin") and the verb ("assassinate"). Very impressive indeed!

But something is seriously wrong here. Since the reader of Drosnin's book is not expected to know Hebrew, the words in quotation marks ("Rabin" and "assassinate") are given on the jacket in English, directly below the Hebrew text. *However, these English words are not what the Hebrew text states!* A glance at the Hebrew text on the jacket shows, to anyone who knows Hebrew, that the topic under discussion in this biblical verse is *accidental death*, and *not* assassination. The words are from Deuteronomy 4:42, where the Bible states that someone who kills another person by accident is obliged to live in one of the designated cities of refuge. Drosnin mistranslates the Hebrew verb "kill-by-accident" as "assassinate." The point becomes very clear if one looks at the entire text of Deuteronomy 4:42: *"There he shall flee,* one who kills his fellow-man by accident, *without intention, and he did not hate him previously; he shall flee to one of these cities and live.*" The emphasized words are the correct translation of the Hebrew words on the book jacket.

In the skilled hands of Drosnin, this harmless biblical verse about accidents has been transformed into a subject of high drama. Assassination! Political intrigue! Murder! The back of the book jacket continues in the same vein: "On November 4, 1995, came the confirmation, a shot in the back … the murder that was encoded in the Bible 3000 years ago." The jacket flaps go even further. "The code may be a warning to the world of unprecedented danger, perhaps the real Apocalypse, a nuclear World War." Such exciting words – "nuclear World War" – while the Bible was merely discussing an accidental death! It is easy to understand why Drosnin's book has become a runaway best-seller.

RABBI JOSEPH B. SOLOVEITCHIK'S ESSAY

What is the attitude of outstanding Torah scholars toward possible proofs for the divinity of the Torah? Rabbi Joseph B. Soloveitchik writes in his famous essay, "The Lonely Man of Faith," that such proofs have never been of any importance to him: "*I have never been troubled by the theories of Biblical criticism which contradict the very foundations upon which the sanctity and integrity of the Scriptures rest … We unreservedly accept the integrity of the Scriptures and their divine character.*"[9]

Rabbi Soloveitchik states that the direct existential encounter and the partner-in-dialogue form the vital link between human beings and God[10]:

> "*The togetherness of God and man is indispensable for the covenantal community. The very validity of the covenant rests upon the principle of free negotiation, mutual assumption of duties, and full recognition of the equal rights of both parties concerned with the covenant.*"

With these words, Rabbi Soloveitchik emphasizes that the primary element of faith is to be found within the human spirit. The "man of faith" is neither seeking nor impressed by logical proofs or esoteric codes. The exhortation "seek and you shall find" is directed *inward*, to the depths of the soul, rather than *outward*, to the logical analysis of the philosophers. Ultimately, it is the Kierkegaardian "leap of faith" that brings mankind into communion with the Almighty.[11]

Conclusion

Our discussion has identified three different approaches to faith. There are those who seek to buttress faith by logical arguments and proofs. This approach of the medieval Jewish philosophers has a modern version in the recent phenomenon of the Bible codes.

A second approach examines the physical universe around us and considers the consistency one finds between the discoveries of modern science and the writings of the Bible and talmudic scholars. The harmony between divine writings and the physical world lends important support to one's faith. This approach, much favored by earlier scholars, such as Francis Bacon in the sixteenth century[12] and Maimonides in the twelfth century,[13] is termed "natural theology," that is, gaining understanding of God through the study of nature.

Finally, there is the approach of Rabbi Soloveitchik, whose faith was absolute and unassailable by the world around him. His mastery of the Torah in all its manifestations provided solid bedrock for his belief. Proofs for the existence of God and for the divinity of the Torah played no role in his deep faith.

NOTES

1. E.T. Bell, 1937, *Men of Mathematics* (Simon and Schuster: New York), p. 175.

2. W. Paley, 1802, *Natural Theology* (vol. 5 of Paley's seven-volume *Works*), pp. 1–2.

3. From the Gaon's commentary to Chapter 5 of the kabbalistic work, *Sifra de-Tzni'uta*.

4. See, for example, D. Witztum, Spring 1998, *Jewish Action*, p. 25.

5. D. Witztum, E. Rips and Y. Rosenberg, 1994, *Statistical Science*, vol. 9, pp. 429–438.

6. S. Sternberg, August 1997, *Bible Review*, pp. 24–26.

7. S. Sternberg, 1997, *Notices of the American Mathematical Society*, vol. 44, p. 938.

8. A. Jackson, 1997, *Notices of the American Mathematical Society*, vol. 44, pp. 935–937.

9. J.B. Soloveitchik, 1965, *Tradition*, vol. 7, pp. 9–10.

10. Soloveitchik, p. 29.

11. S. Kierkegaard, 1848, *Concluding Unscientific Postscript* (transl. D. Swenson and W. Lowrie, Princeton University Press, 1941), pp. 90–97.

12. F. Bacon, *The Advancement of Learning*, First Book I.

13. Maimonides, *Mishneh Torah*, Laws Concerning the Principles of the Torah, 2:2.

6

Evolution: Is There a
Problem Here?

Controversy

EVOLUTION

One of the important news stories of 1999 in the area of science and
religion was the decision of the Kansas Board of Education to remove
the subject of evolution from its high school education standards.
Accordingly, high school students in Kansas would no longer be
tested on the subject of evolution, which of course guaranteed that
they would no longer learn the subject. (As is well known, both
students and teachers tend to view the principal task of teaching as
preparing students for examinations.) An election in Kansas had
produced a Board of Education with a majority of creationists. The
new board opposed teaching evolution as a scientifically established
fact, and held that evolution should be viewed as "merely a theory,"
that is, an unproved speculation. The creationist view of the origin of
the animal kingdom – the separate divine creation of each and every
species – was to be treated as an equally acceptable explanation of
present-day fauna.

We wish to examine here *why* the creationists are so opposed to the
idea of biological evolution. There are certainly many other phenomena for which the standard scientific explanation does not correspond

to the literal text of the Bible, but these other subjects do not cause the creationists to demand changes in the school curriculum.

For example, consider the rainbow. Every science class teaches the Newtonian theory according to which the rainbow is a natural phenomenon, caused by white sunlight being separated into the familiar spectrum of colors by drops of rain which act as a prism.

By contrast, the Bible gives a completely different explanation (Genesis 9:13), namely, that the rainbow is of divine origin, a miraculous creation of God whose function is to give assurance to mankind that all life will never again be destroyed by a flood.

Yet, one never hears of creationists insisting that the Newtonian theory of the rainbow be taught as "merely a theory," and that equal time be devoted in the classroom to the biblical account of the rainbow. What is so offensive in their eyes about biological evolution that generates such spirited opposition?

HELIOCENTRIC SOLAR SYSTEM

There is another scientific issue that, in its time, generated even more controversy. This is the question of whether the sun revolves about the earth, or vice versa. As is well known, the seventeenth-century Italian astronomer Galileo was put on trial by the Catholic Church for championing the heliocentric theory. In addition, Galileo had declared that determining how the heavenly bodied move lay within the domain of the astronomer and his telescope, and not that of the Church. Under threat of death, Galileo was forced to recant. However, even after stating publicly that the heliocentric theory was completely false and that only the Church had the authority to decide on matters of astronomy, Galileo was sentenced by the Inquisition to life imprisonment to do penance.[1] In addition, his books were placed on the *Index*, restricted reading for all good Catholics. It was only his long-time friendship with the pope and his infirm old age that saved Galileo from life imprisonment, when Pope Urban VIII decided to commute his sentence to house arrest.

Opposition to the heliocentric solar system was not limited to the Catholic Church. According to *Encyclopedia Judaica*, "The Jewish

writings on astronomy of the eighteenth century and the rabbinical liter-
ature of the nineteenth century are basically derived from the geocentric
theory. In his book, Ma'aseh Tuvia (Venice, 1708), Tuvia Cohn presents the
geocentric theory in its classic form. The heliocentric view is also analyzed,
but is rejected on religious grounds."[2]

The religious controversy regarding which heavenly bodies are
stationary and which move, is very strange. The Genesis account
of creation does not contain a single word favoring the geocentric
system. Just where in the Bible is it written that the sun revolves
around a stationary earth? This matter is touched upon in a passage in
the Book of Joshua. During the battle in the Valley of Ayalon, Joshua
asked God to command the sun and the moon "to stand still" so
that the battle could be completed victoriously in daylight (Joshua
10:12–13), and these heavenly bodies did so. Since Joshua had asked
God to command the sun and moon to stand still, it follows – so
goes the argument – that under ordinary circumstances, the heavenly
bodies are *not* stationary, but revolve about the earth. On the basis
of this rather flimsy exegesis, the Church condemned Galileo to life
imprisonment and ordered his books to be burned! Surely, there must
be something far deeper here.

AGE OF THE UNIVERSE

The third phenomenon that arouses great passion in the creationist
camp is the age of the universe. Creationists are completely opposed
to the multi-billion-year-old universe of the cosmologists, and insist
that the Six Days of Creation of Genesis are to be taken literally as
six 24-hour periods of time. It is easy to show that the creationist
insistence on this point is not based on their general view that every
word in the Bible must be understood literally.

Consider, for example, the "light" that is mentioned on the First
Day of Creation. In his commentary, Rashi brings the kabbalistic
explanation that the Genesis "light" was not *physical* light at all, but
rather *spiritual* light, set aside for the righteous to enjoy in the World
To Come. No creationist seems troubled by the fact that the literal
meaning of the biblical text has thereby been set aside in favor of

a figurative interpretation. In fact, creationists do not hesitate to interpret many biblical verses as meaning something very different from the literal text.

What do the creationists find so unacceptable about an ancient age for the universe? Why do they refuse to understand the Six Days of Creation *figuratively,* as spiritual days, just as Rashi explains the Genesis light *figuratively* as spiritual light? What impels them to *insist* that the Six Days of Creation *must be understood literally,* as 24-hour periods of time, thus leading to a head-on collision with modern science?

Man's Spirituality

It is a cardinal principle of the Bible that man is the ultimate purpose of God's creation –that human beings are the most important creatures in the universe. This idea, implied in Genesis 1:28–29 and explicit in the Talmud,[3] is an article of faith for the religious person. What are the implications for the *physical* position of human beings? If mankind is of central importance *spiritually,* must the same be true *physically?*

If the answer is in the affirmative – that is, if the spiritual importance of human beings must be reflected in their physical importance – then it would be sacrilegious to believe the principles of evolution, according to which, man developed from a simple bacterium. If mankind shares similar physical origins with cockroaches and crocodiles, this would seem to imply that we are equally devoid of any spirituality.

Similarly, it would follow that the planet we inhabit *must* lie at the very *center* of the universe, with the other heavenly bodies whirling around us. Placing the earth among the other planets as just another astronomical body that revolves around the central sun, would be an affront to the divine dignity of man. As a uniquely divine species, it seems inconceivable that mankind should occupy so undistinguished a dwelling place.

Historically, it is clear that it was not for scientific reasons that the geocentric theory of the solar system went unquestioned for 1400 years. The appeal of this theory was based on other considerations. As one book on the history of science puts it[4]:

"The universal popularity of the geocentric theory of the universe was due largely to the important place it gave man in the general scheme of things. This theory was not developed in order to account for all the observed astronomical facts in a completely satisfactory manner. The geocentric theory added immensely to man's already fairly developed sense of his own importance. As time went on and astronomical observations increased in accuracy, more and more complicated assumptions were simply added to the geocentric hypothesis to explain the astronomical data."

Further support for the view that the medieval geocentric theory of astronomy was not based on scientific considerations, is to be found in the trajectories assumed for the heavenly bodies. It was taken for granted that the sun, moon, planets, and stars all revolved about the central earth in *circular orbits*. Even Copernicus, who proposed the revolutionary idea of a heliocentric solar system, still assumed circular orbits for the planets. What was so attractive about the assumption of circular orbits? The correct shape of the planetary orbits, an ellipse, was a well-known geometric figure, one of the conic sections that had been studied in detail by the ancient Greeks. Why did no one consider the possibility that the heavenly bodies move in elliptical orbits?

The explanation is to be found in the prevailing view of the universe. Since it was assumed that God Himself controlled the motion of the heavenly bodies, their orbits must be "perfect." The ideal geometric figure is the circle. It followed, therefore, that the divinely controlled orbits of the heavenly bodies *must* be circles. Even when it became obvious that circular planetary motion was inconsistent with astronomical observations, the circle was never abandoned. It was still taken for granted that the planets moved in circles, but it was now assumed that the center of the circle (called an "epicycle") moved on a different circle. And when even this more complicated theory proved inadequate to explain the ever more accurate data, it was assumed that the circular epicycle must revolve around yet another circular epicycle which itself moved in a circle. Planetary trajectories could *never* be anything but various combinations of circles, however complicated, because theological considerations restricted medieval astronomers to ideal geometric figures. One historian writes[5]:

> *"By the year 1500, over 80 epicycles were required to account for the motions of the five known planets, the sun, and the moon. That astronomers of that day were able to devise so intricate a picture to account for the observed facts is a tribute to their mathematical ability and ingenuity, but not to their scientific judgment."*

This astronomical theory was but one aspect of a comprehensive theological approach to the physical world, which was assumed to be a window to God. The term "natural theology" was introduced to denote the study of God through the study of nature.

Francis Bacon spoke of the two Books of God: the Book of His word (Bible) and the Book of His works (Nature).[6] Faith in God would be enhanced by studying His universe.

By the 1600s, the scientific community finally came to realize that the geocentric theory simply could not explain the detailed observations, no matter how many new epicycles were added. The heliocentric theory gradually carried the day, and mankind was relegated to a "minor" planet, far from the center of the universe.

Just when the creationists became reconciled to this unhappy state of affairs, another blow fell. In 1859, Charles Darwin published his famous book, *On the Origin of Species*, introducing the theory of evolution by natural selection. This theory asserts that the vast panorama of animals and plants, *including man*, all developed from simpler forms. Scientists had already shown that human beings did not occupy a central planet in the *physical* world. And now scientists were claiming that man is not even a special species in the *biological* world. The creationists eventually did come to terms with the heliocentric solar system; indeed, it would be quite absurd to deny it today. But, with regard to evolution, they continue to assert the biological uniqueness of human beings.

As the preceding discussion makes clear, it is *not* the Genesis text that underlies the creationist opposition to evolution, but a matter of *weltanschauung*.

The creationist perception of human spirituality requires for mankind a different physical origin from that of the "lower" animals. This perception sees human dignity as being degraded by the implication that "man's ancestor was a monkey." The creationist concept places each species in its divinely assigned niche, thus maintaining the unique spiritual position of mankind.

The creationists are also completely opposed to the idea of a very ancient universe. Human civilization, the only subject of interest in the Bible, began only a few thousand years ago. If the universe has existed for more than 10 billion years, then the extremely long period before Adam and Eve accounts for 99.9999% of the history of the universe. This presents a serious problem for the creationist. If man is really so important, as Genesis clearly implies, why was his creation delayed for billions of years?

These questions show how the existence of an ancient universe *appears* to cast doubt on the divinity and spirituality of human beings. Once again, it is *not* the text of Genesis, but the creationist *outlook*, that prevents acceptance of the modern cosmological scenario. This outlook implies that the *physical* absence of mankind over such a large part of the history of the universe indicates that man lacks *spiritual* worth. Moreover, it implies that God permitted the universe to have existed for so very long – many billions of years – without any purpose whatsoever. Thus, it follows that the universe *cannot* be as ancient as the cosmologists maintain.

The conflict over the heliocentric theory differs in a very important respect from the conflict over evolution and an ancient universe. In the twenty-first century, our knowledge of astronomy and our achievements in space flight make it impossible to deny the heliocentric theory. However, the origin of the universe and biological evolution deal with events that occurred in the far distant past, when no human beings were present. Therefore, so the creationists claim, who can know what really happened? Perhaps evolution took place, and perhaps not. It's all "merely a theory," and the creationists will not alter their basic religious beliefs because of an unproven theory.

Physical and Spiritual

All these theological problems disappear if one recognizes that the *physical* importance of an object and its *spiritual* value are *unrelated*. Indeed, Judaism often stresses that spirituality is often found in the most humble surroundings.

The recognition that Genesis deals with the *spiritual* rather than the *physical* qualities of mankind, suggests that the biblical phrase, "*God created man*" refers to the *spiritual* features of man, and *not* to creation in the physical sense (i.e., the creation of something from nothing). Jewish commentators explain the verb "created" (*vayivra*) in reference to mankind (Genesis 1:27), as referring to the unique intellectual and spiritual capabilities that characterize human beings. Rashi, Sa'adiah Gaon, Sforno, Radak, and Ramban all comment that man's superiority lies in the areas of speech, knowledge, intellect, and creativity. Indeed, *physically*, human beings are quite ordinary creatures.

CHIMPANZEES AND HUMAN BEINGS

The importance of distinguishing between physical and spiritual characteristics is well illustrated by a comparison between chimpanzees and human beings. At one time, the physical similarities between different species were determined by morphological studies of tissues, skeletons, and physiological systems. Such comparisons between species could only lead to *qualitative* assessments that were sometimes not much more than educated guesses. In the 1970s, however, advances in molecular biology yielded a *quantitative* method,[7] known as the "molecular clock for DNA," for measuring the physical similarities of different species. Studies in this area have produced some surprises. For example, the primate species most closely resembling human beings (*Homo sapiens*) is now known to be the chimpanzee, whereas previously it was thought to be the gorilla.[8]

We shall now lay the groundwork for explaining the molecular clock for DNA: the new quantitative method for determining the relationship between different species. This method is based on analyzing the molecules found in cells. The major component of a cell is a group of large molecules called proteins, which make up 70–80% of the dry weight of a cell. No cell can exist without proteins. A typical cell contains hundreds of different proteins (enzymes are a type of protein), with each carrying out a specialized task needed for the cell to function as a living entity. Each protein consists of a long chain of several hundred elementary, bead-like units called amino acids, of which there are twenty different types. Proteins differ from one another by the number, type, and order of the specific amino acids in their chain. The production of the protein (stringing the beads on the protein "chain") is orchestrated by an entity called a gene.

Each gene is a specific section of the DNA molecule that consists of a very long chain of elementary units called base-pairs. Unraveling the genetic code, the process by which the DNA base-pairs of the gene control the manufacture of the protein chain, is generally considered to be one of the most important discoveries in molecular biology.

With this background, we can describe the molecular clock for DNA method for determining the similarity between different species. A typical protein is hemoglobin, that is present in the blood of animals and plays a key role in transferring oxygen to the cells. The gene for producing hemoglobin contains 861 DNA base-pairs. By comparing the DNA base-pairs of the hemoglobin gene of two different species, one can determine the similarity between these species *without ever examining the animals themselves*. For example, horses are quite different from humans, and correspondingly, it is found that 20% of the DNA base-pairs of the equine hemoglobin gene are different from those of the human gene.[9] As expected, the hemoglobin genes of humans, orangutans, and chimpanzees are very similar to each other, but differ significantly from the gene of cats, which in turn is quite similar to that of lions.

Such studies of the DNA base-pairs of many different genes have established that the chimpanzee, and not the gorilla, is the primate most similar to humans. In fact, the complete array of DNA base-pairs of chimpanzees is 98.5% identical to that of humans,[10] which demonstrates a close physical similarity between chimpanzees and human beings.

This scientific finding troubles some people, who interpret it as showing that humans are not much different from apes. However, such an interpretation completely misses the point. Anyone can observe the *enormous* differences between humans and apes. In the important spiritual realms of creativity, intellect, understanding, and morality, the accomplishments of chimpanzees are totally negligible compared to those of humans. No chimpanzee has ever written a book, painted a picture, developed a scientific theory, expounded a philosophical thought, or given help of any sort to a different species. Indeed, since the physical characteristics of the apes are so similar to those of human beings, one cannot help wondering why their spiritual characteristics are so different. The idea of humans benefiting from divine input naturally suggests itself.

What can one say about man's *physical* capabilities? Humans cannot run like the deer, cannot fly like the bird, cannot swim like the dolphin, cannot climb like the squirrel, and cannot chisel like the beaver – the list extends forever. Quite obviously, God did not bestow any special *physical* talents upon mankind. Thus, there is a clear distinction between the spiritual and the physical. In the former realm, mankind excels, whereas in the latter realm, we are quite ordinary.

The divine creation described in Genesis maintains this dichotomy between the spiritual and the physical. Thus, there is nothing degrading about the fact that mankind occupies a very ordinary planet that revolves around a very ordinary star, and that humans share a common evolutionary history with all other animal species. Man's uniqueness, *created in the image of God*, is not expressed in the location of his planet or in the genes that reside within his cells. Man's uniqueness is to be found in his spiritual qualities. It follows, therefore, that there is no reason for the devout person to oppose the heliocentric theory or to denounce evolution.

The scientific discovery of a very ancient universe is also not a problem for the believer. The scientific time scale – billions of years

without man, followed by only a few thousand years of human civilization – seems so skewed only because of our human perception
of time. We are all busy people who would consider it extremely
wasteful to wait billions of years before getting to the point. But divine
considerations are very different. It is not at all a defect in human
spirituality if mankind did not exist for the vastly greater part of the
history of the universe. The divine importance of human beings is not
to be measured *temporally* by the length of time until our appearance.
The crucial point is that *now* we are here, and within an amazingly
short time, mankind has assumed the mastery of the physical world,
precisely as commanded by the Almighty in Genesis 1:28:

> *"And God blessed mankind, and He told them to be fruitful and
> multiply, and fill the land and conquer it, and rule over the fish
> of the sea and the birds of the heaven and all the creatures that
> inhabit the land."*

THE SECOND CHAPTER OF GENESIS

This idea of the separation of the physical from the spiritual also
appears in the second chapter of Genesis. This alternate creation story
is discussed by Rabbi Joseph B. Soloveitchik.[11] He emphasizes that
the two versions of creation, which he terms Genesis I and Genesis II,
do not indicate two different traditions later joined by an anonymous
editor, as claimed by adherents of biblical criticism. Rather, the two
versions of creation refer to man's dual nature. Genesis I deals with
the physical – *what* happened? – whereas Genesis II deals with the
spiritual – *why* did it happen?

Consider the following example. If I were asked why the water
boils when the kettle is placed on the stove, the explanation I would
give my physics students in the university lecture hall deals with
the distribution of molecular velocities, intermolecular forces, the
thermodynamic phase transition – all the elements of the scientific
theory of boiling. However, if asked the same question at home, I
reply that the water is boiling because I want to drink a cup of tea. This
example shows that the same person may give differing explanations

to serve different purposes. In the same way, Genesis II, which deals with the *why* of creation, is the natural complement to Genesis I.

CREATION OF MAN

Our discussion of the second chapter of Genesis concentrates on verse 2:7: "*God formed man from the soil of the earth, and He blew the soul of life into his nostrils; and man became a living creature.*"

One cannot understand this verse literally – that God formed man from the materials found in the soil – because the chemicals in the soil (inorganic minerals) are very different from those in the human body (organic hydrocarbons). Therefore, one understands this verse *figuratively*, as expressing the dual nature of man – the physical (*"soil"*) and the spiritual (*"soul"*).

The point of verse 2:7 is that man was formed by adding spirituality (*"soul"*) to a physical creature (*"formed from the soil"*). The *physical* creature, mentioned first, could have been formed by evolutionary processes. That is of no interest. The essential qualities of man lie in his *spirituality*, which was infused into the already existing physical entity (*"He [God] blew the soul of life into his nostrils"*). It is this com-bination –physical *and* spiritual – that constitutes "man".

Are there any signs that human beings possess spiritual unique-ness? In fact, the *uniqueness* of the enormous intellectual and creative abilities of human beings could not be more obvious. This has been illustrated in a very interesting way by the success of primatologist Dr. Sue Savage-Rumbaugh, after considerable effort, in teaching a bonobo chimpanzee (the species most similar to man) named Kanzi to recognize as many words as are learned, *completely effortlessly*, by every human child of two and a half.[12] Such an "intellectual achieve-ment" by this chimpanzee only serves to emphasize the vast chasm that separates the mental capabilities of man from those of *every other species.*

Finally, we note that the word "man" (Hebrew *odom*) in Genesis 1:27 (*"And God created man"*) is a generic term, denoting the human species as a whole, and not referring to a particular person (i.e., Adam). The commentator Sforno points out that throughout the Sixth Day of Creation, and again in verse Genesis 2:7 discussed above, the word "man" always "refers to the species of living creatures known as man."[13]

Genesis and Science

AGE OF THE UNIVERSE

Many biblical passages state explicitly that God's concept of time is very different from that of human beings. For example, consider Psalms 90:4, "*A thousand years in God's sight are like a passing day, like a watch [four hours] in the night.*"

This verse tells us that when a period of time is mentioned in the Bible with reference to God, it need not have the same meaning as when the reference is to mankind. Since the Six Days of Creation relate to the era *before* the appearance of man, the appropriate time-scale would naturally be the one related to the divine conception. The *human* 24-hour day begins only *after* the Six Days of Creation, with the Six Days themselves referring to phases in the *divine* program described in Genesis for the creation and development of the universe.

There is additional support for the idea that the Six Days of Creation were not meant to be understood as 24-hour days. The first three days refer to the period *before* the appearance of the sun. Yet, Genesis states "*And it was morning, and it was evening – the second day,*" and similarly for the first and third days. Morning and evening are astronomical events that are associated with the sun. If there is no sun in the sky, there can be neither morning nor evening nor day in the usual sense. Thus, one *must* understand these terms *figuratively*, at least for the first Three Days of Creation. It is not difficult to extend this understanding to all Six Days of Creation. The idea that God's Days of Creation are not the same as human days of 24 hours pervades the writings of Jewish commentators.[14] In his *Guide for the Perplexed* (2:25), Maimonides states that whenever there are serious difficulties in understanding a biblical verse literally, it should be interpreted figuratively, because "the paths of interpretation are not closed to us."

EVOLUTION

Two different verbs appear in Genesis to describe the origin and formation of the animal kingdom. Regarding the primeval sea creatures, Genesis 1:21 states that God "created" them (*vayivra*), whereas regarding the subsequently formed land creatures, Genesis 1:25 states that God "made" them (*vaya'as*). The verbs "create" and "make" denote two quite different processes. "Creation" implies the formation of something *fundamentally new*, either physically (creation *ex nihilo*) or conceptually (a completely new type of entity, such as *life*). By contrast, the process of "making" implies the fashioning of something *complex* from something *simple* (making furniture from pieces of rough wood).

The foregoing discussion suggests the following interpretation of the Genesis text. The first expression (*God created*) relating to the initial sea creatures, refers to the creation of life itself, which first appeared as marine species. The second expression (*God made*) refers to the land animals, that is, to the later formation of the terrestrial species. This understanding of the biblical text is consistent with the scientific idea that present-day animals developed from earlier species.

This view has been proposed by biblical commentators. Consider, for example, the following analysis of Malbim[15]:

> "Here, [on the Sixth Day,] Genesis does not say "God created," because the formation of living animals had already occurred on the Fifth Day. Rather, [on the Sixth Day,] God "made" the mammals, by infusing them [Fifth Day animals] with properties and capabilities that were not previously present. This process cannot be called "creation ex nihilo" but only "making," by which is meant the completion of an object and its improvement."

Note the consistency between Malbim's explanation of the Genesis account of the formation of the animal kingdom and between the scientific concept of evolution.

Conclusion

We have discussed the two subjects regarding which the creationists adamantly oppose the accepted scientific position: evolution and an ancient universe. To these may be added the sharp dispute in the Middle Ages about the heliocentric solar system. In each case, the creationists' opposition is *not* based on the biblical text, but rather on their worldview, which holds that the spiritual value of human beings requires a corresponding physical importance. By contrast, the Torah views physical and spiritual characteristics as being *unrelated*. It follows that the religious person has no cause to oppose the scientific findings about evolution.

NOTES

1. P. Redondi, 1987, *Galileo: Heretic* (Princeton University Press).
2. *Encyclopaedia Judaica*, 1972 (Keter Publishing House: Jerusalem), s.v. "Astronomy", Vol. 3, p. 805.
3. Talmud, *Sanhedrin* 38a.
4. J. Clarke, 1954, *Man and the Universe* (Simon and Schuster: New York), p. 27.
5. Clarke, p. 28.
6. F. Bacon, 1605, *The Advancement of Learning*, ed. W.A. Armstrong (Athlone Press: London, 1975), First Book, I.3, p. 55.
7. C.G. Sibley and J.E. Ahlquist, February 1986, *Scientific American*, pp. 68–78.
8. A.C. Wilson, October 1985, *Scientific American*, pp. 152–153.
9. Wilson, p. 150.
10. F.B.M. de Waal, March 1995, *Scientific American*, p. 84.
11. J.B. Soloveitchik, Spring 1965, *Tradition*, pp. 5–67, especially p. 10.
12. See March 1992 issue of *National Geographic*, pp. 32–33.
13. Sforno, commentary on Genesis 1:26.
14. A. Carmell and C. Domb, eds., 1976, *Challenge* (Feldheim Publishers: New York), pp. 124–140.
15. Malbim, commentary on Genesis 1:25.

7

Free Will, God, and Science

Obvious Statements

We begin our discussion of free will by making two obvious statements. First of all, human beings feel that they possess free will and have the ability to make decisions. This morning, I decided to wear a blue shirt rather than a green shirt; I decided to drink coffee for breakfast rather than tea; I decided to say morning prayers, while my atheist friend decided not to pray. The feeling of possessing free will is shared by everyone, even by those philosophers who use their free will to staunchly deny its existence.

Second, the possession of free will is an essential prerequisite for religion, at least for the Western religions, including Judaism. Central to our religion is the idea that God's commandments obligate us. However, divine commandments can have meaning *only* if we are *able* to perform them, that is, if we have the *free will* to act in accordance with God's laws, or, if we so choose, to act contrary to these laws. This idea appears explicitly in the Bible, where God tells the Children of Israel: *Behold, I have set before you this day, life and good, and death and evil … therefore, choose life.*[1]

In this chapter, we shall show that classical science seems to indicate that free will is only an illusion, and does not, in fact, exist. We will then explain how more recent scientific discoveries pave the way towards a resolution of this paradox.

Science

In order to appreciate the challenge that science presented to the existence of free will, one must first understand some elements of the history of the scientific enterprise.

In 1687, Isaac Newton published the *Principia*, undoubtedly the most important book of science ever written. In this life's work, Newton presented his new discoveries and proclaimed that all physical phenomena can be explained in terms of a few laws of nature – by no means a generally accepted idea at that time. Newton's greatest successes lay in his formulation of the laws of mechanics – his famous three laws of motion – and his discovery of the law of universal gravitation.

The sun, the moon, and the planets have always attracted and mystified mankind, and they have been the object of continuous star-gazing for thousands of years. But, explaining the motion of the heavenly bodies had long eluded the efforts of astronomers. It was not until Newton's discoveries that it finally became possible to explain planetary motion. However, in order to calculate how the heavenly bodies move across the sky, it was not sufficient to *discover* the laws of nature. New mathematical techniques were required *solve the equations* implied by these laws of nature. This challenge, too, was successfully met by Newton, who developed the mathematics of the calculus, which enabled him to solve the equations that describe the motion of the heavenly bodies.

Because the sun is so very massive (containing 99.86% of the mass of the entire solar system), the primary contribution to the gravitational force acting on each planet is due to the sun. Newton proved that if one ignores the much smaller gravitational force due to the other planets, then each planet will move around the sun in an elliptical orbit, as had previously been deduced by Kepler in the early 1600s on the basis of astronomical observations. In subsequent years, the newly-invented telescope permitted much more precise measurements of planetary motion, and these newer data revealed clear deviations from simple elliptical orbits around the sun. The question then arose: Could Newton's theory of gravity also account for these more accurate measurements?

The great practical difficulty in predicting the details of planetary motion stems from the fact that not only the sun, but *every* heavenly body exerts a gravitational force on each planet. Although the gravitational forces due to the other planets are relatively small, because the mass of the planets is so much smaller than that of the sun, these forces are not negligible and must be included. This leads to a very complicated set of equations for planetary motion, which are extremely difficult to solve.

The French mathematician Pierre-Simon Laplace, born a century after Newton, greatly extended Newton's astronomical calculations, and succeeded in explaining all the details of the observed planetary motion. Before the work of Laplace, it was not even known whether the solar system was stable. Even the great Newton had expressed doubts, thinking that the outer planets would eventually drift away from the sun. It was left to Laplace to provide the definitive proof for the stability of the solar system.

The Clockwork Universe

Laplace's life-work is contained in his masterpiece *Celestial Mechanics*, summarized in 1796 in his classic *The Exposition of the System of the World*. The publication of these two books marked the pinnacle of success in explaining planetary motion. An analogy was often made to a clock. Just as the many parts of a clock – wheels, springs, cogs – all work in harmony according to the craft of the clockmaker, in much the same way, the solar system had been shown to function according to the laws of nature.

In the years following Laplace, the scientific enterprise was extended in many different areas, and the various problems posed by nature all seemed capable of resolution by the concerted efforts of talented scientists. This strengthened the feeling that the laws of nature could provide the explanation for *every* observed feature of the physical world. It therefore became natural to ask why the analogy of a clock should be restricted to the solar system. Perhaps the *entire universe* could be viewed as a gigantic clock, propelled forward by the laws of nature. Thus was born the idea of the "clockwork universe."

One of the most important scientific advances of the nineteenth century was the discovery that there are *only two* forces of nature,[2] gravity and electromagnetism. The force of gravity is most evident with regard to very massive bodies, such as the planets and stars. It is this force that restricts us to the surface of the earth, and causes the planets to orbit around the sun.

Electricity and magnetism were once thought to be two different forces. However, in 1864, James Clerk Maxwell showed that they were really different aspects of a single force, called electromagnetism, which acts on every particle that has an electric charge. Since the most important particles in nature, the electrons and protons, are charged, it follows that electromagnetism is a universal force that acts on every atom.

The two forces of gravity and electromagnetism are responsible for all the numerous diverse phenomena that we observe: light, sound, heat, chemical reactions, magnetism, liquids, gases, electricity, weather, geology, fire, and many more. These myriad phenomena are *not* due to a variety of separate forces and/or different laws of nature, but they can *all* be explained in terms of these two fundamental forces.

An equally important accomplishment of the nineteenth century was the recognition that all materials are composed of submicroscopic particles called atoms. Furthermore, it was discovered that there are relatively few types of atoms, and that the millions of materials found in nature, despite their vastly different properties, are merely different combinations of these few basic atoms. The electromagnetic force bonds the atoms together to form molecules, and the same force bonds the molecules together to form crystals, ceramics, metals, glasses, wood, minerals, and all other familiar materials.

Important support for the concept of a clockwork universe came from these two principles: (1) that there exist only two fundamental forces of nature, and (2) that all the materials in the universe are composed of different combinations of a few basic atoms. Therefore, it was not necessary to invoke numerous laws of nature to explain the many different phenomena that are observed. The universe seemed to be based on simplicity, just like the mechanism of a clock. Nevertheless, explaining the detailed behavior of the universe *in practice* proved to be quite a complicated task, because of the many particles that interact with each other. In this respect as well, nature seemed to resemble a gigantic clock. Therefore, the clockwork universe seemed to be the perfect description of nature.

Determinism

An important by-product of the clockwork universe is the concept of determinism, which was first applied to the solar system. Just as the clock mechanism determines how the clock hands will move in the future, the laws of nature determine the future motion of the planets. In other words, the future positions of all the heavenly bodies *are already determined* by their present positions and the laws of nature. This is the central principle of determinism: *the present determines the future.*

The research of Newton, Laplace and other scientists had shown that the future motion of each planet is completely determined by the planet's present position and the force of gravity acting on it due to the other heavenly bodies. Subsequently, the principle of determinism was used to explain terrestrial phenomena as well. In fact, Laplace himself had emphasized that if one knew everything about a system at any particular time, then its future behavior could be predicted in complete detail.

In practice, of course, it is virtually impossible to predict the future behavior of most systems, because most systems are so extremely complicated that one cannot solve the equations that describe their future motion. However, this inability to predict the future is merely a *technical* problem, due to the mathematical difficulties. *In principle,* determinism seemed to be correct: the future behavior of every physical system is already determined by its present state. The principle of determinism soon became one of the cornerstones of science.

The Vital Force

It did not take long before scientists were discussing whether the principle of determinism could be extended to living entities as well – plants and animals. Here, the implications were disturbing. While it might be acceptable to view trees as mere machines acting blindly according to the laws of nature, it was certainly not so simple to view cats and dogs in the same way. Cats and dogs have long been favored as pets precisely because they display warmth, love, and affection for their human master. No one wants to think of his pet as some sort of automated machine.

This problem was solved by postulating the existence of a new force of nature, the "vital force," possessed by all living creatures. This proposal envisioned the existence of an additional *physical* force in nature, whose activity was limited to plants and animals. The proposal of a vital force is quite ancient, dating as far back as Aristotle, who had first suggested it to explain what gives living creatures the special characteristics that are collectively call "life." The proposal of a vital force also solved another puzzle. What fundamental change occurs in an animal when it dies? The dead animal has the same heart, blood, brain, and other organs that it had when it was alive. Since the living and the dead appear to be exactly the same *physically*, both externally and internally, how can one account for their behaviors being so vastly different? The answer of Aristotle was that living creatures possess the vital force, which left the body upon death.

Human beings, who are on a much higher plane than animals, were presumed to possess the vital force in even greater measure. This would explain why humans are able to display more profound behavior than animals. Another important difference between humans and animals is that human behavior is determined by free will in a much wider range of activities than for animals, who are often guided by mere instinct. In all respects, the vital force seemed necessary to explain the unique features of living creatures, and by the Middle Ages, it had become an accepted paradigm of the biological sciences.

In the nineteenth century, scientists began to carry out systematic

studies of the various systems of the living body, including diges-
tion, excretion, the nervous system, respiration, reproduction, and
metabolism. With these studies came the growing recognition that
none of these systems seemed to exhibit any sign of the vital force.
The principles of chemistry and physics seemed perfectly adequate
to explain completely all aspects of the physiological functioning of
living creatures, including human beings.

Since the vital force did not reveal itself in any physiological study
of living animals, it gradually became clear that this special force does
not really exist, and it was eventually banished from the lexicon of
science. With the demise of the vital force, the disturbing problems
returned. What *is* the fundamental physical difference between the
living and the non-living? Just what material is present in living cells,
but absent in inanimate materials, that gives living creatures their
uniqueness? To put it succinctly, what is life? This question has been
much discussed by scientists, and these very words were used as the
title of a famous book (*What is Life?*) written in 1944 by Nobel laureate
Erwin Schroedinger.[3]

Determinism *vs* Free Will

The relationship between determinism and free will is easily stated:
determinism asserts that *free will cannot exist*. The essence of determinism is that *the present determines the future*, whereas free will is
based on the premise that the present *does not* determine the future.
Having free will means that I am now free, *in the present*, to choose
to do *in the future* whatever I wish to do, because the present *does not*
determine the future.

Consider an inanimate object, such as a stone or a planet or a cloud
or some water. Each of these objects consists of a very large number
of atoms and molecules held together by the two forces of nature:
gravity and electromagnetism. Although the forces acting on each
object depend on all other objects that may interact with it, these
other objects are also completely determined by the laws of nature.

Thus, for each object, its future behavior depends *only* on its present state and on the present state of all the other objects. This is what is meant by the assertion that *the present determines the future.*

Since the vital force does not exist, it follows that all living creatures, including human beings, are not fundamentally different in the physical sense from inanimate objects; they are merely much more complex. In particular, human beings do not differ from inanimate objects in any way that would invalidate the basic principle of determinism, namely, that *the present determines the future.*

It is true that human beings possess certain unique mental characteristics, including thought, consciousness, spirituality, self-awareness, and creativity, whose functioning we do not at present understand. However, these mental characteristics do not change the fact that each of us is basically an "object" consisting of many atoms and molecules, just like a stone. Therefore, it appears that human beings should be subject to the same laws that apply to stones. Just as the laws of science decree that stones have no free will, these same laws would seem to imply that people, too, have no free will. There are some philosophers who dispute this statement, claiming that free will *is* consistent with classical science, but it is not difficult to identify the fallacies in these claims.

We are thus faced with a paradox. Human beings certainly *do* possess free will, as each of us feels in our daily lives. However, the laws of science seem to lead to the conclusion that our free will is merely an illusion. How is this paradox to be resolved?

Quantum Mechanics

The greatest scientific revolution of the twentieth century is quantum mechanics. The previous theory of how particles move is called Newtonian mechanics, or classical mechanics, in contrast to the modern quantum mechanics. The most astonishing aspect of quantum mechanics is that it is a *probabilistic* theory of nature.[4] This means that for any physical system, the most that can ever be known are the *probabilities* that certain events will occur in the future. Through the Schroedinger equation, one can calculate the *exact probability* for the occurrence of each of the possible events. However, *which* of the various possible events will *actually occur* in practice, can *never* be known beforehand.

The probabilistic nature of quantum mechanics leads to an important conclusion that is easily stated: the present *does not* determine the future. This non-determination of the future is called *quantum indeterminacy* and is enshrined in Heisenberg's famous *uncertainty principle.*

It is important to emphasize that quantum indeterminacy of the future is *not* due to lack of knowledge. That is, it is *not* correct to state that the future is already determined but no one is able to predict it. Quantum mechanics states that the future cannot be known *even in principle*, because *it has not yet been determined.* This can be illustrated by the following example: If you simultaneously perform the same experiment twice, with the two experiments being *absolutely identical* in every respect, you may nevertheless obtain different results in the two cases. In other words, the *same present* (the same experiment being simultaneously performed twice) has led to *two different futures* (different results in the two cases). This scenario would be quite *impossible* according to classical science. In fact, this phenomenon violates the very essence of Newtonian mechanics.

These startling results of quantum mechanics heralded the demise of the clockwork universe. The characteristic feature of a clock is that its mechanism determines the future movement of the hands. However, this is no longer the case for the quantum universe.

The reader may be wondering how such a dramatic phenomenon (the present *does not* determine the future) was not noticed earlier by Newton and other great scientists. More to the point, our everyday experience tells us just the opposite; that is, throughout our lives, we observe that the present *does indeed* determine the future. Every soccer player knows that if he kicks the ball in the right direction, in a few seconds (the future) the ball will enter the goal to the roar of the crowd. Why do athletes, as well as all the rest of us, remain unaffected and unaware of quantum mechanics in our daily lives?

The answer is that the effects of quantum mechanics are significant *only* in the description of very minute particles. When dealing with macroscopic objects, such as soccer balls, the difference between the quantum prediction and that of classical science is completely insignificant. (A tiny speck of dust weighing less than a *trillionth of a gram* is considered *large* in this context.) When the soccer ball is kicked in the right direction, classical science predicts a goal with 100% certainty, whereas the quantum prediction is that the chances of the ball entering the goal are 99.99999999….%, with only an *extremely* small chance of the ball missing the goal. Since the difference between these two predictions is unmeasurably small, an athlete needs not be aware of quantum mechanics to become a soccer star. As long as one is dealing with large macroscopic objects, the predictions of classical science are correct.[5]

It should be emphasized that quantum mechanics is of utmost importance for understanding the universe. Many fundamental features of the universe depend *crucially* on the principles of quantum mechanics. In fact, the *very existence* of a stable universe would be impossible if the classical laws of nature were correct.

Whenever one deals with submicroscopic particles, such as electrons and atoms, quantum effects are dominant, and classical science gives a completely erroneous description of nature. Twentieth-century studies of atomic structure led scientists to question the validity of classical science. These studies showed, among other paradoxes, that according to the *classical* prediction, each atom in the universe should *spontaneously collapse* within a billionth of a second! Since it is obvious that atoms are perfectly stable and do *not* collapse, it was clear that the principles of classical science are inadequate to describe the universe. Extensive scientific investigations of these paradoxes eventually led to the development of quantum mechanics.

Quantum Mechanics and Free Will

Let us recall the paradox we posed earlier concerning free will. According to classical science, the present determines the future and, therefore free will cannot exist. Quantum mechanics asserts that the present does *not* determine the future, and so it would seem that the paradox has been resolved. However, matters are not that simple. Human beings are clearly macroscopic objects, and we have explained that classical science is completely adequate to deal with such large objects. If quantum mechanics is not necessary to describe human behavior, the paradox remains unresolved. The paradox would disappear only if quantum theory were *essential* to describing thought processes.

The exercise of free will does not require the functioning of the human body as a whole. Free will is determined by our thoughts, and the organ that controls the activity of thinking is the brain. There has been much progress in our understanding of how the brain functions. Neuro-physiological research has shown that every mental process contains at least one crucial step that occurs through the activity of only a very small number of atoms working in concert.[6] We have previously explained that the behavior of individual atoms lies within the quantum realm. Thus, quantum mechanics may indeed play an essential role in thought processes.

How the workings of the brain are translated into the sensations and thoughts of the conscious mind is still shrouded in deep mystery. Nevertheless, one can already say that the process of thinking apparently cannot be described within the framework of classical science, and quantum mechanics may have to be invoked. This is sufficient to lay aside Laplace's paradox of the scientific impossibility of free will.

Free Will and the Omniscience of God

One of the characteristic qualities of God is His omniscience. The omniscience of God – *that He knows everything* – is generally understood to mean that God not only knows everything that has already happened in the past, but that He also knows everything that will happen in the future. In other words, in the present, God already knows the future. If so, we are once again faced with the paradox regarding the existence of free will.

Knowledge of the future implies the absence of free will. It does not matter whether knowledge of future behavior is acquired through the application of the laws of science or whether it is due to the omniscience of God.

The above assertion is easily demonstrated. Consider the following question. How can I say that I am deciding of my own free will to drink coffee for breakfast, instead of tea, if God already knew last night that I would choose to drink coffee this morning? God's prior knowledge of my choice of morning beverage makes it *impossible* for me to choose tea. Otherwise, God would be in error, and not omniscient. Since my choice *has* to be coffee in accordance with God's omniscience, drinking coffee for breakfast is *not* the result of my free-will decision.

It should be emphasized that this paradox really *does* exist. There are various claims – all incorrect – that this problem is only illusory. For example, one cannot resolve the paradox by saying that God gives us the freedom to choose, although He already knows what our choice will be. Such a statement is self-contradictory.

Another incorrect resolution of this paradox is the following: If I were to say that I *know* that Bob will steal money at the first opportunity, I have not thereby denied free will to Bob. If Bob steals money, he is guilty of theft. Similarly, God's knowledge of the future does not deny us free will, and we remain responsible for all our actions.

The fallacy of the above argument is easily demonstrated. When I assert that Bob will steal money, I do not *know* with absolute foreknowledge what Bob will do. I am merely assessing Bob's character traits, and making an educated guess about what he *probably* will do in the future. It is perfectly possible for me to have guessed wrong. Perhaps, unknown to me, Bob has turned over a new leaf and has decided to stop stealing. This remains up to Bob to decide, and herein lies his free will.

The same scenario cannot be applied to God, because, being omniscient, God *cannot be wrong*. If God knows the future, then He knows *for certain* that Bob will steal the money and therefore, Bob *cannot* decide to do otherwise. Because Bob *must* steal the money, he no longer has free will regarding the crime of theft.

Resolution of the Paradox

GOD EXISTS BEYOND TIME

This paradox can be approached from several angles. First, one can simply state that the concept of time – past, present, and future – does not have the same meaning for God, who is eternal, as it does for man, who is finite. Since God is not a physical entity, the meaning of time for God is not dictated by the laws of science. God exists beyond time. Therefore, God's foreknowledge does not necessarily have anything to do with the human concept of the future, and thus is irrelevant to free will.

While this position is logically unassailable, there is an enormous price to pay. According to this argument, God's knowledge of the future is not foreknowledge in the human sense, because to God, the future is something fundamentally different from what it is for human beings. Divine foreknowledge has thus been reduced to a mystical concept without physical content.

THE FUTURE DOES NOT EXIST TODAY

A different approach, favored by this author, is to examine more carefully what is meant by the term "omniscience." Consider first a related quality of God: His omnipotence – *the ability to do everything.* There is a famous riddle, beloved by all schoolchildren, concerning God's omnipotence. Can God make a stone that He cannot lift? If one replies in the negative, then God is not omnipotent because He cannot make the required stone. If one replies in the affirmative, then once again God is not omnipotent because He cannot lift the stone that He has made. Therefore, goes the riddle, we have proven that God is *not*, in fact, omnipotent!

The resolution of this riddle lies in the recognition that such a stone *cannot exist*, because God can lift every stone. Omnipotence implies the ability to make any object that *can exist*. Being unable to make a stone that *cannot exist* is therefore not a defect in God's omnipotence. For exactly the same reasons, God's inability to prove that two plus two equals five is not a proof that God lacks omnipotence.

Let us now apply the same considerations to God's quality of omniscience – *complete knowledge of everything*. Omniscience means knowing *whatever is possible to know*. However, it is *impossible* for God to know the future, because the future *does not yet exist*. In other words, the future is *not* up ahead, awaiting our arrival; we formulate it as we go along. Since the future has not yet happened, there is nothing that can be known *now* about the events of tomorrow. Therefore, it is *not* a defect in God's omniscience to say that He does not know the future.

Divine Pronouncements

In many places in the Bible, God announces that some particular event will happen in the future. If, as here asserted, God does not know the future, how is it possible for God to state with certainty that a particular event will occur?

The answer is that human beings also possess the ability to make statements about the future. For example, I might announce to my students that there will be a test in physics next Monday. My announcement does not mean that I have suddenly been blessed with the power to predict the future. It simply means that I have the ability to make that event – the test next Monday – happen, and I have decided to exercise that ability. Similar considerations apply to God's pronouncements regarding what will happen in the future.

Summary

Questions regarding the existence of free will are not new. Paradoxes concerning free will have furnished grist for the mills of philosophers throughout the centuries. There are, of course, many more aspects of these complex questions than could be dealt with here. We have chosen to restrict the discussion to those points that can be formulated in terms of science, and have attempted to show that modern science has something of value to contribute to the ancient conundrum of whether or not human beings possess free will.

The Torah relates that God commands us to do good deeds. God bestows upon every human being the ability to decide, *without His interference,* whether to obey God's commandments. This is the essence of free will.

NOTES

1. Deuteronomy 30:15, 19.
2. The two nuclear forces, which were discovered in the 20th century, do not influence the behavior of macroscopic objects, and therefore are not relevant to our present discussion.
3. Schroedinger proposes that the unique features of living organisms are explained by the quantum theory and the ingestion of negative entropy. The former guarantees the stability of the genetic mechanism for heredity (now referred to as the DNA genetic code), and the latter explains why living systems do not decay by reaching equilibrium with their surroundings. Schroedinger explains how the structure of the cell enables it to carry out reproduction and metabolism, the two basic functions that distinguish the cell from inanimate objects.
4. See, for example, R. Feynman, 1985, *QED – The Strange Theory of Light and Matter* (Princeton University Press).
5. There are some special cases for which the behavior of large macroscopic objects is dominated by quantum mechanics, such as liquid helium and radioactive material, but these exceptions do not affect the present discussion.
6. The most widely used description of mental processes is based on the model of neural networks, developed in the 1980s in a series of pioneering articles by Professor John Hopfield of Princeton University. There are crucial steps in the functioning of the neural network that involve the activity of only a few atoms working together.

8

Miracles: Natural and Supernatural

Question

What is a miracle? The obvious answer is that a miracle is a super-natural event – a clear deviation from the laws of nature. The laws of nature determine the functioning of the physical world in "normal" times, but sometimes God sets aside these laws for a special purpose, thus producing a miraculous event. A particularly striking example related in the Bible was the splitting of the Red Sea at the time of the Exodus from Egypt, a divinely ordained event defying the laws of nature, which saved the Children of Israel from the approaching Egyptian army led by Pharaoh.

Miracles and the Laws of Nature

It is the thesis of this chapter that the commonly held perception of a miracle being a supernatural event, incompatible with laws of nature, is not in keeping with Jewish tradition. To demonstrate this, we consider a famous miracle, the miracle of Purim that resulted in the salvation of the Jews from the evil decrees of Haman.

THE MIRACLE OF PURIM

The miracle of Purim is the subject of the Book of Esther, which relates how the beautiful Esther used her position as beloved queen to cause the downfall of the wicked Haman and the cancellation of his murderous decrees against the Jews. Which of the events described in the Book of Esther were supernatural? Was it supernatural for a Jewish woman to be unusually beautiful? Was it supernatural for this beautiful woman to be chosen queen when the king did not know that she was Jewish? The famous sixth chapter in the Book of Esther relates the crucial events that occurred when the king had difficulty falling asleep one night. Was this a supernatural event? Does not everyone occasionally experience difficulty in falling asleep? In his insomnia, the king asked for the royal chronicles to be read to him. Was this supernatural? In fact, it is clear that *none of the events described in the Book of Esther was supernatural*! What, then, is meant by the "miracle of Purim"?

According to Jewish tradition, a miracle is an unusual event whose miraculous aspect lies in the fact that the event occurs *precisely* when needed to accomplish an important result. In other words, miracles are characterized by their *timing*. The Book of Esther describes how the salvation of the Jews came about through a series of unusual events, none of which involved a breach of the laws of nature. The Jews were saved because each event occurred at *exactly* the right time. That was the miracle of Purim.

THE MIRACLE OF THE SPLITTING OF THE RED SEA

The most dramatic miracle recorded in the Torah is surely the splitting of the Red Sea. However, even this greatest of miracles did not involve a deviation from the laws of nature. The event is described in Exodus 14:21: *"Moses raised his hand over the Sea, and God ordered a powerful east wind to pass over the Sea all that night, causing the seabed to become dry land; and thus the waters split."* In other words, we are told that a hurricane struck the Red Sea, driving the waters from the seabed and leaving a path of dry land. This is a natural event which has been observed to occur on occasion in various bodies of water. Therefore, what is miraculous here?

The miraculous aspect of the splitting of the Red Sea resides in the *timing* of the event. With Pharaoh and the Egyptian army fast approaching, and the Israelites trapped by the Red Sea, the hurricane *suddenly* occurred to create a path of dry land in the seabed, thus enabling the Israelites to escape. Moreover, when the Egyptians continued to pursue the Israelites along this newly formed path, the hurricane *suddenly* stopped, causing the waters to return to the seabed, and thus drowning the entire Egyptian army.

The Israelites were saved by the *timing* of these events – the sudden appearance and the equally sudden disappearance of the hurricane, precisely when they were required and it is this fortuitous timing that constitutes the miracle of the splitting of the Red Sea. Indeed, with few exceptions, every miraculous event described in the Torah is depicted as compatible with the laws of nature. The laws of nature were created by God and He does not lightly abandon them. In fact, our tradition emphasizes that *"the world functions in its regular manner"*[1] and that *"one may not rely on miracles."*[2]

God and the Physical World

The above discussion should not be interpreted as implying that God does not interact with the physical world. This is certainly not the case. Indeed, Maimonides emphasizes that one may not believe that the laws of nature *always* apply and that supernatural events *cannot* occur.[3] Such a belief is forbidden because this would imply that God never influences the world – not now and not in the past – a belief that denies basic principles of the Torah. Therefore, the key question before us is not *whether*, but *how*, God influences events.

The Talmud answers this question by saying that divine providence is bestowed upon the world in a manner that is "hidden from the eye."[4] In other words, the framework in which God interacts with the world is *within* the laws of nature. God's intervention does not generally involve overtly supernatural events. Miracles occur, man's needs are provided, problems are solved – and it is all *"hidden from the eye."*

Biblical Miracles

An interesting feature of those biblical miracles that clearly *were* deviations from the laws of nature is that they were invariably performed in private, with no one witnessing the miraculous event, except possibly the recipient of the divine favor. Consider, for example, the famous miracles performed by Elisha.

THE MIRACLE OF THE OIL

One of Elisha's miracles occurs to help a destitute widow who appeals to him to save her from creditors who are about to take her two sons into slavery because she cannot pay her debts (II Kings 4:1–7). When Elisha hears that the widow has nothing in her house except a single jar of oil, he tells her to borrow from her neighbors as many empty vessels as possible, and to fill them from her own jar of oil. The widow does so, miraculously filling all the vessels from her single jar. This provides her with a large supply of oil which she sells, enabling her to pays her creditors and thus save her sons from slavery.

The relevant point for our discussion is that Elisha explicitly instructs the widow *"to close the door behind her and behind her children"* (4:4) before she begins pouring the oil. This strange instruction, which she carries out, ensures that *no one* witnesses this miracle except the widow herself. It was *"hidden from the eye."*

Another interesting point pertains to the question of why oil used as the vehicle for this miracle, with the widow given the bothersome task of borrowing vessels from her neighbors and then selling the oil? Why did Elisha not miraculously provide her with, say, silver and gold? The answer is that the widow *already* had some oil, and therefore increasing the amount would not necessarily appear miraculous to her neighbors, whereas the sudden appearance of silver and gold among the destitute widow's possessions, would be an obvious miracle.

THE MIRACLE OF THE REVIVAL OF THE CHILD

On another occasion, Elisha granted a son to a childless woman in gratitude for her kindnesses to him (II Kings 4:14–36). The fact that this sterile woman gives birth was miraculous. This miracle was *"hidden from the eye"* because there are many recorded cases of women who conceived a child only after many years of barrenness. The story of the woman's child involves a further miracle. One day, while working in the fields with his father, the boy complains of terrible pains in his head. He is carried to his mother and, in her arms, he dies. The mother lays the child down, and rushes to Elisha to complain that she had been given a child only to have him die. Elisha and the distraught mother together hurry to the child, who lies motionless. At this point, the miracle occurs. Elisha restores the child to life and presents the living child to his mother, who is overwhelmed with gratitude.

In relating this event, the Bible states that *"Elisha entered [the room where the child lay motionless] and he closed the door behind him"* (4:33). Thus, *no one* witnessed the restoring of the child to life, *not even his mother.* It was "hidden from the eye."

Even more interesting is what Elisha did behind the closed doors (4:34): *"Elisha lay on the boy, and put his mouth upon the boy's mouth, his eyes upon the boy's eyes, and his palms upon the boy's palms. Elisha thus stretched himself out over the boy, and warmed the boy's body."* These actions of Elisha are clearly reminiscent of artificial respiration, and they raise the possibility that perhaps the boy was, in fact, not dead at all. Perhaps the boy was only thought to be dead because he was not breathing and had no pulse, and Elisha succeeded in reviving him through the application of standard methods of resuscitation. Today, physicians regularly use such methods to revive patients who exhibit no pulse and no breathing. In other words, *even the reader of the Bible* is left in doubt as to whether or not a supernatural event really occurred behind the closed doors, where matters were *"hidden from the eye."*

One could go on and analyze other biblical miracles in the same way. The central point is clear. The purpose of God's miracles is to accomplish some important result, and not to impress the audience with flashy showmanship. Therefore, the Bible invariably *minimizes* the supernatural aspect of its miracles.

Public Miracles

There is one exception to the above principle. Sometimes, public showmanship is the *entire purpose* of the miraculous event. That is, the miracle has no purpose *except* to demonstrate the power and glory of God. In such a case, the *public* dimension of the miracle assumes paramount importance.

THE PROPHETS OF BAAL

The most famous case of a public miracle is surely the challenge of Elijah to the prophets of Baal. Elijah wants to demonstrate that Baal is nothing but a powerless idol, whereas the God of Israel is omnipotent. To this end, he proposes a public contest between himself and the prophets of Baal. Each side is to call upon his deity to produce the miracle of consuming a sacrificial bull through divine fire. The Bible describes in detail how Elijah publicly mocks and ridicules the prophets of Baal for the inability of their deity to produce the required fire (1 Kings 18:19–39). It is then Elijah's turn. He quietly prays to God, who responds with a most dramatic miracle, performed in the presence of everyone, which convinces the Israelites of the glory and truth of the God of Israel.

The purpose of this miracle was to show the Israelites how useless and foolish it would be for them to continue worshipping the impotent Baal. Therefore, the miracle had to be performed publicly to accomplish its aim.

THE TEN PLAGUES

The Ten Plagues, which occurred immediately preceding the Exodus of the Children of Israel from Egypt, are another example of a public miracle. This dramatic series of miracles was not designed to destroy the Egyptians or to punish them. For that purpose, one single plague would have sufficed. The twofold purpose of these miracles is stated explicitly:

> *Pharaoh should know that there is none like Me in all the world…*
> *so that My name may be declared throughout the world.*
>
> (Exodus 9:14, 16)

> *So that you [Israel] may tell your sons and your sons' sons, how I*
> *humiliated the Egyptians and of My wonders with which I afflicted*
> *them, so you may know that I am God.*
>
> (Exodus 10:2)

The Bible thus explains that the purpose of the Ten Plagues was to demonstrate the glory of God to the Israelites, and also to the entire world. Therefore, these miracles had to be performed publicly in order to accomplish their aim.

Other Views

Theologians have long debated the question of how God interacts with the physical world, often referring to the divine mode of inter-action as the "causal joint." One school of thought holds that there is something basically wrong with the idea of God interfering with the laws of nature by performing miracles. The theologians of this school start with the premise that "the existence of an orderly world, having definite laws of nature, is an expression of the faithfulness of God."[5] If one attributes divine meaning to the laws of nature, it might seem to follow that miracles, as deviations from the laws of nature, would constitute a violation of divine faithfulness.

As we have seen, the Jewish tradition is quite different. Maimonides considers belief in the existence of God's miracles to be a basic element of Jewish faith.[6] Moreover, there is no real difference between saying that God does not interact with the physical world and saying that God does not exist. We do not conceive of God as a Great Watchmaker who created this magnificent clockwork universe in the distant past but now leaves it to function on its own. Rather, the God whom we worship is continually sustaining and helping His creatures, usually in a manner that is hidden from the eye, and on occasion openly and directly.

Miracles Today

Do miracles occur today? Jewish tradition asserts that miracles occur all the time, but since they are hidden from the eye, their existence is a matter of belief.[7] The person of faith prays to God for help when he is ill, and, if restored to health, thanks God for His intervention. The non-believer, in the same situation, attributes the cure to medical treatment. The day-to-day miracles of God forever remain *"hidden from the eye."*

NOTES

1. Maimonides, *Mishnah Torah*, Laws of Kings, 12:1.
2. For a complete listing of talmudic sources for this principle, see Rabbis M. Berlin and S.Y. Zevin, eds., 1973, *Talmudic Encyclopedia*, vol. 1, pp. 679–680.
3. Maimonides, *Guide for the Perplexed*, Part II, Chapter 25.
4. Talmud, *Baba Metzi'a* 42a.
5. J. Polkinghorne, 1998, *Science and Theology* (SPCK: London), p. 84.
6. Maimonides, *Guide for the Perplexed*, Part II, Chapter 25.
7. Rabbi M. Feinstein, 1964, *Igrot Moshe – Orach Haim* (Moriah Publishers: New York), vol. 4, Responsum 48, p. 79; vol. 2, Responsum 111, pp. 299–300.

9

Prayer and Divine Providence

Questions

What is the purpose of prayer? Those who pray would probably answer that they are asking God to provide for their needs, both for specific help in times of crisis as well as for the daily needs of every human being. However, a little reflection shows that such an understanding of prayer makes sense only if one equates God to an earthly ruler. A human king is unaware of our specific needs, and hence we must ask him for what we require. But one can hardly apply the same reasoning to God, imagining that He does not know our needs and problems and, therefore, we must inform Him to solicit His help.

Moreover, the framework of our prayers raises additional problems. The basic Jewish prayer, recited three times a day, is called the *amidah* (literally "standing," because the supplicant "stands before God"). The *amidah* consists of eighteen blessings (and therefore is often referred to as *Shemoneh Esreh* – "eighteen").[1] The first three blessings praise God, and the final three thank Him for favors bestowed in the past. In the middle twelve blessings, the heart of the *amidah* prayer, the supplicant asks God to grant physical and spiritual needs (sustenance, health, wisdom, forgiveness of sins, *etc.*).

We have already presented the problem regarding the middle twelve blessings: Why do we have to ask God for our needs? However, there is even greater difficulty in understanding the purpose of the first three and final three blessings. Is God a vain Deity who delights in our praise and expects to hear gratitude for past favors? This is exactly how one would approach an earthly king, because powerful rulers often are vain creatures who are used to hearing lavish praise from their subjects and take offense if such praise is omitted. How dare one attribute such petty qualities to the Almighty!

Thus, we return to our original question: Why does one pray? And why is the text of our prayers formulated in such a seemingly inappropriate way?

The Purpose of Prayer

These questions suggest that one does not pray to God because He needs our prayers. Moreover, the idea that prayers can somehow "influence" God to grant the petitioner good health, long life, and other benefits is utterly divorced from Jewish tradition. The Sages of the Talmud direct severe criticism against those who pray in the expectation that their devout prayers will be answered, thus reducing God to a cosmic vending machine that dispenses benefits upon the insertion of appropriate spiritual tokens in the form of prayers.[2]

The true purpose of prayer is *not* to petition God; instead, our prayers serve to remind *us* that God is the underlying source of all our needs. In other words, it is *we* who require prayer, and not God. As pointed out by Nachmanides[3] and others,[4,5] the purpose of prayer is to emphasize *to ourselves* our dependence upon divine providence, and to help us focus our attention on the deep relationship between ourselves and God.

Maimonides states that if people were on a sufficiently high intellectual and spiritual plane, there would be no need for prayer.[6] In that case, by merely thinking about the central role of God in the universe, we would recognize that it is God who provides all our needs. However, because of our spiritual and cognitive limitations, just thinking about God is not enough. It is also necessary for us to perform the *act of praying to God*. Our thoughts and concentration during an act of prayer enables us to assimilate the fact that God is the true source of our bounty. Emphasizing this point in our prayers helps us to understand and appreciate our dependence on divine providence.

The true purpose of prayer finds expression in the Hebrew word for *"pray."* In all European languages, the word for "pray" means "request" (German *beten*; French *prier*; Russian *molit'sya*). Also in English, the word "pray" is an old form of the word "request." In Hebrew, however, the word for praying, *hithpalel*, means "reflect" or "to think about."[7] This corresponds to the explanation of Maimonides, namely, that one prays in order to reflect upon our dependence on God.

This point also explains the structure and content of our prayers. As explained above, the true purpose of prayer is to enable the *petitioner* to achieve spiritual elevation. Since our prayers are intended to help *us* to better appreciate the centrality of divine providence in our lives, it is most beneficial *to us* to pray in a manner that is familiar.

The accepted manner of petitioning a monarch is to begin with words of praise, then to list one's requests, and to conclude with words of gratitude for past favors. Therefore, this is also the structure of our daily prayers to God.

Spiritual Elevation Through Prayer

The Bible stresses that we should be constantly aware of his or her dependence on God (Deuteronomy 11:10–12). The recognition that God plays a central and essential role in our lives raises us to a higher spiritual level. This is the importance of prayer. Moreover, upon reaching this higher level, we becomes more worthy of receiving God's material and spiritual blessings. This is the sense in which prayers may be said to be "answered." Becoming a better person makes one more deserving of receiving divine blessings, and prayer is an important means of achieving that betterment.

If a man or woman should receive God's bounty through prayer, it is because those prayers made the person more worthy, and *not* because God had been informed of the person's needs. It is very important to understand this subtle but crucial distinction.

Another Question

Underlying the idea of praying to God to obtain our needs is the assumption that God really is the underlying source of our daily needs. Perhaps this assumption implies that if one requires sustenance, then one need do nothing but pray to God? If everything indeed comes from God, then perhaps all our efforts to earn a living have no meaning. Going to work to provide for one's livelihood would be nothing but an exercise in self-deception. Worse! Working for a living could even be understood as a sign of lack of faith, indicating that one questions the rule of God.

This point of view is not without its adherents. There is a non-Jewish religious tradition (well known in the United States) according to which an ill person may do nothing *except* pray to God for the restoration of health. This religion believes that since one's health is determined by God alone, seeking medical aid shows lack of faith and is strictly forbidden. Such beliefs occasionally hit the headlines when a seriously ill child is involved, and his parents refuse to let physicians treat the child on the grounds that rendering medical aid is a violation of their religious beliefs. If the child dies, when his life could have been saved by applying standard medical procedures, then the public is outraged and the police may even file charges of willful homicide against the parents.

But why? The attitude of the parents, so objectionable to the public, would seem to be the natural conclusion to be drawn from the institution of prayer. Indeed, if it is not God who determines sickness and health, then why does one pray to God for health? The parents who have outraged the entire community, religious and irreligious alike, by letting their child die appear to be the only logical persons in the tragic event.

Do Prayers Influence God?

Many people believe that prayers influence God to fulfill the petitioner's requests, and a greater number of prayers leads to greater influence. This implies that someone who has many people praying for his long life should live to a ripe old age. Since church and synagogue services in Britain traditionally include prayers for the monarch's long life, it follows that the British royal family should enjoy marked longevity.

In the nineteenth century, this idea was taken very seriously, and the influence of prayer was investigated quantitatively by the British anthropologist and meteorologist Sir Francis Galton (a cousin of Charles Darwin). Galton compared the longevity of the royal family with that of other groups of Englishmen who were not the subject of prayers (landed gentry, scientists, authors). Not surprisingly, he found no sign of increased longevity among the royals. Quite the contrary. The data showed, for example, that the landed gentry lived an average of six years longer than the members of the royal family. When Galton published his negative results in 1872 (under the title "Statistical Inquiries into the Efficacy of Prayer"[8]), many members of the British public were scandalized.

In recent years, the question of whether prayers influence health has again been taken up, and placed on a "scientific" basis. Indeed, it has become fashionable nowadays to publish statistical studies of the health benefits to seriously ill patients resulting from prayer. One such article, published in 1998 in a reputable medical journal, reports[9]:

> *"A six-month blind study was carried out on 40 patients with* AIDS *who were told that they might or might not be receiving distant healing treatments [prayers for their health] representing a variety of religious traditions. It was found that patients who received such treatments had a statistically significant more benign course than the control subjects, who did not receive such treatments."*

The article states that although *all* the patients were told the same thing – that someone *might* be praying for them – the physicians found improved health *only* for those patients who actually *were* the subject of prayers.

This author has observed rabbis and ministers enthusiastically quoting such results, taking great pains to emphasize their "scientific" authenticity. Needless to say, the typical clergyman's knowledge of statistics leaves something to be desired; and the same can be said of the physicians who publish such findings. The abysmal lack of knowledge of statistics displayed in some of these articles was lamented by Professor William Kruskal, an eminent statistician at the University of Chicago, in a recent presidential address to the American Statistical Association.[10]

The Jewish View

If one sincerely believes that God is the ultimate source of man's worldly benefits, does taking active steps to provide for one's needs indicate a lack of faith?

This fundamental question has been discussed in Jewish writings throughout the generations. For example, Rabbi Moshe Feinstein, a major twentieth-century authority on Jewish law, was asked in 1964 whether there was a prohibition, however slight, in taking out an insurance policy? Does this act show lack of faith in divine providence?

Rabbi Feinstein's answer was quite unequivocal.[11] He stated in no uncertain terms not only that the questioner is permitted to take out insurance to protect his business and property, but that there is even an obligation to do so, in addition to whatever other means are prudent in the normal course of business. One may not neglect a standard business practice and rely instead on divine providence. To do so would violate the talmudic principle that *"it is forbidden to rely on miracles."*[12]

Rabbi Feinstein went on to say that similar considerations apply to all daily needs. Relying on prayers for one's sustenance is completely contrary to Jewish tradition and is strictly forbidden. Rabbi Feinstein emphasized that one must work and earn money for our livelihood. Similarly, a person with a health problem is obligated to obtain the best available medical assistance. Under no circumstances may one avoid medical help, depending solely on miracles and divine providence for the restoration of health.

Rabbi Feinstein's opinions are characteristic of the views of the leading Jewish authorities. For example, in an interesting twelfth-century responsum to the Jews of Provence in southern France, Maimonides sharply criticized, as akin to idolatry, their obsessive interest in astrological and eschatological calculations.[13] He wrote that ancient Israel made the same mistake and paid dearly for it. Because the Israelites were preoccupied with astrological calculations, they neglected to carry out essential military preparations in the face of the impending Roman attack. Maimonides stated that this neglect was responsible for the destruction of the Temple and for the Israelites being driven from their homeland. They should have spent more time and effort in taking the appropriate military and political steps to prepare Israel to meet the Roman military threat. Had they done so, they might have been more successful against the enemy.

The point of Maimonides is clear. When faced with a military threat, the correct response is to make the military and political preparations necessary to confront it. Note that Maimonides did *not* criticize the Israelites for not praying more devoutly or for not doing good deeds. Nor did Maimonides say that one may not pray *in addition* to preparing military defenses. But to rely *only on prayer*, and neglect appropriate preparations, is not the proper way. A *physical* threat is to be countered by *physical* means. This is yet another example of the important talmudic principle: "*It is forbidden to rely on miracles.*"

Divine Providence

As we have seen, prayers do not replace human endeavor in providing for sustenance, health, success on the battlefield, *etc.* What, then, is the role of divine providence in the functioning of the world?

Rabbi Feinstein stressed that it is a fundamental Jewish belief that God is the ultimate provider of all man's needs.[14] Nevertheless, there is no contradiction between this belief and the requirement that people must work for a living. God uses *natural means* to provide us with our needs, blessing *our own efforts* to obtain sustenance, health, and so on, and giving us the wisdom that enables us to take appropriate steps to obtain them. It is through the *interplay* of human endeavor and divine providence that we receive what we require. Were man not to do his part, God's help would not be forthcoming.

The parents of a seriously ill child are *obligated* to take appropriate medical steps. And if they refuse to do so, and confine their efforts to praying to God to restore their child's health, it is the Jewish view that the parents are murderers, at least indirectly. By avoiding medical help, they prevent God from bringing about the cure of the child.

The Talmud emphasizes that divine providence is only bestowed in a manner that is *"hidden from the eye."*[15] God does not invoke miracles in order to solve our problems or to provide for our needs. In fact, the Talmud forbids one to pray to God for an overt miracle, giving the following example.[16] If a person sees from afar that a house is on fire, he is not allowed to pray that the burning house should not be his. The reason is that the people in the town already know which house is burning. Suddenly shifting the fire damage from one house to another house would require a miracle observed by all the townspeople, and this will never happen. Therefore, such a prayer is deemed "in vain" and is strictly forbidden.

Consequences

There is an interesting consequence of the view that God interacts with the world on a daily basis in a manner that is hidden from the eye. Both the devout believer and the morally motivated non-believer may *act* similarly. Each will do his utmost to solve his problems in a morally upright way. The difference between the two lies in their *belief* and in their *understanding* of the involvement of God in the solution to their problems. The man of faith places his trust in God, whereas the non-believer does not.

Prayers to God are an essential element of the Jewish religion, serving as a channel between man and his Creator. However, this does *not* imply that prayers are a means for the petitioner to obtain God's bounty. Jewish belief does not include holy shrines whose visitation brings miraculous cures, nor special prayers and ceremonies whose performance yields divine intercession. The ways of God are – and will forever remain – inscrutable.

The power and importance of prayer lies in its ability to elevate man *spirituality* by enhancing his *recognition* of the central role played by God in human affairs. Such spiritual elevation transforms the petitioner into a better person, and thereby makes him more worthy of receiving divine providence. One merits God's blessings by observing His commandments: those between man and man and those between man and God.

NOTES

1. The current version of the *amidah* actually consists of nineteen blessings. The nineteenth was added after the original formulation, and therefore, the *amidah* is still popularly referred to as *Shemoneh Esreh*.
2. Talmud, Berachot 32b, explanation of *Tosaphot*. See also *Tikunai HaZohar*, p. 22a.
3. Nachmanides, *Commentary on the Torah*, Exodus 13:16, near the end.
4. *Sefer HaChinuch*, Commandment 430 – Blessings, "Reasons for the commandment".
5. *Otzar HaTephilah*, Introduction, Section A, "What is Prayer?", pp. 8–11.
6. Maimonides, *Guide for the Perplexed*, Part III, Chapter 32.
7. The meaning of the Hebrew word for "prayer" is given in Genesis 48:11.
8. F. Galton, August 1872, *The Fortnightly Review*, New Series 12, pp. 125–135.
9. F. Sicher, E. Targ, D. Moore, and H.S. Smith, 1998, *Western Journal of Medicine*, vol. 169, pp. 356–363.
10. W. Kruskal, 1988, *Journal of the American Statistical Association*, vol. 83, pp. 929–940.
11. Rabbi M. Feinstein, 1964, *Igrot Moshe – Orach Haim* (Moriah Publishers: New York), vol. 2, Responsum 111, pp. 299–300.
12. For a complete listing of talmudic sources for this principle, see Rabbis M. Berlin and S.Y. Zevin, eds., 1973, *Talmudic Encyclopedia*, vol. 1, pp. 679–680.
13. Maimonides, "Letter to the Sages of Montpellier" in *Letters of the Rambam*, Part III, Letter 33.
14. Rabbi M. Feinstein, 1964, *Igrot Moshe – Orach Haim* (Moriah Publishers: New York), vol. 4, Responsum 48, p. 79; vol. 2, Responsum 111, pp. 299–300.
15. Talmud, Baba Metzi'a 42b.
16. Talmud, Berachot 54a.

On Science
and the Bible

10

Chaos, Rain, and the Bible

Questions

The economy of ancient Israel depended crucially on rain, as does that of modern Israel. Without sufficient rain in the winter season, the crops could fail, drinking water might be lacking, and disaster would strike. Rain is a matter of great importance in Jewish tradition. Accordingly, at the end of the hot, dry Israeli summer, on the festival of *Shemini Atzereth*, we pray to God for the blessing of rain. Indeed, one of the most moving prayers in our liturgy is the special prayer for rain. The following lines are from this prayer.[1]

> *May God send rain from the heavenly source,*
> *To soften the earth with its crystal drops.*
> *God has named water as the symbol of His might;*
> *Its drops refresh all who have the breath of life,*
> *And revive those who praise His powers of rain.*

In years of drought, the Rabbis would ordain a series of special prayers and fasts, appealing to God to have mercy on His people and send the precious rain. Indeed, an entire tractate of the Talmud, Ta'anith, is primarily devoted to the order of the special prayers and fasts incumbent upon the community when there is no rainfall.

The basic assumption that underlies the special prayers and fasts for rain is that one can never know whether or not the needed rains will come and, therefore, one must appeal to God's mercy. The inability of scientists to accurately predict the next week's rain is very obvious. Just plan a picnic on the basis of last week's weather forecast! However, what about the future? Surely the day will come when the accuracy of weather forecasting is so improved that meteorologists *will* be able to make long-range weather predictions. What, then, will be the meaning and purpose of our prayers for rain?

An example is useful here. Even more important than the rain is the sunshine. It would be absolutely catastrophic if the sun did not rise in the morning and shine during the daytime. Without sunlight, all plants would soon die, and the end of animal life would quickly follow. Nevertheless, the Rabbis of the Talmud never ordained special prayers beseeching God to cause the sun to shine.

The reason that there are no prayers for sunshine is that the shining of the sun is an astronomical event that occurs *with certainty*, in accordance with the laws of nature. It is unnecessary, in fact *inappropriate*, to pray to God to maintain the laws of nature. The laws of nature are *always* operative, unless God decides to invoke a miracle. Therefore, if the prediction of rain were to become a *certainty* as a result of vastly improved weather forecasting, it would become similarly inappropriate to pray for rain.

Weather Forecasting

In the past, weather forecasting consisted of observing cloud patterns, wind speeds, and temperature, and using these data to predict the weather. This method limited forecasting to one day ahead. Beyond that, the weather could not be predicted because the cloud patterns of future days did not yet exist, and there was no way to determine which cloud patterns would form.

There is no *conceptual* difficulty in long-range weather forecasting. Meteorology, the science of weather forecasting, deals with the atmosphere.[2] The atmosphere consists of a known mixture of gases (oxygen, nitrogen, argon, carbon dioxide, and, of course, water vapor), which, under certain circumstances, form rain. The energy input to the atmosphere is known; it comes from the sun and the surface of the earth. The source of atmospheric water vapor is the oceans and the seas. Moreover, for well over a century, meteorologists have understood the equations that govern the interactions among the various ingredients that compose the atmosphere. These equations are Newton's laws of motion and the gas laws, in conjunction with gravity and principles of thermodynamics.

Rain is determined by seven atmospheric parameters (temperature, air pressure, moisture content, amount of cloud cover, and wind speed along the three axes). In order to predict whether it will rain at any particular place and time, one need only use the known atmospheric equations to calculate these seven atmospheric parameters for the specified place and time. It all seems simple. Since everything about the atmosphere is known, why is there such great difficulty in the long-range prediction of rain?

THE WEATHER

The enormous *practical* difficulty in determining future weather stems from the fact that *weather is not a local phenomenon*. The weather in any particular location is strongly influenced by the atmospheric conditions over a surprisingly large area, extending over thousands of kilometers. For example, Chicago's weather two days hence is influenced by today's atmospheric conditions (the seven parameters) *throughout half the United States*. Therefore, to predict the future weather of Chicago, one has to calculate each of these seven parameters *at thousands of different locations*.

It is obvious that performing so many calculations by hand is quite impossible. Therefore, in the days of hand calculations, long-range weather forecasting did not exist, and the prediction of rain was limited to one day in the future. Today's cloud patterns had *already* been visible yesterday, so there was no need to calculate them.

Since the 1950s, all this has changed. Our TV screens routinely show us weather maps containing detailed forecasts for several days in advance. The reason for the radical improvement in weather forecasting can be summarized in two words: electronic computers. It is a trivial task for a modern computer to calculate millions of numbers.

A NUMERICAL EXAMPLE

The great difficulty in weather forecasting can be illustrated by means of a numerical example. The following is a very simplified discussion of the complicated science of meteorology,[3] but it conveys the essence of the subject.

As stated above, in order to predict the future weather in Chicago, one must solve the atmospheric equations at every point over half the United States. In practice, one approximates the area under consideration by using a grid of points placed at intervals of about 100 kilometers and ten to twelve layers deep. This corresponds to more than 7000 points, and, at each point, it is necessary to calculate the seven atmospheric parameters. Thus, over 50,000 numbers must be calculated.

The principle of prediction is to use the present data to calculate what the data will be in the future. The present atmospheric data consists of 50,000 numbers, measured at thousands of weather stations. The current data (these 50,000 parameters) are inserted into equations which are solved by the computer to obtain the atmospheric data at some future time (50,000 new parameters).

How far into the future can the weather be accurately determined by such a computer calculation? The surprising answer is... *only 10 minutes!*[4] Extrapolation beyond 10 minutes is not reliable in weather forecasting. Therefore, to determine what the weather will be 20 minutes from now, one must *repeat* the entire calculation, using the results of the first calculation as input data for the second calculation.

To predict the weather for the day after tomorrow (48 hours, or 2880 minutes, from now), this procedure must be repeated 288 times, which requires the computer to calculate over 10 million numbers! A computer calculates a number by carrying out a series of steps, known as *floating-point operations*. To calculate a single atmospheric parameter requires about 500 floating-point operations. Therefore, calculating the weather two days in the future requires some *5 billion floating-point operations.*

Electronic Computers

We now have an idea of the vast number of calculations necessary for predicting when it will rain. Various tricks, shortcuts, and climate models have been developed that greatly shorten the computations, but at the end of the day, the computer must still perform billions of floating-point operations in order to calculate the future weather.

This leads to the fundamental question of whether computers are up to the job. In other words, can today's computers rapidly perform the many billions of floating-point operations required for long-range weather forecasting?

Before answering this question, it should be mentioned that in addition to great speed, a powerful computer must also have an extremely large memory to store all the numbers computed at each intermediate step during the calculations. However, this aspect of computing will be ignored here, and we shall concentrate on computer speed. A computer's speed is traditionally measured in terms of its ability to perform a certain number of floating-point operations per second, known by the acronym FLOPS. The speed of a computer is given in FLOPS.

The advance in computer speed has been nothing short of phenomenal.[5] In 1965, the fastest computers were capable of a million FLOPS. In 1980, the supercomputer was developed, and, by the late 1980s, billion-FLOPS computation became a reality.[6]

Past experience suggests *"roughly a ten-fold increase in computing speed every five years."*[7] What about future computers? The engineers of the 21st century are already designing and building the next generation of computers, capable of a *trillion* FLOPS.[8]

Predicting the Rain

Because of the great advances in recent years in computing speed, computers are now capable of performing the many billions of calculations necessary for predicting the weather. These make it possible for a TV news program to end with an accurate five-day weather forecast.

As the speed of the computer has increased, the predictive power of the meteorologist has increased correspondingly. The fastest computers available today use sophisticated numerical weather-prediction models.[9] In this way, it is possible to make an accurate prediction of when and where it will rain *for nearly a week in advance.*[10] Armies routinely employ such calculations of future weather to prepare military operations.

ANTICIPATING THE FUTURE

As this trend of faster computers continues, even longer-range weather forecasting can be anticipated. The day will surely come when it will be possible to accurately predict the rain for two weeks in advance, then for a month, and finally, for an entire season. It may require twenty years or perhaps even fifty years, but eventually meteorologists will be able to prepare a chart, for any specific locality, listing *exactly* which days will be rainy and which days will be clear throughout the coming season.

For example, the long-range weather chart might proclaim a rather wet winter for Jerusalem, with nine days of rain for October, fourteen in November, eight in December, eighteen in January, eleven in February, and six in March. The chart would also list exactly *which* days will be rainy, in exact analogy to a sunrise chart that lists the time of sunrise each day for a given locality.

When such a long-range weather chart becomes available, farmers will be delighted. Planning picnics will be simplified. But what will happen to prayers for rain?

Prayers for Rain

Picture the following scenario. The cantor in the synagogue beseeches God to provide rain for the coming season. Meanwhile, the congregants look at the long-range weather chart and learn that the meteorologists have already given assurance that it will rain. Praying for rain when one already knows that it will rain would be equivalent to praying to God to make the sun shine tomorrow. The calendar already tells us when the sun will rise tomorrow. One does not pray for what is already assured by the laws of nature.

Now consider the opposite situation. Suppose the long-range weather chart proclaims that the coming year will, unfortunately, be a year of drought. Would we then pray to God to cause rain to fall, *in contradiction* to the meteorological chart? The answer is no. If one *knows* that it will not rain, then rainfall would be a miracle, and it is *forbidden* to pray for an overt miracle to serve some particular need.[11]

When long-range weather forecasting becomes a reality, will prayers for rain cease?

HIDDEN MIRACLES AND OVERT MIRACLES

Every instance of divine intervention in human affairs is, of course, a miracle. However, the world is so very complex that divine intervention is usually not recognizable as such, and God's miracles are *hidden*. The Talmud explains that divine providence is bestowed in a manner *"hidden from the eye."*[12] Therefore, we are commanded to pray for God's blessings to remind ourselves that God rules the world, even though His rule is not manifest. However, the Talmud explicitly *forbids* praying to God for an *overt* miracle.[13]

Let us return to our comparison between the rain and the sunrise. Like the sunrise, the rain is an event whose occurrence is dictated by the laws of nature. However, from the theological point of view, there is a fundamental difference between these two events. The time of sunrise *can* be predicted accurately, and thus a change in this time would require an *overt* miracle, for which one is *forbidden* to pray. By contrast, the rain *cannot* at present be accurately predicted, and therefore, the occurrence of rain is a *hidden* miracle, for which one is *permitted* to pray. However, if the rain would ever become predictable, then the occurrence of rain would pass from the category of a hidden miracle to that of an overt miracle. As such, prayers for rain would then be forbidden.

Is the Bible Obsolete?

As we have seen, when long-range weather forecasting becomes a reality, it will become necessary to cancel our prayers for rain. However, this need not be a cause for concern. New circumstances require new prayers.

Long-range weather prediction has further consequences. The tractate Ta'anit of the Talmud deals primarily with the special fasts and prayers for rain ordained in times of drought. However, if the extent of the drought is already known, and prayers for rain are therefore forbidden, then this tractate becomes obsolete. This, too, is not a problem. Other talmudic tractates remain for the diligent student to master.

However, when one reads the Bible, one finds that long-range weather forecasting *does* present a problem. Deuteronomy 11:10–12 states that one of the advantages of the Land of Israel over the Land of Egypt is that the water supply in Egypt is assured by the yearly overflow of the Nile, whereas the water supply in Israel depends on the rain and, therefore, is uncertain. The Bible goes on to explain that the advantage of this uncertainty is that it makes the inhabitants of Israel aware at all times that their survival depends on divine providence. Uncertainty regarding the rain deepens one's recognition of the central role that God plays in human affairs.

If the rain can be predicted by meteorological calculations, then Israel has become like Egypt. In *both* countries, scientists will be able to completely determine the state of the national water supply, with no uncertainty whatsoever. Thus, long-range weather forecasting seems to contradict an explicit biblical statement. We can hardly say that the Bible, a book of divine origin, has become obsolete! This would indeed be a problem.

RESOLUTION OF THE PROBLEM

This problem has now been resolved. Recent scientific research into weather forecasting has shown that long-range predictions for the occurrence of rain *will never be possible*. This is not the personal opinion of pessimistic scientists. *One can prove mathematically that at no time in the future* will it be possible to predict rain for significantly more than a week in advance. Moreover, the proof remains valid even if future computers are developed with the speed of a *trillion trillion* FLOPS!

Chaos

The reason for the inability to predict the rain can be expressed in a single word: *chaos* (to be explained presently). Chaos is a completely new branch of science,[14] considered by researchers to be one of the most important scientific discoveries of the twentieth century. *"Chaos is a revolution that is affecting many different branches of science."*[15]

The concept of chaos should *not* be understood as synonymous with confusion. Quite the contrary. Chaos has its own rules, with well-understood consequences. *"There is order in chaos: randomness which has a well-defined underlying form."*[16]

CHAOS AND PREDICTION

The phenomenon of chaos will *forever* limit long-range weather forecasting. Professor David Ruelle, of the Institut des Hautes Etudes Scientifiques near Paris, writes: *"The demonstration that chaos occurs in a system is an important finding. Chaos explains irregular oscillations and limits the predictability of the future."*[17]

Chaos occurs in complex systems whose motion is described by what is technically known as nonlinear dynamics. Although the theory of chaos is very complicated, the central idea is readily explained. Chaotic systems are *extremely* sensitive to even the *slightest* changes in the conditions. To clarify the important implications of this statement, let us compare the behavior of non-chaotic systems with the radically different behavior of chaotic systems.

NON-CHAOTIC SYSTEMS

If you throw a ball, it will eventually land someplace. If you throw a second ball, but this time aim in a slightly different direction, it will land in a slightly different place. Slight changes in the direction of the throw lead to only slight changes in the final landing place. This characterizes a system that is *not* chaotic.

CHAOTIC SYSTEMS

Now consider a system that is chaotic. Fill a balloon with air and release it. As the air rushes out, the balloon lurches and turns erratically in a way that is impossible to predict. If you perform this experiment many times, the balloon will *never* repeat the same jerky trajectory, no matter how carefully you try to duplicate the experiment. The reason lies in the *extreme sensitivity* of the balloon's motion to the initial conditions.

The balloon can never be filled with *exactly the same* amount of air as before, or pointed in *exactly the same* direction. There will always be some *slight differences* between the two experiments, and these *minute* differences are sufficient to cause the second trajectory to be *completely* different from the first trajectory. This almost unbelievable sensitivity to initial conditions is the hallmark of a chaotic system.

The Butterfly Effect

The extreme sensitivity to conditions that characterizes a chaotic system has been given a picturesque name for the case of the weather. Meteorologists refer to this phenomenon as the "butterfly effect."[18] The term graphically expresses the *extreme sensitivity* of the weather to the slightest changes in atmospheric conditions *anywhere* in the world. It means that if a butterfly in Tokyo flutters its wings, this absolutely trivial event will eventually have a *major effect* on the weather in Tel Aviv, on the other side of the planet.

It is obviously impossible to include in the data base for a weather forecast the fluttering of the wings of every single butterfly in the world (and all such other tiny events that influence the atmosphere). Therefore, it is *impossible* to make a long-range prediction of the weather and of the rain.

Note that the butterfly effect does *not* imply that extreme meteorological events will occur. For example, a butterfly flying in Tokyo *will not* cause rain to fall in Tel Aviv in August, because it *never* rains there in the summer. But on January 15th, Tel Aviv could experience *either* a sunny and warm day *or* a cold and rainy day. Japanese butterflies *do* play a role in determining which of these two possibilities will occur.

It should be emphasized that the term "butterfly effect" is not just a figure of speech. It is *literally true* that the motion of a *single* butterfly will eventually cause large-scale changes in the weather *everywhere* on our planet. This illustrates how extremely sensitivity the weather is to the details of atmospheric conditions.

Our discussion of the butterfly effect shows that developing much faster computers will not solve the problem of long-range weather forecasting. The fastest computer imaginable will not be able one to input all the data that influence the weather, including the slightest movement of every living creature in the entire world. This explains why long-range predictions of rain will not be possible even for a trillion-trillion-FLOPS computer.

Characteristic Time for Chaos

There is a feature of chaotic systems that is very important for our discussion. If the balloon experiment described above were repeated under the exact same conditions, the second balloon's trajectory *would*, in fact, be almost identical to the first balloon's trajectory for an initial *short* time. After about *one second*, however, the second balloon would begin to move on a somewhat different trajectory from the first balloon, and soon afterwards, its trajectory would be *totally* different.

This experiment teaches us the following. The extreme sensitivity of a chaotic system takes effect *only after* a certain characteristic time – about one second in the case of the balloon experiment. Therefore, it *is* possible to predict the motion of the balloon during the first second after its release, *before* this characteristic time. However, after the first second, it is no longer possible to predict the balloon's motion. The existence of such a characteristic time is a central feature of chaos.

THE SOLAR SYSTEM

The motion of the planets is well understood. Each planet moves in an elliptical orbit around the sun, forever tracing out the same ellipse. The time required for one complete orbit of the earth around the sun defines our year of approximately 365 days.

The scenario laid out above is not exact. It is based on the approximation of considering each planet as being attracted *only* by the sun. In fact, the solar system is a highly complex system of interacting bodies, consisting of the sun, planets, their moons, asteroids, and billions of comets. All these masses interact in a very complicated manner.

Because the solar system is complex, the possibility of chaos must be considered. If the solar system is *not* chaotic, then one may make the standard approximation of analyzing *separately* the elliptical motion of each planet around the sun, and simply adding the very minor influences of the other bodies comprising the solar system. On this basis, many phenomena can be predicted, such as the occurrence of eclipses far into the future.

It has recently been discovered that our solar system *is*, in fact, a chaotic system.[19] Chaotic systems in nature are now known to be far more widespread than was once assumed. However, for the solar system, the characteristic time is about 10 million years. This explains why it is possible to make accurate predictions of planetary motion, eclipses, and phases of the moon *even though* the solar system is chaotic. As long as the prediction refers to an event occurring less than 10 million years in the future – before the characteristic time – chaos does *not* limit prediction. However, chaos makes it *impossible* to predict planetary motion *beyond* the characteristic time. As Professor Jacques Laskar of the Bureau des Longitudes in Paris writes: "*Predictability of the orbits of the planets, including the Earth, is lost within a few tens of millions of years.*"[20]

The Atmosphere as a Chaotic System

We may apply these principles to examine the implications of chaos for long-range weather forecasting. It has been shown that the atmosphere is a highly complex system and the equations that govern atmospheric behavior satisfy the conditions for a chaotic system. Therefore, there exists a characteristic time which sets a limit on accurate long-range weather forecasts. For shorter times, accurate weather predictions *are* possible, whereas for longer times, prediction is *not* possible.

The key question is the magnitude of the characteristic time. We recall that this time can be as short as one second (the balloon experiment) or as long as 10 million years (the solar system). What is the characteristic time for predicting the weather?

Scientists have discovered that the characteristic time for atmospheric chaos is about *two weeks*.[21] In other words, accurate weather predictions are possible for only two weeks in advance. Of course, such predictions require powerful supercomputers and sophisticated numerical weather models. However, chaos guarantees that long-range weather forecasting will forever remain impossible.

The Biblical Text

Deuteronomy 11:10–12 states that the occurrence of rain in Israel will forever remain uncertain, and therefore the eyes of the Israelites will always be directed toward God, the ultimate source of rain. It was once thought that as supercomputers become ever faster, the day would eventually come when it would be possible to accurately predict the occurrence of rain for an entire season in advance. Such a prediction would contradict these biblical verses.

Recent scientific findings have established the chaotic nature of the atmosphere. As a result, it will *never be possible* to predict the occurrence of rain for more than about two weeks in advance, in accordance with the verses in Deuteronomy. Thus, the rain is yet another example of how modern science provides an explanation of the biblical text.

NOTES

1. Translation by Phillip Birnbaum, 1977, *Daily Prayer Book* (Hebrew Publishing: New York) p. 698.
2. R.A. Houze, Jr., 1993, *Cloud Dynamics* (Academic Press: New York), pp. 26–30.
3. J.P. Peixoto and A.H. Oort, 1992, *Physics of Climate* (American Institute of Physics: New York).
4. A.P. Ingersoll, September 1983, *Scientific American*, p. 119.
5. R.W. Hockney and C.R. Jesshope, 1988, *Parallel Computers 2* (Adam Hilgor: Bristol), pp. 2–53.
6. E. Corcoran, January 1991, *Scientific American*, pp. 74–83. The number billion is used in the American sense to mean a thousand million.
7. Hockney and Jesshope, p. 3.
8. T. Fukushige, P. Hiet and J. Makino, March/April 1999, *Computing in Science and Engineering*, pp. 12–16.
9. K.E. Trenberth, 1992, *Climate System Modeling* (Cambridge University Press).
10. D.G. Andrews, 2000, *Introduction to Atmospheric Physics* (Cambridge University Press), pp. 207–209.
11. For a complete listing of talmudic sources for this principle, see Rabbis M. Berlin and S.Y. Zevin, eds., 1973, *Talmudic Encyclopedia*, vol. 1, pp. 679–680.
12. Talmud, *Baba Metzi'a* 42b.
13. Talmud, *Berachot* 54a.
14. J. Gleick, 1988, *Chaos: A New Science* (Cardinal: London).
15. J.P. Crutchfield, December 1986, *Scientific American*, p. 38.
16. Crutchfield, p. 38.
17. D. Ruelle, July 1994, *Physics Today*, p. 26.
18. Gleick, pp. 20–22.
19. J. Laskar, 1989, *Nature*, pp. 237–238.
20. Laskar, p. 238.
21. Ruelle, p. 28.

11

The Extreme Longevity
of the Early Generations
in Genesis

Questions

One of the most difficult questions in the Book of Genesis relates to the extreme ages ascribed to the twenty generations from Adam to Abraham. Genesis speaks of people in this period living for more than 900 years, culminating in the record holder, Methuselah, who reached the unbelievable age of 969. How are we to understand such longevity? Anyone who has had close contact with the very elderly has observed that the human body literally deteriorates when approaching the age of 100. Thus, the biblical accounts of people living for many hundreds of years seem completely impossible.

There is yet another difficulty. After the Exodus from Egypt, extreme longevity disappears and the life span of subsequent generations becomes normal by present-day standards – completely consistent with the traditional 120-year maximum life span. What happened to cause this dramatic decrease in longevity?

There are the questions to be addressed here. It will be shown that recent scientific advances regarding the process of aging pave the way to understanding the thousand-year life spans of the early generations in Genesis, as well as the contemporary life spans of those who lived after the time of the Exodus.

Living Longer

Why do human beings age? Until quite recently, no one really knew. However, in the last few decades, there have been enormous advances in our understanding. In fact, the study of aging has become the focus of such intense scientific effort that one of the leading authorities speaks of *"a revolution in aging research."*[1] Some of the findings of this research have been so completely unexpected that scientific journals aimed at the educated layman now abound with articles that describe these exciting discoveries. Some examples will illustrate the point.

From the cover of *New Scientist*: "Life at 200: Will We Always Grow Old?" The cover story, dramatically entitled "Death of Old Age," begins as follows: *"We can live healthy lives well into our hundreds, researchers claim."*[2]

A news item in *Scientific American*, entitled "Immortality Gene Revealed," states: *"Two teams of scientists have cloned the gene for telomerase, known as the 'holy grail' of aging research ... Cells that produce telomerase are immortal."*[3]

Professor Michal Jazwinski, director of the Center on Aging at Louisiana State University, a major figure in aging research, asserts that *"the maximum human life span might go as high as 400 years."*[4]

Why Do We Age?

Aging is one of the universal human experiences. Aging and death seem as natural as breathing, and just as inevitable. Although aging was long regarded as a mysterious aspect of life, scientific research has now revolutionized our knowledge about what causes it.[5] Scientists continue to make breathtaking progress and gain new insights about the basic mechanisms responsible for aging. More important, they now have the ability to intervene in the aging process and thereby extend the human life span. This newfound knowledge strongly suggests that biomedical advances will eventually enable us to delay and even to eliminate many of the causes of aging and death.

The characteristics of aging are many. The body produces chemicals (free radicals) that destroy tissues by a process called oxidation. The immune system weakens and is no longer able to defend the body against disease. Structural proteins become altered, leading to rigidity of the heart muscle, lungs, ligaments, and tendons. Cataracts form in the eyes. Certain cells (fibroblasts) lose their ability to divide (Hayflick limit). DNA molecules, which are vital for cellular replication, become damaged by mutations. Cancers develop as cells suddenly proliferate out of control. Hormonal changes occur that cause the gradual destruction of the bones (osteoporosis). Critical enzymes cease functioning. Strokes attack the brain. Arthritis appears in the joints. Nerve cells in the brain degenerate (Alzheimer's disease). Blood vessels lose elasticity (arteriosclerosis) and cease to function properly. Parkinson's disease and diabetes develop. Memory declines. And so forth, and so on.

It now appears that there is a common cause for the seemingly endless list of afflictions of old age. Although still subject to some controversy, a scientific consensus is emerging that the root cause of all aging processes is genetic. According to Professor Caleb Finch of the Department of Neurobiology of Aging at the University of Southern California, *we are convinced that the rate of aging is under genetic control.*[6] The body *does not wear out* in the way that a car or washing machine wears out after years of faithful service. Rather, the human body contains certain genes that cause all the havoc of old age listed above.

In other words, we all suffer from genetic defects. If our defective genes could be identified, and their effects neutralized through genetic engineering, the human life span could be extended, perhaps very considerably. This exciting possibility, discovered by scientists who study aging, is responsible for the dramatic pronouncements quoted above.

The idea that genes cause aging has received important support from the research of Professor Mark Azbel, formerly at Moscow State University and now at Tel Aviv University. In a series of pioneering articles, Professor Azbel showed that the extensive mortality data for human beings can all be explained by assuming a genetic basis for aging and death.[7] He emphasized that *"there exists a genetically programmed probability to die at a given age ... and this age may be genetically manipulated."*[8]

Experiments that alter the genetic structure of laboratory specimens have already produced striking results. A favorite subject for study is a small nematode worm (*Caenorhabditis elegans*) that has 13,000 genes. Professor Tom Johnson of the University of Colorado found that changing a single gene, aptly named *age-1*, doubles the life span of this nematode.[9]

Professor Michael Rose of the University of California has genetically engineered a new strain of fruit flies (*Drosophila melanogaster*) that live almost twice as long as standard laboratory-reared flies. Moreover, these "superior" flies are *"more robust at every age. Even when old, many are stronger than ordinary young specimens."*[10]

Similarly, Professor Michal Jazwinski has identified several genes that prolong the life of brewer's yeast (*Saccaromyces cerevisiae*). Introducing the gene LAG-1 significantly extends the life span, and he also found that *"yeast cells that bear this gene maintain their youth longer."*[11]

For readers who find incredible the suggestion that genetically engineered living creatures could have enormous life spans, we point out that *even now*, there are many animals that do not exhibit any signs of aging, their low mortality rate of youth never rises, and they continue to bear offspring for as long as they live. Professor Leonard Hayflick of the University of California explains[12]:

> *"Some animals do not seem to age at all. If they do age, it occurs at such a slow rate that their aging has not been demonstrated. These non-aging animals experience a peak in their physiological functions, but these functions then do not seem to decline ... Non-aging animals do not live forever because of accidents, disease and predation."*

Perhaps the most astonishing data comes from the field studies of the Scottish ornithologist George Dennet, who has spent a lifetime observing a colony of marine birds called fulmars (*Fulmarus glacialis*) on the Orkney Islands. Dennet reports that *"fulmars show no increase in mortality rate and no decline in reproduction up to at least 40 years. Certainly no species of similarly sized mammals or birds maintain their fertility at a comparable age. Do these birds avoid aging altogether? We do not know."*[13]

As of 1990, the Milwaukee zoo and the Moscow zoo each possessed an Andean condor (*Vultur gryphus*) that was nearly 80 years old, but continued to lay eggs and showed no signs of aging.[14] Studies of tortoises and certain fish yielded similar results[15]:

> *"One specimen of Marion's tortoise (Geochelone gigantea) died accidentally at age 150 years in a British military fort on Mauritius. Studies in progress on other tortoise species suggest that they remain fertile throughout their long life and that their mortality rate remains low."*

The longevity record for fish is held by the sturgeon (*Acipenser fulvescens*), which reaches 150 years of age, as confirmed by the number of rings on their scales. The very old individuals of rock fish (*Sebates aleutianus*) studied by Bruce Leaman of the Pacific Biological Station of Fisheries produced egg masses and showed no sign of the tumors and other pathological lesions found in mammals at advanced ages.[16]

A World Without Aging

In the light of the facts presented above, it should not be too difficult to imagine a world in which human beings do not age. This does not mean that no one will ever die. Lives would still be cut short by the usual hazards of traffic accidents, virulent diseases, and violent crime. But the *rate* at which people die would not increase with age. For example, the chances of dying in a car accident are the same at age 60 and at age 20.

The safest age for human beings is ten to fifteen year. The period of dangerous childhood diseases is past and the infirmities of old age have not yet begun. In the United States and Western Europe, the mortality rate, defined as the chance of dying with one year, of a ten-year-old boy is about 0.05%. That is, only 1 in 2000 male youngsters will die within a year (Young girls do somewhat better.) This is the minimum mortality rate observed for human beings. By contrast, the mortality rate for hundred-year-olds is 50%. Half of the centenarians will not survive the year.

What can one say about the human life span in a world without aging? If people did not age, then everyone would remain forever young, and the minimum mortality rate of a ten-year-old child would persist throughout one's entire life. Professor Caleb Finch has shown that under these circumstances, the average life span would be about 1300 years.[17] Moreover, chronologically extremely old, but biologically still young, men and women would be able to sire children throughout their thousand-year lives. This is how society would be if one could eliminate all the genetic defects that cause aging.

The Biblical Text

Having presented the scientific advances regarding aging, we return to the account in Genesis of the extreme longevity of the early generations. The life spans of the first twenty-six generations are given in the accompanying figure. It is clear that there is a marked difference between the life spans before Noah and after Noah. Up to and including Noah, the life spans are nearly the same (about 900 to 950 years), except for Enoch, who is explicitly described in Genesis as having died young and may therefore be removed from consideration. After Noah, however, the life span decreases steadily, falling from 959 years for Noah (tenth generation) to the "traditional" value of 120 years by the time of Moses (twenty-sixth generation).

THE 900-YEAR LIFE SPANS BEFORE THE TIME OF NOAH

Consider the following scenario. When Adam and Eve were in the Garden of Eden, they were destined to live forever. We propose that this immortality was the result of Adam and Eve not possessing any of the genetic defects that nowadays cause aging (discussed above). Moreover, Adam and Eve were not subject to the non-genetic causes of mortality that are unrelated to aging. In the Garden of Eden, there presumably

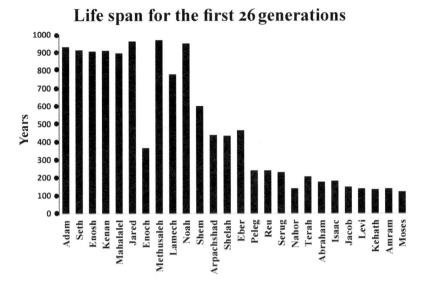

were no traffic accidents, no virulent diseases, and no violent crime. Therefore, it follows that Adam and Eve would live forever.

When Adam and Eve ate the "forbidden fruit," they were banished from the Garden of Eden and forced into the outside world. Of course, once they were outside the Garden, they became subject to the usual non-genetic causes of death that afflict us all (accidents, diseases, etc.), and thus they became mortal. Indeed, this is precisely what God meant when he told Adam and Eve that *"on the day that you eat of the tree of knowledge, you will die"* (Genesis 2:17). Not that Adam and Eve would *die* on that day, but rather, they would become *mortal* – subject to dying.

The key point of our proposal is that even after leaving the Garden of Eden, *Adam and Eve still did not have the genetic defects that cause aging and, therefore, they did not age.* This explains both their great longevity (930 years for Adam) and their ability to bear children at a very advanced age.

We have already seen that in the absence of aging, the average human life span would be about 1300 years. Thus, we really have to explain why the early biblical life spans were so short! In this regard, we note that there is no reason why the non-aging life span should be the same today as it was in early biblical times. Back then, they had fewer traffic accidents, but they also did not have antibiotics to cure diseases. Indeed, the difference of only 40% between the contemporary non-aging life span (about 1300 years) and the early biblical life span (900–950 years) should be viewed as good agreement.

This approach also explains the advanced age of childbearing listed for the early generations in Genesis. Methusaleh and Lamech were nearly 200 years old when they sired children, and it is explicitly mentioned that they had other children even later in life. Similarly, Noah was 500 years old when his three children were born. Moreover, at the age of 600 years (Genesis 7:6), Noah was placed in charge of the complicated enterprise of building and outfitting the Ark, hardly a task that could be assigned to a doddering old man. Thus, it is clear that Noah not only lived extremely long, but that he remained young throughout his life.

The ability to bear offspring until the end of life is characteristic of animals that have unusually long life spans. Recall the 80-year-old Andean condors and the 150-year-old sturgeon, discussed earlier. Moreover, long life spans are associated with the absence of the other signs of aging. Thus, the unusually long life spans of the early generations in Genesis are consistent with their ability to sire children at an advanced age and the lack of signs of aging.

There is another point to be made. Recent discoveries have shown that it is not possible for a human being to be completely free of genetic defects. The same gene that is necessary for an important physiological function early in life may occasionally be harmful to the body in later life.[18] This important finding, called antagonistic pleiotropy, was introduced by Professor George Williams of the State University of New York at Stony Brook.

In the light of the above discussion, it is reasonable to assume that the early generations in Genesis did possess a small number of genes that produced some signs of aging. These few genes eventually led to death at some advanced age (say, 900 years), far beyond the contemporary life span (about 80 years) but still shorter than the enormous life span (about 1300 years) predicted in the absence of any aging genes. Moreover, this approach also why the life spans of almost all the early generations were so similar. (Of the nine persons mentioned in Genesis who lived up to the time of Noah, all but one had a life span in the restricted range of 895–969 years.[19]) Genes for aging can be shown to produce such an effect.

THE STEADY DECREASE IN LIFE SPAN
AFTER THE TIME OF NOAH

Genesis records the following important differences between the generations who lived immediately after the time of Noah (tenth generation) and those who lived earlier:

- As the figure shows, the life spans decreased steadily after Noah (959 years), with no one living longer than 240 years after Eber (fourteenth generation). After Moses (twenty-sixth generation), there is no instance recorded in the Bible of anyone living significantly longer than 120 years, which remains to this day as the maximum human life span.
- Men no longer sired children at an advanced age. After Shem (eleventh generation), the age of having children dropped to the thirties, just as today. Indeed, when Abraham and Sarah (twentieth generation) became parents at ages 100 and 90 years, respectively, Genesis describes the event as miraculous.
- For the first time, people are described in Genesis as becoming old and infirm. Aging in later life is a characteristic feature of the Patriarchs and Matriarchs (twentieth to twenty-second generations). This applies to Abraham and Sarah (Genesis 18:11–13), to Isaac (27:1–2), and to Jacob (48:10).

Clearly, something happened at the time of Noah that caused these important changes in later generations – changes that are all associated with *aging*. The biblical text reveals this event. In Genesis 6:3, we are told that God was extremely displeased with the corrupt behavior of people at the time of Noah and, therefore, He decreed that the maximum human life span would be reduced to 120 years ("*Therefore, man's life span shall be one hundred and twenty years*"[20]).

The human life span did not, in fact, immediately decrease to 120 years. A full ten generations after this divine pronouncement, Abraham still live to age 175, with similar life spans for the other Patriarchs.

In the light of our earlier scientific discussion of aging, we propose that the divine pronouncement of Genesis 6:3 can be understood as follows. At the time of Noah, the genes for aging were introduced into the human gene pool. It would, of course, take several generations for these aging genes to propagate throughout the entire human population. This explains why another sixteen generations had to pass (from the time of Noah to the time of Moses) until the maximum life span finally became reduced to the divinely decreed value of 120 years. The human life span decreased steadily during this transition period (from 959 years for Noah to 120 years for Moses).

This proposal also accounts for the fact that after the time of Shem (Noah's son), there are no further (non-miraculous) instances in Genesis of people having children at an advanced age. Finally, this also explains why the usual infirmaries of old age were exhibited by the Patriarchs, whereas they were absent in earlier generations.

Conclusion

The recent dramatic scientific discoveries regarding aging provide the basis for a comprehensive explanation of all aspects of the extreme longevity of the early generations described in Genesis.

NOTES

1. S.M. Jazwanski, *Science*, vol. 273 (1996), p. 54.

2. D. Consar, *New Scientist* (22 June 1996), p. 24.

3. "News in Brief," *Scientific American*, October 1977, p. 14.

4. R.L. Rusting, *Scientific American*, December 1992, p. 95.

5. For excellent popular accounts of the many recent advances in aging, see R.E. Ricklefs and C.E. Finch, *Aging* (New York: Scientific American Library, 1995) and L. Hayflick, *How and Why We Age* (New York: Ballantine Books, 1994). For an encyclopedic treatment, see C.E. Finch, *Longevity, Senescence, and the Genome* (University of Chicago Press, 1990).

6. Ricklefs and Finch, p. 176.

7. M. Ya. Azbel, *Proceedings of the National Academy of Sciences (USA)*, vol. 91 (1994), pp. 12453–12457; *Proceedings of the Royal Society of London*, vol. 263B (1996), pp. 1449–1454; *Physics Reports*, vol. 288 (1997), pp. 545–574; *Physica A*, vol. 249, pp. 472–481.

8. M. Ya. Azbel, *Physics Reports*, vol. 288 (1997), p. 545.

9. T.E. Johnson, *Genetics*, vol. 118 (1988), pp. 75–86.

10. Rusting, p. 87.

11. *Ibid.*, p. 91.

12. Hayflick, pp. 21–22.

13. G.M. Dunnet, in *Reproductive Success: Studies of Individual Variations in Contrasting Breeding Systems*, ed. T.H. Clutton-Brock (University of Chicago Press, 1988), p. 268.

14. Finch, p. 148.

15. R.E. Ricklefs and C.E. Finch, *Aging*, p. 8.

16. *Ibid.*, p. 10.

17. *Ibid.*, p. 2.

18. G.C. Williams, *Evolution*, vol. 11 (1957), pp. 398–411.

19. Recall that we have eliminated Enoch from consideration because it is explicitly stated in Genesis that he died young.

20. This verse is often interpreted in a non-literal midrashic sense (*e.g.*, see Rashi). However, in the present analysis, we concentrate on the literal meaning of the Genesis text.

12

"May You Live to 120!"

A Blessing for Long Life

The traditional Jewish blessing for long life, the title of this chapter, is not just an item of ethnic folklore. The source for this blessing is a verse in Genesis (6:3), in which God decrees the maximum human life span to be 120 years (*"man's days shall be one hundred and twenty years"*). Since everyone presumably wants to live for as long as possible, it has become traditional for one to wish a friend the maximum number of years – in good health, of course.

We here examine the scientific basis for this number, asking whether there is any justification for assuming that 120 years is the maximum human life span.

It should be mentioned at the outset that the source for the traditional 120 years *cannot* be empirical. It is simply not true that the oldest people have always lived to about the age of 120. Before the twentieth century, anyone living for more than 100 years was an extreme rarity, and absolutely nobody reached the age of 110. In fact, until quite recently, the scientific literature quoted the figure of either 105 years[1] or 110 years[2] for the maximum human life span. Therefore, on the basis of observation alone, there would never have been any reason to consider the higher figure of 120 years.

In this context, it should be emphasized that there is no factual basis whatsoever for the widely-quoted anecdotal reports of remote mountain villages of the Caucasus region of Georgia or in Ecuador or in Colombia or in Pakistan where many people supposedly live longer than 120 years. Such reports are, of course, very beneficial to the tourist trade, but investigation invariably reveals that these claims of extreme longevity are groundless.[3]

To promote the publicity value of such claims, both Russia and Colombia issued postage stamps in 1956 to honor their longest-lived citizen.[4] The Colombian stamp depicts a man said to be 167 years old, whereas the Russian stamp is somewhat more modest, claiming only the age of 148 for its most senior citizen. It is usually implied that the healthy atmosphere of the mountains, the relaxed life style and simple diet – a certain type of yogurt is often mentioned – are responsible for these fictitious ages!

The Maximum Human Life Span

It was only in the latter part of the eighteenth century that systematic birth records began to be kept on a widespread scale, thus making it possible to establish reliably the age of the oldest human beings. Based on such records, scientists had until recently accepted[5,6] that the "oldest person in history" was a Japanese man listed in the 1987 *Guinness Book of World Records*, Shigechiyo Izumi, who died in 1986 at the age of 120.

This record has been broken[7] by a Frenchwoman, Madame Jeanne Calment, born in 1875 and died in 1997 at the age of 122. For the first time in post-biblical history, we have authenticated cases of persons reaching the age of 120, thus confirming the divine pronouncement of Genesis 6:3.

Let us now consider the reverse question. Perhaps the biblical figure of 120 years is, in fact, *too low* for the maximum human life span? With improved health care for the elderly and modern medical miracles, perhaps the day will come when people will live to the age of 130 or 140 or even beyond? Is there any scientific evidence that supports the biblical figure of *only* 120 years for the maximum human life span?

Making accurate estimates of the largest possible values of various quantities on the basis of previous experience is a new and active branch of statistics. For example, it is important to be able to determine how destructive the next earthquake or flood will be, based on the history of earthquakes and floods in the region. This field of statistics, known as extreme value theory, has received renewed impetus through the research work of Professor Richard Smith of the University of North Carolina.[8]

One of the most intriguing applications of extreme value theory is to the question of human longevity, a subject of great interest to biologists and actuaries.[9] An analysis was recently carried out by Professor Laurens de Haan and his colleagues at the Erasmus University in Rotterdam, Holland. Using all the available data on human longevity, Professor de Haan finds the value of 119±6 years for the maximum human life span.[10] This result is clearly consistent with the Biblical value of 120 years.

The Oldest Old

Most of us have an unfavorable image of extremely old people. We tend to think of nonagenarians and centenarians (often called *"the oldest old"*[11]) as physically infirm and mentally debilitated. Thus, the traditional blessing of living to 120 seems of doubtful value. Why should anyone want to live so long only to end up as a burden to his or her children?

Recent studies of the oldest old demonstrate that this unfavorable image has no basis in fact. Professor Thomas Perls, geriatrician at Harvard Medical School, explains[12]:

> *"The prevailing view of aging as advancing infirmity is wrong… The oldest old are often the most healthy and agile of the senior people in my care … Centenarians, with few exceptions, report that their nineties were essentially problem-free. As nonagenarians, many were employed, sexually active, and enjoyed the outdoors and the arts. They carry on as if age were not an issue. Accumulating evidence indicates that we must revise the common view that advancing age inevitably leads to extreme deterioration."*

Similar views are expressed by Professor Richard Suzman of the National Institute of Aging at the NIH, who emphasizes that the pessimistic expectations of infirmity for the oldest old are being revised in the light of new studies.[13]

> "National data show that a surprisingly large percentage of the oldest old require no personal assistance on a daily level, and are also physically robust ... Health-service research is revealing that a large percentage of those in old age remain low-cost users of medical services."

Other authorities confirm these views[14]:

> "New scientific evidence regarding physiological aging shows that we had overestimated the age rate of decline for the oldest old in various physiological functions. More recent studies of healthy survivors to advanced ages show that physiological functions of many types decline much more slowly than previously thought. For example, the cardiovascular function of healthy 80-year-olds was found to be not much different from that of 30-year-olds."

VERY OLD PERSONS

A recent article, entitled "The Oldest Old," contains a photograph of Madame Jeanne Calment, the world's oldest person of confirmed age, at a party to celebrate her 116th birthday.[15] Madame Calment is shown drinking a glass of wine (after all, she is French!) and she appears to be thoroughly enjoying herself. She lived for another six years after that party, finally dying at the age of 122, basically in good health until near the very end.

I would like to add a personal testimony. In 1984, I had the privilege and pleasure of meeting Charlotte Hughes, then Great Britain's second oldest person at the age of 111. Mrs. Hughes was physically fit and completely lucid throughout our conversation. She told me that she reads from Shakespeare and the Bible every day. On the occasion of her 110th birthday, she had been flown to New York City on a supersonic jet as the personal guest of the mayor. Mrs. Hughes enjoyed life fully until she died in her 114th year.

This optimistic view of the vitality of the oldest old is fully supported by recent statistical data on human mortality. Throughout most of life, human mortality increases with age at a steady pace (called the Gompertz law of mortality). However, upon reaching the age of the oldest old, the rate of increase in mortality slackens and then stops altogether. The data for centenarians show that their mortality rate actually *decreases*. *"After the age of 105 years, the one person in a million still alive has a greater chance of reaching age 106 than an individual aged 104 has of reaching age 105."*[16]

Professor Kenneth Manton of the Center for Demographic Studies of Duke University, an authority in demographic patterns of aging, has reached similar conclusions[17]:

> *"The vital statistics data show very little increase in mortality above age 100 … There is a decline in mortality above age 104, based upon the British population registry data, which have extremely accurate reporting. Similar patterns have been found in the United States, Sweden and France."*

Conclusion

The conclusion to be drawn from all these recent scientific findings is that if one merits the traditional blessing of extremely long life, it is usually accompanied by good health. Divine favor is not marred by physical or mental infirmities.

150 · FOSSILS AND FAITH

NOTES

1. F.A. Lints, 1978, *Genetics and Ageing*, vol. 17 of *Interdisciplinary Topics in Gerontology*, series editor: H.P. van Hahn (S. Karger AG: Basel), p. 29.
2. L.C. Campanelli, 1985, in *Aging*, ed. C.B. Lewis (E.A. Davis: Philadelphia), p. 7.
3. L. Hayflick, 1994, *How and Why We Age* (Ballantine Books: New York), pp. 196–202.
4. A. Lindenbaum, 1970, *Stamps That Tell a Story* (Sabra Books: New York), p. 15.
5. D.W.E. Smith, 1989, *Biological Reviews*, vol. 64, p. 9.
6. R.E. Ricklefs and C.E. Finch, 1995, *Aging* (Scientific American Library: New York), p. 181.
7. T.T. Perls, January 1995, *Scientific American*, p. 52.
8. See, for example, R. Smith, 1990, *Extreme Value Theory*, in *Handbook of Applicable Mathematics: Supplement* (Wiley: New York).
9. Extreme value theory determines the maximum value of a particular parameter by extrapolating known data for a given system, assuming that no new feature has been introduced. Thus, if genetic engineering were used to "improve" human beings, then the maximum life span calculated by extreme value theory would no longer be valid, since this calculated age refers to "unimproved" human beings.
10. R. Matthews, 12 October 1996, *New Scientist*, p. 40.
11. R.M. Suzman, D.P. Willis and K.G. Manton, editors, 1992, *The Oldest Old* (Oxford University Press).
12. Perls, p. 50.
13. R.M. Suzman, 1992, in *The Oldest Old*, ed. R.M. Suzman, D.P. Willis and K.G. Manton (Oxford University Press), p. 343.
14. K.G. Manton, 1992, in *The Oldest Old*, ed. R.M. Suzman, D.P. Willis and K.G. Manton (Oxford University Press), p. 157.
15. Perls, pp. 50–55.
16. Ricklefs and Finch, p. 6.
17. Manton, pp. 160–161.

13

The Spread of Languages and the Tower of Babel

The Tower of Babel and the Noahide Languages

One of the most interesting events in Genesis is the incident of the Tower of Babel. The Bible relates (Genesis 11:1–9) that at one time everyone spoke the same language and they assembled together to build a mighty structure – the Tower of Babel. God was displeased with this plan, however, and He dispersed the people and confounded their language. This population dispersal led to the development of different nations and gave rise to the various languages of the ancient world.

The account of the Tower of Babel offers no details about which peoples and languages developed as a result of the dispersal of the population. This information is given in Chapter 10 of Genesis, which is devoted to the genealogy of Noah's three sons: Shem, Ham, and Japheth. Each of Noah's sons is described as the progenitor of more than ten nations,[1] and a list of nations is given for each son. Of specific interest is the fact that the dispersal of Noah's descendants did not simply result in separate peoples, but also led to the development of separate languages, as explicitly stated in Genesis:

> From these [descendants of Japheth] … each according to his language (10:5).

These are the descendants of Ham ... according to their languages
(10:20).

These are the descendants of Shem ... according to their languages
(10:31).

Scholars do not agree on the exact geographical location of the
various Noahide languages, but such differences in detail are not
relevant for our discussion. The locations of the Noahide languages
given in the *Hammond Atlas of the Bible*[2] are reasonably similar to
those given in *Carta's Atlas of the Bible*.[3]

We shall here compare the development of the Noahide languages,
as related in Genesis, with the latest findings in linguistic research. In
the eyes of many, the biblical description of the spread of languages
reads more like a mythological tale than a realistic account of past
events. However, in contrast to this widespread misconception, we
shall see that the Genesis text is, in fact, in agreement with recent
discoveries in comparative linguistics.

The Languages of Shem and Ham

The Semitic and Hamitic languages, attributed to the descendants of
Noah's sons Shem and Ham, are all related, and linguists classify them
as belonging to the Afro-Asiatic family of languages (in the linguistic
context, "Afro" means North African and "Asiatic" means the Middle
Eastern).[4] The Afro-Asiatic languages of the ancient world included
Hebrew, Assyrian,[5] Egyptian, Babylonian, Aramaic, Amorite, Moabite,
and Cushite. All these names are familiar from the Book of Genesis.

Because of the close correspondence between these ancient languages and the names appearing in Genesis, they were previously
called the Hamito-Semitic family of languages. However, linguists
now prefer the term Afro-Asiatic family.

It is the Japhethide languages that raise difficult questions about
the Genesis account of the spread of languages. These will be discussed in this chapter, and it will be seen that the Bible and modern
linguistics are, in fact, in close agreement.

The Languages of Japheth

The most interesting feature of the Japhethide languages is their vast geographical extent. As the accompanying map shows (next page), the Japhethide languages were spoken throughout Europe and deep into Asia. The European branch of the Japhethide languages extends from Greece through Germany and as far west as Spain, whereas the Asian branch extends from Persia through the ancient Kingdom of the Medes (present-day Northern Iran and Afghanistan) and as far east as ancient India (present-day Pakistan).

The Genesis account of Japhethide languages implies the following:

- There should be a linguistic relationship between the various Japhethide languages, including ancient Greek and German (European) and ancient Persian and Indian (Asian).
- The Japhethide languages should show signs of having originated near Turkey, since they all developed during the dispersal of Noah's descendants after the Flood. Recall that Noah's ark landed on Mount Ararat, in eastern Turkey.
- The most ancient of these languages should have originated around the date of the Flood, about 4000 years ago.
- The languages of Japheth did not spread by conquest. Genesis implies that the descendants of Japheth developed new languages as they peacefully migrated into previously unoccupied lands in Europe and Asia.

We shall see that all these statements agree with current findings in linguistics.

European Languages

There are about 6000 languages in the world today. Most widespread are the languages of Europe. Although European languages comprise only 3% of the world's languages, they are the native tongue of nearly half the world's population.[6]

The classification of the world's languages is a major area of

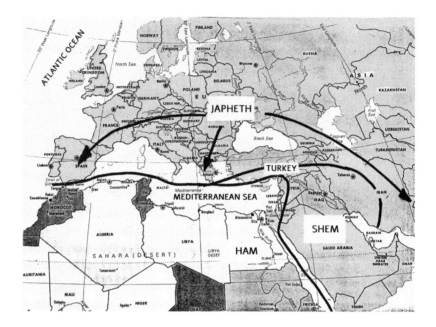

linguistics research. Scholars compare various languages, seek correspondences between them, and group related languages into families.

It has long been obvious that almost all the European languages are related. French, Italian, and Spanish stem from Latin; the Scandinavian languages are very similar; German, Dutch, and English share many words, as do all the Slavic languages. Careful studies of vocabulary, syntax, and phonology have established that, with four exceptions,[7] *all* the languages currently spoken in Europe belong to one single family.

When leaving Europe, the situation changes. The languages of the neighboring countries of Turkey, Georgia, and the Middle East are unrelated to those of Europe.

THE PROBLEM

In the eighteenth century, linguistic opinion was at variance with the Genesis account of the Japhethide languages. At that time, linguists believed that there was *no connection* between the ancient languages of Asia and Europe, whereas Japhethide languages include *both* Asian languages (e.g., ancient Persian and Median) *and* European languages (e.g., the ancient languages of Germany and Greece). Moreover, between the Asian Japhethide languages and Europe are the countries of Turkey, Georgia, Azerbaijan, Iraq, and Syria. In none of these intervening countries is a European language spoken.

These facts clearly present a problem, because they seem to be inconsistent with the statement in Genesis that all the Japhethide languages are related.

The Indo-European Family of Languages

SANSKRIT: A LINGUISTIC SURPRISE

One of the most important events in the history of linguistics was the shattering of the belief that there is no relation between European and non-European languages. The linguistic bombshell fell in 1786, when Sir William Jones, an English oriental scholar serving as a judge in India, made an extraordinary discovery.[8] Jones had taken up the study of Sanskrit, the extinct language of the earliest literary and religious texts of India. Even after it was no longer spoken, Sanskrit continued to be the language of scholarship and literature, similar to the role of Latin in the West during the Renaissance.

In his "Third Anniversary Discourse" to the Asiatic Society of Bengal, Jones said the following regarding Sanskrit and its relation to European languages[9]:

> "The Sanskrit language has a wonderful structure; more perfect than Greek and more copious than Latin. It bears to both of them a strong affinity, both in the roots of verbs and in the forms of grammar... so strong that no philologist could examine these three languages without believing them to have sprung from a common source. Also Gothic [ancient German] and Celtic had the same origin as Sanskrit, and old Persian should be added to the same family."

Jones recognized the fact that there was a deep connection between the ancient languages of Europe and those of Asia. This brilliant observation was subsequently studied and developed by many linguists. In 1813, the English scholar Thomas Young introduced the term "Indo-European" for this widespread family of languages. The Asian branch of the Indo-European languages is not restricted to Sanskrit, ancient Persian, and a few other languages. Asia is the homeland of over 40% of the Indo-European languages.

THE LANGUAGE OF ANCIENT TURKEY:
ANOTHER SURPRISE

An important discovery in the study of Indo-European languages was the deciphering of the language of ancient Turkey. The course of events has been described as follows[10]:

> "In the late nineteenth century, excavations in Turkey uncovered thousands of tablets in an unknown language. These tablets remained a mystery until 1917, when scholars were astonished to find that this language belonged to a previously unknown ancient branch of the Indo-European family. This language, called Anatolian, is the earliest Indo-European language discovered to date."

THE PROBLEM SOLVED

At one time, it was thought that there was no connection between the European languages and those of Asia. However, according to Genesis, the Japhethide languages include both European and Asian languages. Thus, there was a discrepancy between Genesis and linguistics regarding the relationship between the European and the Asiatic languages.

Today, linguists recognize that the Indo-European family of languages links ancient Asian languages with ancient European languages, in precise accord with the Genesis list of Japhethide languages. Moreover, the ancient Anatolian language of Turkey (also called Old Hittite) was also found to be an Indo-European language. (In modern Turkey, an unrelated Altaic language is spoken.) Therefore, we see that *all the Japhethide languages belong to the same Indo-European family of languages*, in agreement with the description given in Genesis.

The Ancestral Homeland of the
Indo-European Languages

Once it became clear that Indo-European languages are found in both Asia and Europe, scholars naturally began to wonder about the origin of this widespread linguistic family.

Had it originated somewhere in Asia and then spread westward to Europe? Had it originated in Europe and then spread eastward to Asia? Perhaps it had originated near the European-Asian border, say in Turkey, and then spread *both* eastward into Asia *and* westward into Europe? The last scenario corresponds to the account given in Genesis.

The effort to locate the original homeland of the Indo-European languages – the so-called Indo-European problem – has occupied generations of linguists.

The deep similarities between the various Indo-European languages clearly indicate that all of them derived from a single ancestral language, older than Sanskrit, Greek, or Latin. This ancestral language, called "proto-Indo-European" or PIE, was reconstructed by studying cognate words (words of common origin) in the various Indo-European languages. For example, a comparison of the English word *birch*, the German *birke*, the Lithuanian *berzas*, the Old Slavonic *breza*, and the Sanskrit *bhurja* indicates that there existed a parent word for birch tree in PIE. From the vocabulary of PIE that was thus constructed, linguists developed a picture of the world inhabited by its original speakers and their environment before their dispersal from their original homeland.

From such studies, it is possible to estimate when PIE was last spoken. Professor Jared Diamond of the University of California emphasizes that the words that appear in PIE, and, even more important, the words that are absent, serve as an indication of which items were used by these ancient people. The absence of a word indicates that the object in question was unknown to the speakers of PIE. For example, there is no word in PIE for "iron," suggesting that iron was unknown until after the breakup of PIE. Combining these results with archaeological evidence about the time when various items first came into use, Diamond has estimated that PIE began to develop into daughter languages about 4500 years ago.[11]

We note that this time period estimated by Professor Diamond corresponds closely with the date of the biblical Flood.

Such considerations are also helpful in determining the location of the ancestral homeland of PIE speakers. Many possible homelands have been proposed, including Central Asia, Northern Europe,[12] Central Europe, and north of the Black Sea.[13]

A NEW PROPOSAL FOR THE ANCESTRAL HOMELAND OF PIE

Colin Renfrew, Professor of Archaeology at the University of Cambridge, is a leading authority on Indo-European languages. In his book, *Archaeology and Language: The Puzzle of Indo-European Origins*, Renfrew stresses the importance of archaeological evidence in determining the ancestral homeland of the proto-Indo-Europeans. Critically reviewing the various suggestions and explaining their shortcomings, Renfrew asserts that: *"these proposals do not provide the solution to the Indo-European problem."*[14]

Professor Renfrew marshals the evidence in favor of his new proposal that the first speakers of proto-Indo-European lived in Turkey. He concludes that *"in central and eastern Anatolia [present-day Turkey], the early form of Indo-European was spoken. The distribution of the language and its successors into Europe was associated with the spread of farming."*[15]

In his article, "The Origins of Indo-European Languages," Renfrew writes[16]:

> *"Almost all European languages are members of a single family [of languages] that spread by peaceful diffusion ... The traditional view holds that the ancestral PIE language was spread by nomadic horsemen who lived north of the Black Sea. These mounted warriors conquered indigenous peoples and imposed their PIE language, which eventually evolved into the European languages*

we know today … I here offer a different view, based on new insights. According to this view, the spread of the Indo-European languages did not require conquest. It was a peaceful diffusion from its origins in Anatolia [Turkey] and the Near East."

CURRENT STATUS OF RENFREW'S PROPOSAL

As of this writing, Renfrew's proposal is still the subject of debate. Some scholars continue to support the older, traditional view that the northern coast of the Black Sea was the ancestral homeland of the Indo-Europeans.[17] Renfrew himself states[18]:

> *"It would be wrong to assume that the last word on this topic has been spoken. My proposal of an Anatolian origin of the Indo-European languages does find validation in recent research, but the final picture will no doubt be more complex. Yet, I predict that when a more complete understanding is achieved, the spread of farming from Turkey into Europe will prove to be a significant part of the story."*

The Biblical Text

Having presented the linguistic evidence regarding the Indo-European family of languages, we return to the questions posed earlier regarding the Japhethide languages.

- The Genesis list of Japhethide languages is completely consistent with the Indo-European family of languages. These include many European languages, as well as the Asian languages of Persian, the language of the Kingdom of the Medes, and the ancient language of Turkey. All these appear on the Genesis list of Japhethide languages.
- Professor Colin Renfrew identifies Anatolia (present-day Turkey) as the location of the original homeland of the Indo-European languages. This location agrees with the landing site of Noah's ark on Mount Ararat.

The rival theory suggests the northern shore of the Black Sea as the place of origin of these languages. This locale is not far from Turkey, which lies on the southern shore of the Black Sea. Thus, the rival theory is also in reasonable agreement with Genesis.

• The date proposed for the beginning of the separation of proto-Indo-European into daughter languages (about 4500 years ago) is close to that of Noah's Flood.

In conclusion, we find that current knowledge in linguistics is in good agreement with the Genesis account of the languages of the descendants of Japheth.

> "God said, 'Behold, they are one people with one language, and this is what they begin to do. What they propose to do should be withheld from them. Let us descend and confuse their language, so that they will not understand each other.' And God dispersed them from there over all the earth, and they stopped building the city. That is why it was called Babel, because from there God confused their language and scattered them over the earth." (Genesis 11:6–9)

NOTES

1. The term "nation" is not intended to imply a modern nation-state, but a chiefdom or a tribal society.

2. C.S. Hammond, 1959, *Atlas of the Bible* (Hammond: New York), map on p. B-4.

3. Y. Aharoni, 1974, *Carta's Atlas of the Bible* (Carta: Jerusalem), map 15 on p. 21.

4. D. Crystal, 1997, *The Cambridge Encyclopedia of Language*, 2nd edition (Cambridge University Press), p. 318.

5. The Assyrians spoke the ancient Semitic language known as Akkadian. There were two dialects of Akkadian, the Assyrian dialect spoken in northern Mesopotamia and the Babylonian dialect spoken in southern Mesopotamia. For this reason, the Akkadian language is also referred to as Assyro-Babylonian.

6. Crystal, pp. 286–287.

7. Finnish, Hungarian, and Estonian are Uralic languages from Asia, whereas the Basque language, spoken in parts of northeast Spain, is an "isolate," that is, unrelated to any other known language.

8. Crystal, p. 288.

9. W. Jones, 1807, *The Collected Works of Sir William Jones III* (John Stockdale: London), p. 23.

10. J. Diamond, 1991, *The Rise and Fall of the Third Chimpanzee* (Vintage: London), p. 236.

11. Diamond, pp. 237–238.

12. The search for the proto-Indo-European homeland has not always remained an academic discussion. For most of the 20th century, German scholars favored an ancestral homeland in Northern Europe, and they referred to the original PIE speakers as Aryans, a term introduced by Gordon Childe in his 1926 book, *The Aryans: A Study of Indo-European Origins*. The Nazis perverted this idea into the concept of a master race of pure-blooded Aryans who had lived in ancient Germany (Northern Europe) and who were responsible for everything worthwhile in Western civilization. The Nazis regarded themselves as the twentieth-century descendants of the Aryans, assuming for themselves the role of guardians of the "purity" of Western civilization, with the task of destroying all non-Aryan influences. The result was the Holocaust.

13. Crystal, p. 298.

14. C. Renfrew, 1987, *Archaeology and Language: The Puzzle of Indo-European Origins* (Jonathan Cape: London), p. 98.

15. Renfrew, p. 205.

16. C. Renfrew, October 1989, *Scientific American*, p. 82.

17. Diamond, pp. 241–247.

18. Renfrew, October 1989, *Scientific American*, p. 90.

Fossils

14

Misreading the Fossils

Fossils

Anyone who deals with the subject of science and religion will, sooner or later, be confronted with the question of fossils, those ancient relics of prehistoric plants, animals, and men. The common assumption is, of course, that the scientific evidence regarding fossils is basically reliable and need not be seriously questioned by the layman. In other words, one's job is *to deal* with these facts – not to cast doubt on their veracity. Other than the creationists, who reject the entire scientific enterprise, one naturally assumes that the fossil evidence and its interpretation have been presented by serious scientists who were objective in their pursuit of knowledge and who used accepted standards of scientific rigor.

In this chapter, we shall see that *nothing could be further from the truth*. In fact, the record will show that evolutionary biologists have a dismal record when it comes to interpreting hominid fossils (fossils of prehistoric man). Blunder after blunder has been made in the course of "scientific work." Moreover, these absurd interpretations of hominid fossils were *not* published by third-rate workers, but *by world-famous scientists*. Indeed, it is precisely because of the unquestioned authority of these scientists that it often required decades to correct their errors. It has become clear that the reason for this shoddy work is that the evolutionists in question were often motivated by subjective considerations, such as national pride, professional jealousy, and preconceived notions.

To establish this thesis, only the *leading authorities in evolutionary biology* will be quoted. This is a very important point, because in recent years, a plethora of books and articles criticizing Darwin and evolution has been published, written by lawyers, journalists, physicians and other laymen in the field of evolutionary biology. It cannot be emphasized strongly enough that such books will *not* be quoted here. The sources presented here were all written by recognized experts in evolutionary biology and hominid paleontology – Darwinists to a man. Moreover, the gross errors in fossil interpretation that will be pointed out are no longer subjects of controversy. They are admitted by all – with acute embarrassment.

Neandertal Man – the Brute That Wasn't a Brute

A few introductory remarks are in order before one discusses Neandertal Man, the prehistoric men who immediately preceded us ("us" being, of course, Modern Man, whose scientific designation is *Homo sapiens*). The word "Neandertal" (literally, Neander Valley) derives from a valley near Dusseldorf, Germany, where the first fossil skull was discovered in 1856. Such fossils have since been discovered throughout Europe, the Middle East and even farther afield, with hundreds of nearly complete skeletons now available for study.

The Neandertals first appeared about 200,000 years ago (the date is uncertain) and then, for unknown reasons, they abruptly disappeared from the fossil record about 30,000 years ago. Since that time, *only* Modern Man appears in the hominid fossil record, with the oldest Modern Man fossil skeletons being physically identical in every respect to the skeletons of contemporary people. It is relevant to the believing person to point out that there is no "family connection" between Modern Man and Neandertal Man.[1] Professor Steven Stanley of Johns Hopkins University, emphasizes that *"out of nowhere, Modern Man appeared in the fossil record with particular features that are utterly unpredictable on the basis of what preceded them."*[2]

The question that interests us here is this: What did the Neandertals look like? How would one characterize them? In a recent discussion of this question, the British journal *New Scientist* points out that *"those who rail at the conduct of football hooligans or rowdy parliamentarians often describe the objects of their ire as 'behaving no better than Neandertals,' conveying an image of uncouth and uncivilized conduct. 'Neandertal' has become a convenient term of abuse to describe all that is brutish and boorish."*[3]

These assertions of *New Scientist* are amply confirmed by *Roget's Thesaurus*, in whose list of synonyms for the adjective "Neandertal," one finds such terms as savage, brutal, bestial, animal, troglodytic."[4] The popular image of the Neandertal is that of a coarse-featured, stooped-walking, long-armed brute whom no one would want to meet in a dark alley.

It has now recognized that this description of Neandertal Man is *completely and utterly false.* Scientists now understand that Neandertal Man looked remarkably similar to Modern Man, so similar, in fact that, to translate a current scientific joke into Israeli terms, if a Neandertal Man wearing a *kova tembel* were to board an Egged bus, his fellow passengers would probably not even be aware that sitting next to them was a member of a different species!

How did this complete misrepresentation of Neandertal Man come about? Why did all the leading scientists misunderstand the facts for so long? These are the questions that we shall explore in this chapter. More details can be found in the definitive treatise[5] on the Neandertals that has recently been published by Professor Erik Trinkaus, one of the leading authorities on Neandertal Man.

In relating the strange history of Neandertal research, *New Scientist* asks: *"What did the Neandertals do to acquire their reputation for brutality and stupidity?"* Trinkaus answers that *"Neandertals have hardly ever been interpreted objectively. They have suffered a range of scientific abuse that can only be understood in its historical context."*[6]

The "villain" of our story is the world-renowned scientist, Professor Marcellin Boule. In the early decades of the twentieth century, Boule was Director of the Institute for Human Paleontology of the famous Museum National d'Histoire Naturelle of France and editor of the major journal *L'Anthropologie*. No one had more impressive scientific credentials in the field of prehistoric man than Marcellin Boule, "the doyen of human paleontology in France between the world wars."[7] He made Neandertal Man his special field of expertise and, after a long and detailed study, Boule published his definitive monograph on the Neandertals in the 1911–13 issues of *Annales de Paleontologie*. As Trinkaus points out, *"the monograph was immediately a classic, a study of such thoroughness and merit that it established the paleontology of humans – paleoanthropology, it would be called – as a scientific discipline."*[8]

Unfortunately, Boule's "classic monograph" *was wrong in every respect*. In his book on hominid paleontology, appropriately entitled *The Myths of Human Evolution*, Professor Niles Eldredge explains that *"every feature Boule stressed in his analysis had no basis in fact ... To Boule, the premier French paleontologist of his day, we owe the shambling brutish image of the Neandertals immortalized in a thousand comic strips."*[9]

Trinkaus has emphasized the same point[10]:

> *"What is remarkable is that Boule's monograph is astonishingly wrong in many of its conclusions.... Boule reconstructed the vertebral column of Neandertals as much straighter [than it was], giving rise to a stooping posture and slouching gait, a forwardly thrust head and perpetually bent knees. The drawing in his monograph imprinted itself on the minds of anthropologists everywhere. It was the perfect troglodyte: the brute, the savage."*

How could a famous scientist such as Professor Marcellin Boule come to make such gross errors? The explanation lies in the extreme subjectivity with which Boule approached his study of Neandertal Man. The complete story is long (for details, see Trinkaus), but the following paragraphs summarize the main points of this almost unbelievable episode.

Boule had a hated foreign rival, a well-known Swiss paleontologist named Otto Hauser, *"much despised by the French for his boorish personality and his habit of finding prize fossils on French territory ... Boule was to remain Hauser's arch-enemy for life."*[11] Moreover, Boule was intensely jealous of two French colleagues, Gabriel de Mortillet and Leonce Manouvrier, professors at a rival institution, the Ecole d'Anthropologie. Therefore, for Boule, *"embarrassing de Mortillet was always a welcome outcome to a study."* [12]

Boule began his research with the definite preconceived notions of what the Neandertals should look like. *"He was inclined to believe that Neandertals had nothing to do with human ancestry, and his anatomical analysis succeeded in expelling these brutish forms from the human family tree."* [13]

The combination of national pride, professional jealousy and preconceived notions led Boule to make an incredible series of errors. As Trinkaus explains, *"Boule did not deliberately and knowingly slant his results; it was only that he saw, readily, that which was agreeable, and was oblivious to elements that suggested uncomfortable implications."* [14]

The results were inevitable. Worst of all was the effect on his colleagues of Boule's grossly erroneous work, for as Eldredge notes, *"Boule's authority was so close to absolute that his conclusions strongly affected paleontological thinking for several decades."* [15] Trinkaus adds that *"his conclusions were to have a more lasting effect on the image of Neandertals than any previous work."* [16]

Piltdown Man: The Ape That "Became" a Man

Professor Stephen Jay Gould of Harvard University, a renowned evolutionary biologist, characterizes Piltdown Man as *"the most famous and spectacular fraud of twentieth-century science."* [17] The facts are as follows (for more details, see *The Piltdown Forgery*[18]).

In 1912, an amateur fossil collector named Charles Dawson announced that he had found, in a Piltdown gravel pit on the Sussex coast of England, parts of the fossil head of a prehistoric man that soon came to be known as Piltdown Man. Before his sudden death in 1916, Dawson "discovered" a few more pieces of Piltdown Man's skull and jaw. This fossil was accepted as genuine by the entire scientific community, and was given the scientific name *Eoanthropus dawsoni* ("Dawson's dawn man") in honor of its discoverer.

In fact, Piltdown Man was an outright fraud. What Dawson had done was to combine a contemporary human skull with the jaw of a contemporary ape (orangutan), both of which he stained to match the color of the Piltdown gravel pit. Dawson broke off the parts of the bone where the skull attaches to the jaw to hide the fact, otherwise obvious, that the (human) skull did not fit the (ape) jaw. Finally, he filed down the ape's teeth a bit to make them look more human, and in various ways contrived to make the bones look ancient, as befits a prehistoric fossil.

What is important here is *not* the fact that a fraud was perpetrated; every profession has its cheats. What is central to our discussion is the assessment of this fraudulent fossil by the leading members of the scientific community. One would have thought that as soon as this jaw of an ape reached the hands of professional anatomists, the game would be up. How could any skilled anatomist fail to recognize immediately that the Piltdown jaw was identical in every respect to that of a modern orangutan, and that the Piltdown skull was identical in every respect to that of a contemporary man, without any indication of those features that characterize "prehistoric man"? Surely, Dawson's fraud would be exposed by leading scientists within a matter of minutes.

But that is not what happened at all. In fact, this fraud remained undetected *for forty years*! Piltdown Man created a sensation in the British paleontological community; it was England's earliest prehistoric man, and it was universally accepted as genuine.

From 1912 until 1953, every scientific reference book and encyclopedia informed its readers of the great importance of Piltdown Man in establishing the evolutionary history of Modern Man. We were told that, unlike Neandertal Man, who was nothing but a "savage brute" unrelated to Modern Man (as Professor Boule had so firmly established in his famous monograph!), Piltdown Man (the "Dawn Man") was our earliest direct ancestor, as was clearly proven by the very modern appearance of his skull.

The sorry "trio of heroes" in the Piltdown farce were Sir Grafton Elliot Smith, Sir Arthur Keith and Sir Arthur Smith Woodward, variously characterized as *"the great names of the British school of paleontology of the 1920s and 1930s,"*[19] and *"the three leading lights of British anthropology and paleontology.*"[20] Each man was a recognized world authority; the first two were the foremost British anatomists of their day and the third was an expert on hominid paleontology. Each man had been knighted by his monarch as a sign of the esteem accorded him by the scientific community. And each man was convinced that the Piltdown fossils were genuine!

"*The great trio of British paleontologists were in agreement ... The combined influence of Smith Woodward, Keith and Elliot Smith ensured that Piltdown Man became the standard by which other hominid fossils were to be measured.*"[21]

How could such leading authorities have made such gross blunders? Having preconceived notions goes far to ensuring that one sees what one wants to see.

It was quite obvious to anyone who examined the Piltdown fossils that the skull (which, we recall, belonged to a Modern Man) appeared much more human-like and much less ape-like than the jaw (which was, in fact, the jaw of an ape). To explain this anomaly, scientists invoked the principle of "mosaic evolution," which asserts that different parts of the body may evolve at different rates. However, which part of the body evolved first remained a matter of sharp debate. The British school of paleontology insisted that the brain (skull) of Modern Man should have evolved relatively rapidly, whereas the jaw should have evolved more slowly. Thus, according to the British school, it was expected that our prehistoric ancestors would, at some early stage, have a relatively modern human-like skull while still sporting a relatively primitive ape-like jaw. When Piltdown Man displayed precisely these characteristics, he was welcomed with open arms by the British paleontologists. "*Proof positive at last that man's large brain had characterized his line from the earliest times.*"[22] And when one adds the happy fact that the Dawn Man was discovered in England, the joy of the British scientists knew no bounds.

But there still remained one problem. If the British experts were right, then the basically human skull should have displayed some clearly ape-like features, and the basically ape-like jaw should have displayed some clearly human features. After all, Piltdown Man was supposed to be a fossil in transition – on the way to becoming a completely Modern Man. And these expected, but completely non-existent features were exactly what each of the three leading British scientists claimed to have seen in the Piltdown fossils! We can illustrate this phenomenon by quoting the world-famous anatomist Sir Grafton Elliot Smith[23]:

> "The Piltdown skull, when properly reconstructed, is found to possess strongly simian [ape-like] peculiarities. In respect to these features, it harmonizes completely with the jaw, the simian features of which have been exaggerated by most writers ... The outstanding interest of the Piltdown skull is the confirmation it affords of the view that in the evolution of man, the brain led the way."

In other words, Britain's leading anatomist claimed to see distinctly human anatomical features in the jaw of a modern orangutan and distinctly ape-like anatomical features in the skull of a contemporary human being, when, in fact, *none of these anatomical features really existed*. One should never underestimate the power of wishful thinking when hominid fossils are being examined by scientists with strongly held preconceived ideas. Professor Donald Johanson, director of the Institute of Human Origins in Berkeley, California, wryly comments: "Anthropologists dealing with prehistoric man tend to get very emotionally involved with their fossils."[24]

Hesperopithecus: The Man Who Was a Pig

The final fossil we discuss bears the scientific designation *Hesperopithecus* ("western anthropoid") to emphasize that this was the first anthropoid fossil ever discovered in the Western Hemisphere (near Snake Creek in the state of Nebraska). It will be the rare reader who has ever heard of *Hesperopithecus*. The history of this fossil has been shoved deep under the rug by almost all paleontologists (an exception is Professor Stephen Gould, who has written an amusing essay about the fossil[25]), and its story has been carefully excised from all scientific writings – and with good reason. Of all the blunders committed by evolutionary biologists during the 20th century in their various "scientific studies" of hominid fossils, none can compare with *Hesperopithecus*.

Our story takes place in America in the 1920s, a decade marked by an ongoing battle between creationists and scientists. Nowadays, creationists make much more modest demands; they merely insist that their views be taught in the schools side-by-side with standard evolutionary theory. In the 1920s, however, their demands were considerably more far-reaching; they insisted that *only* their ideas be taught. In fact, the creationists succeeded in passing laws in several states, including Tennessee, making it a criminal offense to teach Darwin's theory of evolution in the public schools. The opposition convinced a high-school teacher in Tennessee named John Scopes to openly teach Darwin's theory in order to challenge the law.

The resulting Scopes trial became a national sensation, pitting the foremost trial lawyer of the day, Clarence Darrow, against one of America's leading creationists, William Jennings Bryan (who was nearly elected President of the United States!). It is necessary to understand this background and the mood of the country to properly appreciate the story of *Hesperopithecus* and its impact on scientific thinking.

The "hero" of the *Hesperopithecus* fiasco was Henry Fairfield Osborn, a leading evolutionary biologist. Once again, we encounter a scientist motivated by intense personal rivalry and preconceived notions, features which paved the way for yet another scientific disaster. Osborn was universally recognized as "a great paleontologist"[26] and served as the director of the world-famous American Museum of Natural History in New York. His feelings for Bryan were *"pure venom and contempt ... In Osborn's view, Bryan was perverting both science and the highest notions of divinity."*[27] Osburn hated Bryan with a passion, setting the stage for a vicious confrontation between the two men in the arena of "Science and Religion."

The Osburn-Bryan confrontation began in February 1922, when the *New York Times* published an article by Bryan attacking Darwin's theory of evolution, soon followed by a reply from Osburn which defended the scientific principles of evolution and argued that the concept of evolution was, in fact, completely compatible with the Bible. To ridicule Bryan's rejection of fossil evidence, Osborn cited a biblical passage: *"Speak to the earth and it shall teach you"* (Job 12:8). Osborn was referring, of course, to the fossil evidence.

In the month following this sharp exchange of articles in the *New York Times*, a geologist sent Osburn a fossil tooth that he had discovered. Osburn quickly created a sensation by claiming that it was the first anthropoid fossil ever found in America. This claim was to lead to Osborn's downfall. Professor Gould describes the events[28]:

> *"Osborn's enthusiasm warmed as he studied the tooth and considered its implications. An American anthropoid would certainly be a coup for Osborn's argument that the earth spoke to Bryan in the language of evolution ... Therefore, Osborn proclaimed the momentous first discovery of a direct human ancestor in America. Osborn named the fossil Hesperopithecus and presented it to the scientific world in a paper published in the April 1922 issue of the prestigious Proceedings of the National Academy of Sciences."*

Osborn exulted in the uncannily happy coincidences of both time and place. Not only was this fossil discovered at the very time that Bryan was denying fossil evidence. The crowning irony was that *Hesperopithecus* was found in Nebraska, Bryan's home state! No fossil could have had a greater potential to embarrass Bryan; no fossil could have bettered *Hesperopithecus* for rhetorical impact. The precious irony of the situation was not lost on Osborn, who inserted the following gloat of triumph into his article for the staid *Proceedings of the National Academy of Sciences*:

> *"It has been suggested humorously that the fossil should be named Bryanopithecus after the most distinguished primate that the State of Nebraska has ever produced. It is certainly singular that I had advised William Jennings Bryan to consult a certain passage in the Book of Job, "Speak to the earth and it shall teach you" and it is a remarkable coincidence that the first earth to speak on this subject is the sandy earth of Snake Creek in western Nebraska."*

For several years after the discovery of *Hesperopithecus* in 1922, Osborn missed no opportunity to use the fossil to heap public abuse on Bryan. On the eve of the Scopes trial in 1925, Osburn published a book devoted primarily to ridiculing Bryan and chose a biting parody of Job as his title: *The Earth Speaks to Bryan.*

In addition to using *Hesperopithecus* to attack Bryan, Osborn publicized the prize fossil in his American Museum of Natural History, commissioning *"a graphic reconstruction of a Hesperopithecus couple in a forest surrounded by other members of the Snake Creek fauna, prepared by the well-known scientific artist Amadee Forestier."*[29] This reconstruction was a marvelous example of the lifelike three-dimensional exhibits for which this museum is justly famous. Looking at a photograph of the well-known *Hesperopithecus* exhibit, one is amazed by the many details of the physical appearance and the cultural behavior of this prehistoric man and woman that Osborn and "the well-known scientific artist" claimed to have deduced *from one single tooth.*

Five years later, Osborn's world collapsed. Additional fossil evidence discovered in the Snake Creek beds in Nebraska showed conclusively that the *Hesperopithecus* fossil was, in fact, the tooth of a *pig.* Osborn's long-standing claim that *Hesperopithecus* was an anthropoid was officially retracted in the 16 December 1927 issue of *Science.*

As a sorry comment on Osborn's integrity, it should be noted that his name does not appear in the retraction article. He left to a colleague the embarrassing task of admitting publicly that their famous *Hesperopithecus* "prehistoric man" was really a pig. Gould explains: *"Osborn simply shut up and never mentioned Hesperopithecus again in his numerous succeeding articles on human ancestry."*[30]

Once again, we ask: How could this farce have happened? Why were America's leading hominid paleontologists so ready to accept the absurd idea that a *single tooth* – so worn that it could not even be properly identified as belonging to a pig – was sufficient to establish a new class of prehistoric men? To answer this question, one must be aware of the situation at that time in hominid paleontology. By the 1920s, hominid fossils had been found worldwide, everywhere but in America. England had Piltdown Man; France and Germany had

Neandertal Man, Cro-Magnon Man, and Heidelberg Man; Asia had Java Man and Peking Man; Africa had *Australopithecus*. Hominid fossils were being discovered everywhere – except in the United States.

American paleontologists had been relegated to being mere spectators in the prestigious game of hominid paleontology. Therefore, when the *Hesperopithecus* fossil was discovered, they eagerly jumped onto Osborn's hominid bandwagon. It would have required more scientific integrity than the American paleontologists could muster for them to have taken a more cautious stance. In spite of his unquestioned scientific talents, objectivity was not a strong feature in the character of Henry Fairfield Osborn.

Among the results of this scientific fiasco was the fact that during years, a million visitors to the American Museum of National History in New York were enthralled by the brilliantly executed reconstruction of the *Hesperopithecus* prehistoric man and woman living in the Nebraskan forest. Few of these visitors would ever read the scientific literature which revealed the truth about *"the man who was actually a pig."*

Conclusions

In our account of hominid paleontology during the twentieth century, we encountered the gentle man who was described as a savage brute (Neandertal Man), we then moved on to the modern orangutan who was mistaken for our prehistoric ancestor (Piltdown Man), and finally we met the pig who was misrepresented as a man (*Hesperopithecus*). And all these almost unbelievable mistakes were made by the most prominent names in hominid paleontology: in France (Marcellin Boule), in England (Sir Arthur Smith Woodward, Sir Grafton Elliot Smith, Sir Arthur Keith), in the United States (Henry Fairfield Osborn). Moreover, two of these gross errors remained universally accepted by the scientific community for *nearly half a century.*

Upon viewing this incredible parade of scholarship, one is sorely tempted to cry out, *"But the Emperor has no clothes on!"* Professor David Pilbeam of Harvard University, has recently discussed this lamentable situation at length and made the following remarks: *"Our theories have often said far more about the theorists than about what actually happened ... All our theories about human origins were relatively unconstrained by fossil data ... Many evolutionary schemes were dominated by theoretical assumptions that were largely divorced from the data derived from fossils."*[31]

Has the situation improved? At the present time, the origins of Modern Man are the subject of sharp controversy in scientific circles, with the champions of the two competing theories accusing each other of lacking scientific rigor. One can almost hear history repeating itself, leading one to wonder what comments future scientists will make about the current debates surrounding hominid paleontology.

Final Comment

In addition to their intrinsic interest, the bizarre examples of the misinterpretation of hominid fossils in this chapter carry an important message pertaining to the question of contradictions between Torah and science. As a professional scientist, I greatly respect the scientific enterprise. However, one must remember that scientific research is carried out by human beings, who are subject to the shortcomings of prejudice, professional jealousy, and national pride that afflict us all. The history of science has shown that subjective behavior has plagued some of the most famous scientists. Therefore, current contradictions between Torah and science may well melt away as new scientific understanding emerges. [32]

NOTES

1. It is also very relevant for the believing person to compare the *cultural achievements* of Modern Man and Neandertal Man. For such an analysis, see N. Aviezer, 1990, *In the Beginning: Biblical Creation and Science* (Ktav: New York), pp. 94–102.

2. S.M. Stanley, 1981, *The New Evolutionary Timetable* (Basic Books: New York), p. 151.

3. B. Wood, 3 July 1993, *The New Scientist*, p. 38.

4. P.M. Roget, 1977, *Thesaurus*, 4th edition (Harper & Row: New York), p. 702.

5. E. Trinkaus, 1993, *The Neandertals* (Jonathan Cape, London).

6. Wood, p. 38.

7. Trinkaus, p. 181.

8. *Ibid.*, p. 190.

9. N. Eldredge, 1982, *The Myths of Human Evolution* (Columbia University Press: New York), p. 76.

10. Trinkaus, pp. 190.

11. *Ibid.*, pp. 175, 181.

12. *Ibid.*, p. 194.

13. *Ibid.*, pp. 194–195.

14. *Ibid.*, p. 194.

15. Eldredge, p. 76.

16. Trinkaus, p. 190.

17. S.J. Gould, 1983, *Hen's Teeth and Horse's Toes* (Norton: New York), p. 202.

18. J.S. Weiner, 1955, *The Piltdown Forgery* (Oxford University Press).

19. R. Lewin, 1987, *Bones of Contention* (Penguin Books: London), p. 31.

20. S.J. Gould, 1980, *The Panda's Thumb* (Penguin Books: London), p. 97.

21. Eldredge, p. 79.

22. *Ibid.*

23. Lewin, pp. 72, 73.

24. *Ibid.*, p. 300.

25. S.J. Gould, 1991, *Bully for Brontosaurus* (Penguin Books: London), pp. 432–447.

26. *Ibid.*, p. 433.

27. *Ibid.*

28. *Ibid.*, pp. 434–436.

29. *Ibid.*, p. 444.

30. *Ibid.*, p. 442.

31. D. Pilbeam, 1980, in *Major Trends in Evolution*, ed. L.K. Konigson (Pergamon Press: London), pp. 262, 267.

32. See Aviezer, *In the Beginning*.

15

The Scientific Quest for the Origins of Man

Paleoanthropology

The most fascinating topic in fossil research is surely the scientific quest to understand the origins of *Homo sapiens,* our own species. Scientists who study the origins of mankind are called paleoanthropologists (*paleo* means "ancient" and *anthropos* means "man"). In this chapter, we shall trace the erratic and controversial history of research in paleoanthropology.

The basic classification unit of animals and plants is the *species.* Groups of similar species form a *genus* (plural: genera), and similar genera form a *family.* Man-like species belong to the hominid family. Bipedal locomotion is their most important distinguishing feature. Hominids walk upright on two legs. Scientists can generally determine from the knee joints and pelvic structure of a fossil, whether or not a particular prehistoric creature walked on two legs.

Errors of the Past

Studies of the evolutionary development of mankind have been characterized by profound misunderstanding and many erroneous assumptions. Until 1960, paleoanthropologists still believed in the single-species hypothesis. According to this hypothesis, the most primitive hominid species gradually evolved into a somewhat more advanced species, which in turn gradually evolved into a still more advanced species, and so on. This process was repeated several times, until it resulted in the most advanced hominid species of all: Modern Man. As new hominid species were discovered, they were interpreted as representing additional phases in the straight-line evolutionary development from the earliest ape-man-like species to Modern Man.

The single-species hypothesis was finally discarded on the basis of extensive fossil evidence. Professor Niles Eldredge, curator at the American Museum of Natural History, refers to this hypothesis as *"the great evolutionary myth of slow, gradual, and progressive change. So bewitched were the single-species people by the linear elegance of this myth, that they were reluctant to see it marred."*[1] In his book, appropriately entitled *The Myths of Human Evolution*, Eldredge emphasizes that *"the standard expectation of evolution – slow, steady, gradual improvement and change through time – is indeed a myth."*[2]

GENUS AUSTRALOPITHECUS

By the 1980s, a picture of human evolution that is now known to be erroneous was generally accepted. The hominid family was described as containing two genera, the extinct *Australopithecus* and the present-day *Homo*. The older genus, *Australopithecus* ("southern ape"), consisted of only four species, *Australopithecus afarensis*, *A. africanus*, *A. boisei*, and *A. robustus*. The ancestral relationship between various australopithecine species was a subject of dispute.

During the 1990s, anthropologists identified three additional australopithecine species, and even more dramatic, they discovered a third hominid genus, *Ardipithecus*.[3] The relationships between these different australopithecine species are vigorously debated, with almost as many theories as there were paleoanthropologists.

The significance of these recent findings does not lie in merely increasing the number of australopithecine species that once existed, though the doubling of their number within only a few years is surprising enough. The real importance of these new findings is that they totally change our understanding of the history of prehistoric man.

An example will illustrate the point. In 1994, Professor Yves Coppens, of the College of France in Paris, published an article entitled "The Origins of Humankind."[4] In this article, Professor Coppens, a member of the French Academy of Sciences and a recognized authority on human evolution, described a new theory to explain the evolutionary history of humankind. The basic idea was that geographical isolation in Africa had triggered the evolution of hominids, and that *"the Rift Valley in Africa holds the secret to the divergence of hominids from the great apes and to the emergence of human beings."*

The theory did not survive for long. Only three years later, Coppens's explanation was demolished by new fossil evidence. An article published in 1997 by two well-known authorities (Professor Alan Walker of the American Academy of Sciences, and Professor Meave Leakey, head of paleontology at the National Museums of Kenya) explained that Coppens's theory had been "debunked" by the newly discovered *bahrelghazali* hominid fossils.[5] These fossils showed that there was, in fact, *no* geographical isolation and that African hominids had lived on *both sides* of the African Rift Valley.

So it goes in the study of human evolution. Today's new theory for the origins of humankind is discarded on the basis of tomorrow's fossil discoveries.

Professor David Pilbeam of Harvard University laments the large number of dramatic upheavals in the scientific understanding of human evolution that have occurred within so short a time. After describing a complete change in scientific consensus that took place within a span of only five years, Pilbeam asks: *"Why had the hominid fossil record been so misinterpreted?"* and answers: *"The early hominids were markedly different from any living species. In many instances, however, these differences were ignored and early hominids have been made to seem too much like modern humans."*[6]

GENUS HOMO

We now turn to the contemporary hominid genus, *Homo*. Since the *Homo* fossils are more recent and more plentiful than the australopithecines, one would expect the scientific picture to be less confused.

Unfortunately, this is not the case. As we shall see, the same scientific uncertainty and confusion that characterizes the older hominid fossils is also present regarding the *Homo* fossils.

Until quite recently, the genus *Homo* was thought to consist of only three species, *H. habilis*, *H. erectus*, and *H. sapiens* ("wise man"), with the last species (characterized by a large, modern brain) subdivided into two subspecies: Neandertal Man and contemporary Modern Man, the only living hominid.

Within a single decade, this picture totally changed. The genus *Homo* is now believed to consist of *seven* species.[7] New fossil discoveries have added the species *H. ergaster* and *H. rudolfensis*, and reclassification has added *H. heidelbergensis* and *H. neandertalensis*. The lack of understanding regarding the early *Homo* fossils was the subject of an article appearing in the respected British journal *Nature*.[8] The article, carrying the satirical title, "Who is the 'Real' *Homo habilis*?", describes the confusion surrounding the discovery of the hominid fossil known as OH-62 and then concludes: *"The new fossil rudely exposes how little we know about the early evolution of Homo."*

HOMO SAPIENS

The most interesting scientific questions relate to *Homo sapiens* – our own species. Since *Homo sapiens* is the contemporary hominid species, one might expect the scientific evidence to be reasonably clear. In fact, however, strident arguments regarding the origins of our species are quite common among paleoanthropologists.

There are currently two opposing theories, each claiming to have found the correct explanation for the evolutionary history of contemporary human beings. These two competing schools of paleoanthropology use completely different methods of research. One school emphasizes traditional studies of the prehistoric fossils, whereas the opposing school uses modern methods of molecular biology to study the DNA sequences of different races to determine their evolutionary history. It might be expected that the two complementary approaches to the study of human origins would lead to similar results, with each method confirming the findings of the other. However, this has not been the case. The opposing schools have been at loggerheads for over a decade, with vociferous arguments continuing unabated to this very day.

One theory designated "Out of Africa" claims that all human beings alive today descend from a single African woman ancestor, who lived about 200,000 years ago. The opposing theory designated "Multiregional" claims that the various human races arose independently at different times and at different sites around the world, roughly where these races are living today. To clarify the positions of the competing schools, *Scientific American* invited each side to present its case in consecutive articles.[9,10]

These articles make very instructive reading for the following interesting reasons. First, each pair of distinguished authors claims that their theory has now been established *with absolute certainty*.

The "Out of Africa" scientists write: "*After years of disagreement, we won the argument; the paleontologists admit that we had been right and they had been wrong.*"

The "Multiregional" scientists counter: "*The fossil record is the real evidence for human evolution … we describe a theory that synthesizes everything known about modern human fossils, archaeology, and genes.*"

The reader may be wondering how it is possible for two distinguished scientists to examine the *very same data*, and yet arrive at diametrically opposite conclusions! In fact, such occurrences are quite common in the study of human origins. Professor David Pilbeam notes that "*virtually all theories of human origins are relatively unconstrained by the fossil data.*"[11]

Another interesting feature of the *Scientific American* debate on the origins of *Homo sapiens* is that each side claims that the methods used by the opposing camp are *completely erroneous*, and are based on incorrect scientific procedures.

The "Multiregional" scientists write of their opponents' methods of analysis: "*Their evidence was based on a flawed 'molecular clock' … their hypothesis must be rejected because their reasoning is flawed.*"

The "Out of Africa" scientists describe their opponents' fossil data as follows: "*Fossils cannot, in principle, be interpreted objectively …*

Paleontologists' perspective contains a built-in bias that limits its power of observation ... The fossil record is infamously spotty ... the fossils examined may lead down an evolutionary blind alley."

How is one to relate to these contradictory claims by well-known scientists? Is the genetic evidence *"inherently flawed"* or is it *"convincing"*? Are fossil remains *"a monumental body of much more reliable evidence"* or do they *"contain a built-in bias"*? Are the genetic data *"complete and objective"* or do they *"rely on a long list of assumptions"*? Whatever happened to accepted standards of scientific objectivity?

To assess the reliability of the data, it is useful to examine the opinions of other scientists who are not directly involved in the debate and therefore presumably more objective in their views.

Discussing the genetic and DNA data used by the "Out of Africa" scientists, Professor Alan Templeton, of the University of Washington, is bitterly critical: *"It is likely that this ["Out of Africa"] hypothesis would never even have been proposed if a proper analysis had been performed on the original data set."*[12]

Regarding the fossil analysis of the "Multiregional" scientists, Professor Erik Trinkaus of the University of New Mexico, a leading authority on Neandertal Man, is very critical of relying heavily on fossil data. He points to the tendency of different scientists to look at the *same* fossils and come to *opposite* conclusions, with each scientist seeing the data as supporting his own theory. Trinkaus writes: *"The Saint-Cesaire [Neandertal] fossil was a perfect mirror, reflecting back into each viewer's eyes the convictions that he brought to it ... they constructed their hypotheses so flexibly that no evidence could possibly disprove them."*[13]

Conclusion

Perhaps the correct conclusion to draw from all these claims and counterclaims is that *both* groups of scientists are right in their dismissal of their opponents' methods of analysis, and therefore *neither* side has reliable arguments – or a reliable theory.

The reader should keep these thoughts in mind the next time

a well-known professor announces a new theory for the origins of mankind, and claims that only his theory is supported by *"clear and convincing"* scientific evidence. As we have seen, evidence that seems clear and convincing to one distinguished scientist may be described by his equally distinguished colleague as *"inherently flawed, and relying on a long list of assumptions."*

In view of this bizarre situation, it is easy to understand the lament of Professor Trinkaus about the tendency of paleoanthropologists to see whatever they want to see in the fossil data. He writes: *"What is uncanny – and disheartening – is the way in which each side can muster the same fossil record into utterly different syntheses for human evolution. Reading their papers side by side gives the reader a distinct feeling of having awakened in a Kafka novel."* [14]

NOTES

1. N. Eldredge and I. Tattersall, 1982, *The Myths of Human Evolution* (Columbia University Press: New York), p. 120.
2. Eldredge and Tattersall, p. 2.
3. T.D. White, G. Suwa, and B. Asfaw, 1995, *Nature*, Vol. 375, p. 88.
4. Y. Coppens, July 1994, *Scientific American*, pp. 62–69.
5. M. Leakey and A. Walker, June 1997, *Scientific American*, pp. 60–65.
6. D. Pilbeam, March 1984, *Scientific American*, pp. 63–69.
7. B. Wood, 1987, *Nature*, Vol. 327, pp. 187–188.
8. I. Tattersall, January 2000, *Scientific American*, pp. 38–44.
9. A.C. Wilson and R.L. Cahn, April 1992, *Scientific American*, pp. 22–27. The article is entitled, "The Recent African Genesis of Humans."
10. A.G. Thorne and M.H. Wolpoff, April 1992, *Scientific American*, pp. 28–33. The article is entitled, "The Multiregional Evolution of Humans."
11. D. Pilbeam, 1980, in *Major Trends in Evolution*, ed. L.K. Konigson (Pergamon Press: London), p. 267.
12. A.R. Templeton, 1992, quoted in *Scientific American*, May 1992, p. 80.
13. E. Trinkaus and P. Shipman, 1993, *The Neandertals* (Jonathan Cape: London), p. 379.
14. Trinkaus and Shipman, p. 390.

16

Darwin's Theory of Evolution

Over 150 years have passed since Charles Darwin published his famous book, *On the Origin of Species*. Nearly a century has passed since the formulation of neo-Darwinism, the modern version of Darwin's theory of evolution. This theory is also known as the synthetic theory of evolution, because it is a *synthesis* of Darwin's original ideas (natural selection, survival of the fittest, struggle for existence, adaptation) with modern genetics and population biology. During this period, Darwin's theory of evolution has become one of the best known theories in the realm of science, taught in every school, discussed by every intelligent person, the subject of innumerable articles. Today, there is hardly anyone, however minimal his education, who has not heard of Darwin's theory.

In view of this long history, one would expect to find overall agreement among evolutionary biologists regarding the content of Darwin's theory and the basic facts about evolution. In science, unlike other disciplines, there are objective methods of examining data and arriving at conclusions that are accepted by the entire scientific community.

Therefore, one would have thought that during the past half-century, scientists would have succeeded in sorting out the basic principles of the evolution of the animal kingdom and, more particularly, of Darwin's theory of evolution. However, this is by no means the case. In fact, it is quite astonishing to witness the strident arguments that persist to this day among leading authorities concerning even the most fundamental principles of evolution.

It should be emphasized that the sharp disputes over long-standing questions of evolutionary biology are *not* the critical comments of religious biologists with creationist tendencies, who raise questions in order to cast doubts and aspersions on evolution. Only *mainstream biologists* will be quoted here, scientists who publish their articles in the *most prestigious scientific journals* in the field. The controversies about major issues in evolutionary biology are *real,* and they deal with most fundamental matters that have been debated for decades without achieving a scientific consensus.

Controversies

WHAT IS A SPECIES?

The question posed here is surely strange. Why do evolutionary biologists not know what a species is? The title of Darwin's famous book, *On the Origin of Species,* would seem to imply that scientists *do agree* on what is meant by a *species* of animal. Otherwise, what was Darwin talking about? In view of this, it will probably come as quite a surprise to many readers to learn that it is not clear to biologists just what constitutes an animal species or, even more astonishing, whether the concept of a species has any meaning.

It should be emphasized that we are *not* discussing the existence of a few unclear borderline cases, as happens with every definition. Rather, there exists a fundamental ambiguity about what is meant by the word *"species."*

The considerable controversy regarding this question has persisted for many decades[1] and has come to be known as the "species problem."[2] The fact that the species problem continues to vex biologists, can be inferred from the *Proceedings* of the First International Symposium on Biology, held at the University of Tokyo in November 1985. The first two papers in the *Proceedings* present the diametrically opposing views of leading authorities.

Professor Peter Raven, Director of the Missouri Botanical Gardens, argues[3]:

> *"One should turn away from the biological species as a unit of fundamental evolutionary significance... species do not have an objective reality in nature... It is the population, not the species, which should be the focus of evolutionary studies. We have embarrassingly little evidence for some widely-held notions in systematics and evolutionary biology."*

In complete contrast to these views, Professor Walter Bock of Columbia University argues[4]:

> *"Species have an objective reality ... Species and speciation play a very important role in macro-evolutionary change ... Interactions between species are the major source of the directional selective pressures that drive evolutionary changes."*

The standard textbook definition of a species is a group of animals that form an interbreeding population.[5] In other words, the criterion for determining whether or not two animals belonging to the same species is whether or not they interbreed in the wild to produce fertile offspring. In a laboratory or a zoo, one can artificially cause interbreeding among different species (lions and tigers, for example), but this never occurs in the wild.

Unfortunately, this standard criterion for a species has been shown to be incorrect. It is now recognized that there are, in fact, many examples of animals that belong to different species, but nevertheless interbreed quite freely in the wild to produce fertile hybrids. According to Professor James Mallet of University College, London: *"About a quarter of all species of ducks, gamebirds, and pheasants hybridize in the wild ... For coral reef fish, the figure is 20% ... Blue whales hybridize with fin whales ... A quarter of all Heliconius species of butterflies hybridize in the wild."*[6] Mallet emphasizes that the recognition of widespread hybridization in nature *"is nothing less than a completely new way of looking at the animal kingdom ... ignoring these genetic leaks by mainstream biological opinion has created a myopic view of evolution."*[7]

ARE MUTATIONS RANDOM?

An animal is determined by its array of genes – segments of long thread-like molecules (DNA) found in every cell of every living creature. Elephants have elephant genes; cockroaches have cockroach genes; kangaroos have kangaroo genes. In sexual reproduction, the genes of the parents are copied before transmission to the offspring. An error, called a *mutation,* occasionally occurs in the biological process of copying the genes. The resulting offspring is said to have undergone a genetic mutation.

One of the cornerstones of evolutionary biology is that all mutations are *random.*[8] Mutations are not *directed* by any agency to solve some problem faced by the organism. There is no connection whatsoever between the occurrence of a mutation and its being beneficial or harmful to the organism. Mutations are always the result of *pure chance.*

Random mutations constitute the raw material on which natural selection operates. Darwin's theory of evolution is based on the twin pillars of *random* mutations forming genetic variety among a population of animals, followed by *non-random* natural selection that "selects" which of these different individual animals is more fit to survive. Thus, evolution is driven by the *interplay* between random processes (mutations) and non-random processes (natural selection). This is the essence of the theory of evolution.

In view of this fundamental understanding of Darwin's theory, it came as quite a surprise to evolutionary biologists when some experiments suggested that mutations may not be random after all. In 1988, Professor John Cairns and his colleagues at the Harvard University School of Public Health reported in the influential journal *Nature* "*that cells may have mechanisms for choosing which mutations will occur.*"[9]

In their experiment, Cairns and co-workers developed a strain of bacteria that could *not* digest lactose (milk sugar), and then fed them *only* lactose. In the absence of food that they could digest, these bacteria were not expected to multiply. However, instead of remaining inert, some of these bacteria *mutated* one of their genes to make the enzyme that *could* digest lactose, and these mutated bacteria then flourished. The researchers were utterly astonished by what they had discovered (*"That such events ever occur seems almost unbelievable"*[10]), and emphasized the far-reaching implications[11]:

> *"The main purpose of this paper is to show how insecure is our belief in the randomness of mutations. This idea [of random mutations] seems to be a doctrine that has never been properly put to the test. We describe here some experiments and give evidence suggesting that bacteria can choose which mutations they should produce."*

The revolutionary nature of these findings, termed "directed mutation," can be gauged from the fact that a full decade later, the usually staid *Scientific American* was characterizing these results as "sensational experiments" leading to an "incendiary idea." *Scientific American* entitled their article "Evolution Evolving," with the subtitle, *"New findings suggest that mutation is more complicated than anyone thought,"* and proclaimed that the experimental results of the Harvard University team diametrically opposed the accepted principles of evolutionary biology: *"This radical proposal [of directed mutation] collided head-on with the sacrosanct principle that mutations occur at a rate that is completely unrelated to whatever consequences they might have [for the organism] ... This incendiary idea ignited a firestorm of debate."*[12]

The idea of directed mutation is so unthinkable to evolutionary biologists that in the years following the Cairns experiments, explanations for these results have been proposed that mimic the appearance of directed mutation. Professor Barry Hall of Rochester University states that whatever explanation finally solves this startling puzzle, *"the mechanisms that produce the ghost of directed mutation could shake up biology."*[13]

WHAT FACTORS CONTROL EVOLUTION?

Readers who doubt that biologists are still arguing about what factors control evolution, are invited to read *Causes of Evolution*. Here is how the editors explain the purpose of the volume[14]:

> *"We wanted to see what would happen if paleobiologists were asked to identify what they believed were the causal factors controlling evolution ... We asked them to comment on the relative roles of biotic and abiotic, intrinsic and extrinsic factors ... We hoped that identifying and categorizing the causal factors proposed by evolutionary biologists could contribute to better understanding of the role that different factors play in evolutionary processes."*

Is this question central to evolutionary biology? Professor Stephen Gould of Harvard University writes that *"the two largely orthogonal dichotomies selected by the editors have been central to evolutionary biology ever since Darwin – and never resolved. Darwin's own treatment of these issues illustrates their crucial character."*[15]

Gould's assessment is shared by Professor Norman Gilinsky of Virginia State University: *"When discussion and debate over an issue continue for a century and a half with little prospect for resolution, it's time to re-evaluate the question ... This emphasizes the need to rethink our entire conceptualization of organism and environment and, thereby, the entire question of biotic versus abiotic causes."*[16]

It is surely strange to read of *"the need to rethink our entire conceptualization"* of a problem that *"has been central to evolutionary biology ever since Darwin."*

HAS THERE HAS BEEN ANY EVOLUTIONARY PROGRESS OVER THE HISTORY OF THE ANIMAL KINGDOM?

The question that serves as the title of this section must seem astonishing. We are taught that Darwin's motivation for proposing his theory of evolution was to provide a mechanism to explain *how* progressive biological change came about. Therefore, how could anyone suggest that evolutionary progress has never occurred? Moreover, why can this question not be settled by simply examining the extensive fossil record for signs of evolutionary progressive change? Why is there any dispute at all? But dispute there is!

Richard Dawkins and Stephen Jay Gould are respected evolutionary biologists. Both are professors at world-famous universities (the former at Oxford, the latter at Harvard); both have introduced important scientific concepts in the field of evolutionary biology (Dawkins: the selfish gene; Gould: punctuated equilibrium); both are eloquent and prolific writers who have authored best-sellers on evolutionary biology. But here the similarity ends. These two biologists *completely disagree* about some of the most basic questions regarding evolutionary biology, *including* the question posed above.

Has evolutionary progress occurred in the animal kingdom? Dawkins answers with an unequivocal "Yes!" whereas Gould answers with an equally unequivocal "No!"

To stimulate debate, the editor of *Evolution*, the premier scientific journal in the field, decided to pit these two famous biologists against each other, by having each man review the other's most recent book (*Climbing Mount Improbable* by Dawkins, and *Full House*[17] by Gould). The editor notes with satisfaction that *"we expected – and received – two frank and provocative articles about important issues in our field."*[18]

Chief among the important issues was the question of whether or not there has been any evolutionary progress over the history of the animal kingdom. Gould maintains that *"the notion of 'progress' in evolution is an illusion based on anthropomorphic bias."*[19] In complete contrast, Dawkins maintains that *"evolution is clearly and importantly progressive ... adaptive evolution is deeply, indispensably progressive."*[20]

Professor David Depew of the University of Iowa has published an amusing article about this controversy, entitled "Are Evolutionists Still Hooked on Progress?"[21]

An Astonishing Situation

One can only wonder at such controversies. Here we have a situation in which two famous scientists (Dawkins and Gould) look at the same data, bring equally competent expertise to the analysis, and come to diametrically opposite conclusions! The editor of *Evolution* writes[22]:

> *"Throughout the past half century, our journal has witnessed many controversies, but none more persistent than the debate about the roles of random versus deterministic forces in evolution. Stephen*

Jay Gould has constantly emphasized the importance of chance and contingency, [whereas] Richard Dawkins embraces a deterministic world view, emphasizing the power of natural selection."

A further source of wonderment is that each of these famous evolutionary biologists informs the readers of *Evolution* that his equally famous colleague does not understand even the most basic principles of evolutionary biology!

Dawkins writes of Gould that *"his argument is flawed ... Gould is wrong ... Gould's attempt to reduce all progress to a trivial artifact constitutes a surprising impoverishment and a demeaning of the richness of evolutionary processes."*[23]

Gould writes of Dawkins that *"his logic is seriously flawed by an ill-chosen metaphorical apparatus developed to carry the book's central logic ... such imagery is especially misleading ... the conceptual foundation of Dawkins' book is deeply invalid at its core."*[24]

It should be emphasized that Gould and Dawkins are not arguing about some of the latest scientific results, regarding which disagreement would be natural. Their differences center on the very essence of their discipline – matters that have been discussed in detail for decades. Only in evolutionary biology does one find this bizarre situation that even the most fundamental principles are still subject to sharp dispute.

In contrast to this, consider my own scientific field, theoretical physics. Can one imagine two famous physicists totally disagreeing about the content of Einstein's theory of relativity or Maxwell's theory of electromagnetic radiation or the Schroedinger-Heisenberg quantum theory? Can one imagine a famous physicist accusing an equally famous colleague of not understanding one of the basic theories of physics?

I have mentioned the quantum theory in particular because there are disputes about the *interpretation* of the quantum theory,[25] which is an extremely weird theory[26] with important philosophical implications. However, there is no difference of opinion at all about how this theory explains the phenomena observed in nature.[27] However, such arguments lie at the heart of the controversies that rage in evolutionary biology.

More Controversies

The controversies discussed so far are only the tip of the iceberg. One need merely read recent scientific books or articles published in the leading journals to become convinced of how many of the central issues in evolutionary biology remain shrouded in confusion. The two following examples will serve to illustrate this important point.

NATURAL SELECTION

Professor John Endler of the University of California writes[28]:

> *"Those who think that natural selection is the most important factor in evolution, work primarily with morphological traits in natural populations, whereas those who consider natural selection to be unimportant tend to work with molecular or biochemical traits in laboratory populations."*

Professor Jeffry Mitton of the University of Colorado adds[29]:

> *"We find that natural selection means many things to many people… Differences of opinion concerning the nature and importance of natural selection contribute to several unresolved issues."*

An article in the journal *Evolution*, entitled "Controversies over the Units of Selection," begins as follows[30]:

> *"One of the most enduring problems in evolutionary biology has been the identification of the levels and units which form the targets for natural selection."*

SPECIATION

Professor Bradley Shaffer of the University of California describes the many scientific controversies associated with speciation, which is clearly one of the central issues of evolutionary biology[31]:

"Speciation, modes of speciation, mechanisms, hybrid zones, iso-lating mechanisms, reinforcement. These words, and many others associated with speciation research, often bring fear to practicing evolutionary biologists, and certainly to us who try to teach evo-lution. No one seems to be able to agree even on the terminology associated with speciation, let alone the proper way to study the process... Ultimately, I find myself simply saying [to my students] that there are lots of opinions, little resolution, and several ways of looking at the problem, and moving on before anyone gets even more frustrated. What an unfortunate way to deal with the topic that was of primary concern to Darwin, and has been a central focus of evolutionary biology ever since."

Conclusion

One stands in awe at the welter of confusion and mystery that abounds in evolutionary biology. Although this field has been the subject of intensive research for many decades, the expected scientific consensus regarding the basic principles has not yet materialized.

NOTES

1. See, for example, the many books and articles on this subject over the years by the eminent evolutionary biologist, Professor Ernst Mayr of Harvard University: 1942, *Systematics and Origin of Species* (Columbia University Press: New York); 1957, *The Species Problem* (American Association for the Advancement of Science: New York), Publication No. 50; 1963, *Animal Species and Evolution* (Harvard University Press: Cambridge, MA).

2. See, for example, D.J. Howard, 1988, *Evolution*, vol. 42, pp. 1111–1112.

3. P.H. Raven, 1986, in *Modern Aspects of Species*, ed. K. Iwatsuki (University of Tokyo Press), pp. 11–29.

4. W.J. Bock, 1986, in *Modern Aspects of Species*, ed. K. Iwatsuki (University of Tokyo Press), pp. 31–57.

5. See, for example, the widely-used university textbook by E.P. Solomon, L.R. Berg, D.W. Martin and C. Villee, 1996, *Biology*, 4th ed. (Harcourt Brace College Publishers: New York), p. 434.

6. J. Mallet, 3 July 1999, *New Scientist*, pp. 32–36.

7. Mallet, p. 33.

8. See, for example, the widely-used university textbook by E.P. Solomon, L.R. Berg, D.W. Martin and C. Villee, 1996, *Biology*, 4th ed. (Harcourt Brace College Publishers: New York), p. 423.

9. J. Cairns, J. Overbaugh, and S. Miller, 1988, *Nature*, vol. 335, pp. 142–145.

10. *Ibid.*, p. 145.

11. *Ibid.*

12. "In Focus", September 1997, *Scientific American*, p. 9.

13. B.G. Hall, September 1997, *Scientific American*, p. 12.

14. R.M. Ross and W.D. Allmon, eds., 1990, *Causes of Evolution: A Paleonto-logical Perspective* (University of Chicago Press), p. 1.

15. S.J. Gould, in Ross and Allmon, Foreword, p. vii.

16. N.L. Gilinsky, 1992, *Evolution*, vol. 46, pp. 578, 579.

17. Gould's book was published in England under the different title of *Life's Grandeur*.

18. J. Coyne, 1997, *Evolution*, vol. 51, p. 1015.

19. *Ibid.*, p. 1015.

20. R. Dawkins, 1997, *Evolution*, vol. 51, p. 1017.

21. D. Depew, 1998, *Evolution*, vol. 52, pp. 921–924.

22. Coyne, p. 1015.

23. Dawkins, pp. 1015, 1018, 1020.

24. S.J. Gould, 1997, *Evolution*, vol. 51, pp. 1021, 1022.

25. See the article entitled, "Quantum Theory Needs No Interpretation" by C.A. Fuchs and A. Peres, March 2000, *Physics Today*, pp. 70–71.

26. See the article entitled, "Is the Moon There When No One is Looking? – Reality and Quantum Theory" by D. Mermin, April 1985, *Physics Today*, pp. 38–47.

27. R.P. Feynman, 1985, *QED – The Strange Theory of Light and Matter* (Princeton University Press).

28. J.A. Endler, 1986, *Natural Selection in the Wild* (Princeton University Press), p. 239.

29. J.B. Mitton, 1989, *Evolution*, vol. 43, p. 1339.

30. J.B. Mitton, 1987, *Evolution*, vol. 41, p. 232.

31. H.B. Shaffer, 1990, *Evolution*, vol. 44, p. 1711.

17

Non-Darwinian Theories
of Evolution

The title of this chapter may strike the reader as a contradiction. It is widely believed that Charles Darwin's theory of evolution, formulated in 1859, is the *only* scientific theory that explains the evolution of the animal kingdom. In fact, however, several other theories have been proposed to account for the vast panorama of animal and plant life that we observe today. These competing theories will be discussed in this chapter.

Darwin held that each animal of a given species has different physical characteristics, and as a result, some members of the species are better able to survive (*"more fit"*) than others. In each generation, many more offspring are produced than can possibly survive to the next generation. The individuals that survive long enough to reproduce will be those having the characteristics that enable them to better adapt to the local environment. Animals that do not possess these characteristics are not *"adaptive,"* and will perish in the *"struggle for existence."* This process by which nature weeds out the "less fit" is known as natural selection. In the course of very many generations, the less fit animals disappear, whereas the more fit become dominant in each area. In this way, new species gradually evolve and previously existing species become extinct. This, in a nutshell, is Darwin's theory of evolution.

The competing theories of evolution are non-Darwinian in the sense that their explanation for biological evolution is *unrelated* to the basic Darwinian ideas of survival of the fittest, adaptation, and natural selection.

Before discussing some of the important non-Darwinian theories of evolution, we wish to explore the following question: Why does Darwin's theory continue to hold such sway on the public mind, while the competing theories of evolution remain unknown? Why is the very existence of non-Darwinian theories of evolution almost a trade secret among evolutionary biologists?

As we shall see, the reason for the widespread unawareness of non-Darwinian theories of evolution lies in the manner that evolution is explained to the general public. We are told over and over, in the most emphatic terms, that Darwin's theory offers a *complete* explanation of *all aspects* of evolution. If that is the case, it naturally follows that alternative non-Darwinian theories of evolution do not exist.

"DARWIN'S DANGEROUS IDEA" BY DANIEL DENNETT

In recent years, evolution has become an exciting topic to the general public – the subject of numerous television science programs, as well as several books that have reached the best-seller lists. Most of these books have a common theme, namely, that Darwin's theory of evolution explains *absolutely everything* about the development of the animal kingdom, as well as many other features of the universe.

Anyone who thinks this statement is an exaggeration is invited to read the 1995 best-seller by Daniel Dennett, *Darwin's Dangerous Idea*. Dennett compares Darwin's basic idea to a universal acid (*"so corrosive that it will eat through anything!"*), writing:

> *"Darwin's idea bears an unmistakable likeness to a universal acid: it eats through just about every traditional concept, and leaves in its wake a revolutionized worldview … transformed in fundamental ways."*[1]

> *"If I were to give an award for the single best idea that anyone ever had, I'd give it to Darwin, ahead of Newton and Einstein and everyone else."*[2]

Rare praise indeed, since Newton and Einstein are universally considered the two greatest physicists who ever lived. Dennett explains[3] the reason for his unbounded admiration for "Darwin's magnificent idea":

> "Darwin's idea had been born to answer questions in biology, but it [also] offers answers to questions in cosmology and psychology … It unifies the realm of life, meaning and purpose, with the realm of space and time, cause and effect, mechanism and physical law … And if mindless evolution could account for the breathtakingly clever artifacts of the biosphere, how could the products of our minds be exempt? … Darwin's idea also dissolved the illusion of our own authorship, our own divine spark of creativity and understanding."

We are here told that Darwin's idea is not limited to explaining evolution, but also answers fundamental questions in fields as far apart as cosmology and psychology, including the very workings of the human mind. Since these dramatic assertions were made by a Distinguished Professor of Arts and Sciences and Director of the Center for Cognitive Studies at Tufts University (titles held by Daniel Dennett), the layman may be excused for not imagining that there are respected scientists who seriously doubt whether Darwin's ideas are even sufficient to explain the evolution of the animal kingdom.

Consider, for example, the words of Professor Stuart Kauffman, a leading authority of the new discipline of complexity theory[4] (to be discussed presently):

> "Darwin's natural selection captivates us all. But is it right? Better, is it adequate? I believe it is not … Darwin's appeal to a single force – natural selection – ignores that complex biological systems exhibit order spontaneously."

How trustworthy are Dennett's far-reaching claims? *Darwin's Dangerous Idea* was reviewed by a well-known evolutionary biologist, who filled several pages with a detailed critique of the many scientific errors, gross omissions, and other defects of the book.[5] The review was sarcastically entitled "Dennett's Dangerous Idea."

What interests us here is not the lack of scientific accuracy of Dennett's book (*"marred by factual errors"*). Rather, we ask how Dennett deals with the non-Darwinian theories of evolution. How accurately and fairly are they presented?

In fact, Dennett so blatantly and completely ignores all non-Darwinian theories, that the reviewer could not contain his amazement, writing[36]: *"Consider this remarkable omission. Although a full third of his book examines challenges to evolution by natural selection 'that have arisen within biology itself,' Dennett never once utters the words 'neutral theory' or 'Kimura'! What can account for this astonishing omission?"*

The reference is to the neutral theory of molecular evolution (to be discussed presently) proposed by the Japanese geneticist, Professor Motoo Kimura. *"This theory ranks among the most interesting and powerful adjuncts to evolutionary explanation since Darwin's formulation of natural selection."*[7] And yet, Dennett ignores it entirely! No wonder the reviewer expresses amazement at *"this astonishing omission"* and concludes that *"Dennett apparently sees red whenever adaptation is questioned, undermining any hope of a balanced presentation."*[8] Adaptation is, of course, a central feature of Darwinian natural selection.

Particularly perceptive is the reviewer's comment regarding a possible *reason* for Dennett's *"remarkable omission"* of the important non-Darwinian theories of evolution: *"Dennett may not want to let the cat out of the bag, and inform the layman reader that many biologists believe that non-Darwinian evolution is common."*[9]

The reviewer's point is easily understood. After asserting unequivocally and repeatedly that Darwin's theory of evolution is *"the single best idea anyone has ever had,"*[10] Dennett is not going to devote much time to discussing competing ideas that tend to diminish its importance.

"THE BLIND WATCHMAKER" BY RICHARD DAWKINS

Richard Dawkins's best-selling books on the subject of evolution, felicitously written, have gained for him an academic chair at the University of Oxford as Professor of the Public Understanding of Science. We here consider one of the most famous of his books about evolution, *The Blind Watchmaker*, and ask how Dawkins deals with the important subject of non-Darwinian theories of evolution. The answer is given right in the preface, where Dawkins *denies the very possibility* of a non-Darwinian theory of evolution! *"I want to persuade the reader that the Darwinian world-view is the only known theory that could, in principle, solve the mystery of our existence."*[11] And why do some people, nevertheless, refuse to accept Darwin's theory? Dawkins asserts that lack of acceptance must be due to a defect in the functioning of the brain! *"It is almost as if the human brain were specifically designed to misunderstand Darwinism, and to find it hard to believe."*[12]

Dawkins wastes no time in stating his position. The very first sentence of *The Blind Watchmaker* asserts that Darwin's theory has finally solved the "mystery of evolution." *"This book is written in the conviction that our own existence once presented the greatest of all mysteries, but that it is a mystery no longer because it is solved."*[13]

The reader of these dramatic words would hardly imagine that Darwin's theory *fails* to account for important features of the evolutionary history of the animal kingdom – features which *are explained* by non-Darwinian theories. Consider the impact theory (to be discussed presently), proposed by Nobel laureate Luis Alvarez and his son Walter. The bulletin of the American Physical Society refers to this theory as *"tremendously important."*[14] Gould calls it *"one of the two most important paleontological discoveries of the past twenty years."*[15] But the impact theory is *never mentioned* in *The Blind Watchmaker*.

If this is how evolution is presented in a best-seller, then it is not surprising that the public remains unaware of the very existence of non-Darwinian theories of evolution.

PROFESSOR ERNST MAYR

The opinion that Darwin's 1859 theory of evolution requires no revision today is not limited to the authors discussed above. Even major figures in evolutionary biology are afflicted with the idea that nothing of significance has ever happened that might change our understanding of how evolution works.

Ernst Mayr is Professor of Zoology at Harvard University, and one of the principal architects of the neo-Darwinian synthesis. On the occasion of his 90th birthday, Mayr was interviewed by *Scientific American*. When asked about changes in thinking that have taken place in evolutionary biology over the many years, Mayr made the astonishing declaration that *no changes at all* had occurred during the past 150 years! He said bluntly: *"In 1859, Darwin published his theory of descent through natural selection. Look at it now. It stands there, not a dent in it."*[16]

The interviewer was moved to comment that: *"Mayr believes that the existing framework of the evolutionary synthesis is unshakable."* A strange view for a scientist!

These extreme opinions of Ernst Mayr would naturally prevent any recognition that important contributions to evolutionary biology have been made by non-Darwinian theories. Some of these concepts will now be described.

Complexity Theory

One of the most exciting discoveries in recent years is known as complexity theory (also called self-organized criticality). Scientists have found that it is characteristic of complex systems to remain static for a long period of time, and then *suddenly* undergo a fundamental change – *spontaneously and without any driving force.*[17] The implications of complexity theory are quite widespread, including the physical sciences, the life sciences, and even the social sciences. For example, it is now widely thought that the reasons underlying the stock market crash of 1987 are not connected with economics, but that the market crashed *spontaneously*, because of the complexity of the system of stock trading.

The new findings of complexity theory were deemed so important that in 1984, George Cowan and three Nobel laureates, Philip Anderson, Murray Gell-Mann, Kenneth Arrow, established the Sante Fe Institute in New Mexico as an interdisciplinary research institution devoted to the study of the many implications of complexity theory for a wide variety of disciplines.

An explanation of the remarkable behavior of complex systems is far beyond the scope of this book. Reading even the simplified "popular" versions of complexity theory can be a daunting experience for the layman. For those who like a challenge, excellent introductions to complexity theory are given in *How Nature Works* by Per Bak, and in *At Home in the Universe: Laws of Self-Organization and Complexity* by Stuart Kauffman. Both authors are among the founders of this new science.

COMPLEXITY THEORY AND EVOLUTION

Scientists were not slow to recognize that living systems – animals and plants – satisfy the criteria of complexity. Moreover, the fundamental changes that have occurred over time in living creatures – what we call evolution – are reminiscent of the *spontaneous* changes that characterize almost every complex system. Therefore, biological evolution *may not be due* to the Darwinian mechanisms of survival of the fittest and adaptation. The natural behavior of complex systems may be the correct explanation for the evolutionary changes observed in the animal kingdom.

The most striking similarity between biological evolution and complexity theory lies in the phenomenon known as punctuated equilibrium. This concept expresses the fact that the fossil record indicates that evolutionary changes tend to occur *suddenly*, exactly as predicted by complexity theory, rather than gradually. *"The history of most fossil species includes features particularly inconsistent with gradualism."*[18] Indeed, this fundamental prediction of complexity theory (that complex systems remain *static* for a long period of time before suddenly undergoing a fundamental change) is a precise description of the fossil record. *"The fossil record reveals that species typically survive for a million generations or more without evolving very much."*[19]

COMPLEXITY THEORY AS A NON-DARWINIAN THEORY OF EVOLUTION

The preceding discussion suggests that many features of the evolution of the animal kingdom are better explained in terms of complexity theory than by the Darwinian mechanisms of natural selection and

206 · FOSSILS AND FAITH

adaptation. It is very instructive to quote a few of the leading authorities on the relationship between Darwin's theory and complexity theory.

Professor Stuart Kauffman of the Santa Fe Institute seriously doubts whether Darwin's theory offers the correct explanation of the evolution of the animal kingdom:

> "We live in a world of stunning biological complexity. Where did this grand architecture come from? For over a century, the only existing explanation was natural selection. Darwin taught us that the order of the biological world arose as natural selection sifted among random mutations for the rare, useful forms. Recent research has shown that this dominant view of biology is incomplete. Self-organization is the root source of order ... Darwinism is not enough."[20]

> "Since Darwin, we have thought that without natural selection, there would be nothing but incoherent disorder. I shall show that this idea is wrong ... Complexity spontaneously generates much of the order of the natural world."[21]

Kauffman's conclusion is that Darwin's theory is *not* the correct explanation for the evolution of the animal kingdom. His conclusion is strikingly different from the unequivocal claim made in *The Blind Watchmaker* that *"the Darwinian world-view of slow, gradual, cumulative natural selection is the explanation for our existence."*[22]

Professor Henrik Jensen of Imperial College emphasizes that many observed features of the evolutionary development of the animal kingdom are quite typical of the features exhibited by all complex systems, physical and well as biological[23].

> "Since the 1970s, it has been known that evolution takes place through bursts of activity, separated by calm periods ... Species survive for long periods of time, and then disappear within a relatively short span of years. Moreover, the extinction of one species often occurs simultaneously with the extinction of many other species. When evolution and extinction are portrayed in this fashion, we immediately spot the similarities with other examples of the dynamics of complex systems."

The quotations presented above could easily be multiplied by including the articles of Professor Per Bak of the Brookhaven National Laboratory,[24] Professor Leo Kadanoff of the University of Illinois,[25] and Professor Philip Anderson of Princeton University.[26] All these leading authorities suggest that complexity theory may be the principal reason for the important changes that have occurred in the evolutionary history of the animal kingdom.

In the last few decades, many scientists have recognized that Darwin's mechanisms – survival of the fittest and adaptation – may only be of secondary importance in explaining the development of the animal kingdom. The full range of fossil evidence seems to be explained primarily by complexity theory, but supplemented and fine-tuned by Darwinian natural selection.

Neutral Theory of Molecular Evolution

Another important non-Darwinian theory of evolution is the neutral theory of molecular evolution, proposed in 1968 by Professor Motoo Kimura of the National Institute of Genetics in Japan.[27] This theory asserts that the genetic mutations that become incorporated into the gene pool are "selectively neutral." In complete contrast to the Darwinian theory of natural selection, the neutral theory holds that new mutated genes are neither more nor less advantageous than the genes they replace. Kimura explains[28]:

> "For more than a decade, I have championed a view different from Darwin … My theory holds that at the molecular level, most evolutionary change and most of the variability within a species are not caused by selection, but by the 'random drift' of mutant genes that are selectively neutral."

On the basis of a mathematical analysis of the molecular changes needed to explain observed evolutionary development, Kimura came to the conclusion that the Darwinian mechanisms were not adequate to explain the data. He writes[29]:

"The picture of evolutionary change that emerged from molecular studies seemed to be quite incompatible with the expectations of neo-Darwinism ... Intrinsic evolutionary rates are essentially determined by the structure and function of molecules, and not by environmental conditions ... Selectionists consider environmental conditions to be the major determinant of genetic variability. This prediction seemed logical and plausible, but it failed to account for the data."

Especially interesting is the question of how his colleagues responded to Kimura's radical departure from the orthodox Darwinian approach to evolution, based on survival of the fittest and adaptation – the ability of an animal to adapt to its local environment. Kimura's description of his colleagues' reaction to his research is the most astonishing statement that I have ever read in a *Scientific American* article[30]:

"People have told me, directly and indirectly, that the neutral theory of molecular evolution is not important because neutral genes are not involved in adaptation. My own view is that what is important is to find the truth, and that if the neutral theory is a valid investigative hypothesis, then to establish the theory, to test it against the data and to defend it, are worthwhile scientific enterprises."

One can imagine the great pressures that must have been exerted on Professor Kimura to abandon his research into non-Darwinian evolution, if he felt moved to conclude his article with those words.

Impact Theory

One of the long-standing puzzles of evolutionary biology is the sudden demise of all the world's dinosaurs and all other dinosaur-like species. These gigantic reptiles were among the most successful animals that ever lived, inhabiting every continent, the air (flying dinosaurs – pterosaurs), and the seas and oceans (marine dinosaurs – ichthyosaurs, plesiosaurs, mosasaurs). Then, after terrorizing all other forms of animal life for well over 100 million years (their name means "terrible lizard"), the dinosaurs abruptly disappeared from the fossil record, and together with them, about 70% of all other animal species. What catastrophe struck down all these enormous creatures that for so long had been so fit in the Darwinian sense?

This question is not new. For many decades, biologists have struggled with this conundrum, and the array of proposed explanations is truly staggering. No idea seemed too far-fetched to prevent some biologist from championing it. Gould has written an amusing account of the various bizarre hypotheses suggested in the course of time to explain the sudden destruction of all of the world's dinosaurs.[31]

The puzzle was finally solved in 1980, when Professors Luis and Walter Alvarez of the University of California showed that this mass extinction was caused by the impact of a meteor falling with tremendous speed from outer space and colliding with our planet with devastating results.[32] The meteoric impact occurred in the Yucatan Peninsula in Mexico. The overwhelming scientific evidence that now supports this explanation, known as the impact theory, was the subject of a detailed article in *Physics Today*.[33]

IMPORTANCE OF THE IMPACT THEORY

The importance for evolutionary history of the mass extinctions that have struck our planet in the course of time can hardly be overemphasized. This most famous of the mass extinctions, the one that led to the destruction of all the world's dinosaurs, has been the subject of many scientific articles. Gould describes[34] how very different the present-day animal kingdom would be, had this meteor not collided with the earth.[35]

> *"Without the great Cretaceous extinction [the mass extinction caused by the Alvarez meteor], the dinosaurs might still dominate the earth. Mammals might still be a small group of rat-like creatures casting about for an occasional bit of protein in a dinosaur egg. Primates would probably not have evolved.*
>
> *We owe our evolution to the great Cretaceous dying that cleared*

a path, yet spared our ancestors' lives to tread it. That meteor may well have been the sine qua non of our present existence."

The crucial importance of this meteoric impact and the subsequent mass extinction has also been pointed out by Alvarez[36]:

"From our human point of view, that impact [that destroyed all the dinosaurs] was one of the most important events in the history of our planet. Had it not taken place, the largest mammals alive today might still resemble the rat-like creatures that were scurrying around then, trying to avoid being devoured by dinosaurs."

NON-DARWINIAN CHARACTER OF THE IMPACT THEORY

The impact theory is non-Darwinian because the *cause* of the world-wide catastrophe was *extraterrestrial*, and hence *unrelated* to the local environment. It follows that the species that perished in the meteoric impact were *not less fit* than the survivors. The Darwinian principle of survival of the fittest is not relevant to a mass extinction of this kind.

The above explanation is the thesis of a widely-quoted article[37] (subsequently expanded into a book[38]) by Professor David Raup of the University of Chicago. Raup's article and book, both bearing the pithy title, "Extinctions: Bad Genes or Bad Luck?", discuss the important distinction between species being unable to adapt to local conditions ("bad genes," that is, *Darwin*) and extinctions due to events unrelated to species fitness ("bad luck," that is, *Alvarez*). As Raup explains[39]:

"If the extinction of a given species is more bad luck than bad genes, then the conventional Darwinian model is not correct ... pure chance would then favor some biologic groups over others – all in the absence of Darwinian natural selection between species."

Gould points out the non-Darwinian character of the impact theory, emphasizing that the survival of species is often caused by random events: contingency (what Raup calls luck) rather than by Darwinian fitness. In Gould's words[40]:

"Many people feel that conventional Darwinian reasons must rule the grand ebb and flow of major groups in the history of life ... Dinosaurs must have been bad at something that the surviving mammals could do well ... The facts of a mass extinction prove the fallacy of this argument. If some groups [of animals] slowly replaced other groups, some gaining in species over millions of years while others losing just as steadily, then a scenario of natural selection might seem irresistible. The groups that survived a mass extinction must have survived for a reason. They were the tough guys, the good competitors. But recent data on the extent of mass extinctions calls this comforting explanation into question. If nearly 96% of all species died, leaving as few as 2000 species to propagate all subsequent life, then it is clear that some groups died, and others survived, for no particular reason at all. Organisms can muster few defenses against a catastrophe of such magnitude. The survivors may simply be among the lucky 4% ... Evolutionary theory is stirring from the strict Darwinism that previously prevailed. Randomness has become a central focus because Darwin's dichotomy is breaking ... This is an exciting development in evolutionary theory."

I have quoted at some length from Raup and Gould to demonstrate that these leading authorities leave no doubt that the Alvarez impact theory constitutes a clear deviation from the Darwinian paradigm of survival of the fittest and natural selection.

It is important to make this point because there are biologists who still maintain that a mass extinction caused by a meteoric impact can be understood within the framework of Darwinian natural selection, and that nothing fundamentally new has occurred in our understanding of the mechanism for evolution.

For example, Professor Raphael Falk of the Hebrew University believes that the Alvarez meteoric impact and the accompanying mass extinction is simply an example of the Darwinian principle of the survival of the fittest. In fact, Falk is so convinced of this that he writes that to think otherwise is "stupid"![41]

The reluctance of some biologists to admit that a new paradigm has occurred in evolutionary biology is a marvelous example of the phenomenon described by the philosopher of science Thomas Kuhn in his well-known book, *The Structure of Scientific Revolutions.* Professor Kuhn points out that when a scientific revolution takes place leading to a new paradigm, many scientists find themselves unable to accept the new results. They continue to insist that the revolutionary ideas "fit under the rubric" of the older ideas, and that no change in thinking is required.

Charles Darwin

In 1859, Darwin formulated one of the most important theories ever proposed in biology, accounting admirably, in the best scientific tradition, for all the evidence known *at that time.* But 150 years have passed, our store of knowledge has vastly increased, and new, non-Darwinian ideas have taken their place upon the scientific stage. Men like Kimura, Alvarez, Raup, Anderson, Kadanoff, Kauffman, Gould, Stanley, and Bak are serious scientists of the first rank. When they tell us that Darwin's theory is insufficient to explain important aspects of the evolution of the animal kingdom, we would do well to lay aside our biases and to listen. It is time to move forward.

NOTES

1. D.C. Dennett, 1995, *Darwin's Dangerous Idea* (Penguin Books: London and New York), p. 63.
2. Dennett, p. 21.
3. Dennett, p. 63.
4. S.A. Kauffman, 1993, *The Origins of Order* (Oxford University Press), p. xiii.
5. H.A. Orr, 1996, *Evolution*, vol. 50, pp. 467–472.
6. Orr, p. 468.
7. S.J. Gould, 12 June 1997, *The New York Review*, p. 36.
8. Orr, p. 468.
9. Orr, p. 469.
10. Dennett, p. 21.
11. R. Dawkins, 1986, *The Blind Watchmaker* (W.W. Norton: New York and London), p. x.
12. Dawkins, p. xi.
13. Dawkins, p. ix.
14. *Physics Today*, January 1985, p. 11.
15. S.J. Gould, 1989, *Wonderful Life* (W.W. Norton: New York and London), p. 280.
16. "Profile – Ernst Mayr," August 1994, *Scientific American*, p. 15.
17. P. Bak, C. Tang, and K. Weisenfeld, 1987, *Physical Review Letters*, vol. 59, pp. 381–384.
18. S.J. Gould, *The Panda's Thumb*, 1980 (W.W. Norton: New York), p. 151.
19. S.M. Stanley, *New Evolutionary Timetable*, 1981 (Basic Books: New York), p. xv.
20. S.A. Kauffman, 1995, *At Home in the Universe: the Laws of Self-Organization and Complexity* (Oxford University Press), pp. vii, viii.
21. Kauffman, p. 8.
22. Dawkins, p. 318.
23. H.J. Jensen, 1998, *Self-Organized Criticality: Emergent Complex Behavior in Physical and Biological Systems* (Cambridge University Press), p. 27.
24. P. Bak and K. Chen, 1989, *Nature*, vol. 342, pp. 780–782; January 1991, *Scientific American*, pp. 26–33.
25. L.P. Kadanoff, March 1991, *Physics Today*, pp. 9–11.
26. P.W. Anderson, March 1990, *Physics Today*, pp. 9–11; July 1991, *ibid.*, pp. 9–10.
27. M. Kimura, February 1968, *Nature*, pp. 624–626.
28. M. Kimura, November 1979, *Scientific American*, p. 94.
29. Kimura, pp. 95, 98, 101.
30. Kimura, p. 104.

31. S.J. Gould, 1983, *Hen's Teeth and Horse's Toes* (W.W. Norton: New York and London), pp. 320–324.
32. L.W. Alvarez, W. Alvarez, *et al.*, 1980, *Science*, vol. 208, pp. 1095–1108.
33. L.W. Alvarez, July 1987, *Physics Today*, pp. 24–33.
34. Gould, pp. 320–331.
35. Gould, p. 329.
36. Alvarez, p. 33
37. D.M. Raup, 1981, *Acta Geologica Hispanica*, vol. 15, pp. 25–33.
38. D.M. Raup, 1991, *Extinctions: Bad Genes or Bad Luck?* (Oxford University Press).
39. Raup, pp. 26, 29.
40. Gould, pp. 333, 334, 338, 340.
41. R. Falk, Spring 1994, *Alpayim* (Am Oved Publishers: Tel Aviv), p. 139.

18

Darwinian Fundamentalism

An interesting phenomenon has occurred in the past few years. A surprisingly large number of books dealing with science have been published. Aimed at the educated layman, some of these books have proved so popular that they have become best-sellers. One would think that professional scientists would applaud this development, but popularity is not always the most desired goal. Unfortunately, many of these best-selling science books have their science seriously in error. Nowhere is this problem more acutely felt than in the field of evolutionary biology, as will be seen in this chapter.

Criticism

The title of this chapter, "Darwinian Fundamentalism," is also the title of an article written by Professor Stephen Gould of Harvard University, a leading authority on evolutionary biology.[1] In his article, Gould attributes unscientific traits to some of today's most famous writers of evolutionary biology, accusing them of practicing *"a self-styled form of Darwinian fundamentalism ... pushing their line with an almost theological fervor."* The dictionary relates the term *"fundamentalism"* to religious belief, where it refers to *"the strict and literal adherence to divinely revealed principles."* For the devout, divine revelation is the basis for belief. However, scientific knowledge is derived from other sources. Thus, the term "fundamentalism" applied to a scientist indicates an unwillingness to accept scientific facts and the uncompromising advocacy of preconceived notions. Professor Gould comments wryly that *"Darwin has attained sainthood, if not divinity, among many evolutionary biologists."*[2]

Gould uses the words *"Darwinian fundamentalism"* to denote a complete lack of scientific objectivity regarding evolutionary biology, as well as a serious distortion of Darwin's writings. The evolutionary biologists he especially singles out for criticism include Richard Dawkins and Daniel Dennett, both of whom have written books that have reached the best-seller lists. According to Gould, what is presented to the public as the "science of evolution" would be more accurately described as the *"religion of evolution."*

Gould is not alone in criticizing the prevalence of fundamentalism in evolutionary biology. Similar criticisms have been voiced by Professor Niles Eldredge, curator at the world-famous American Museum of Natural History in New York, and recognized authority on evolutionary biology. In his recent book, appropriately entitled *Reinventing Darwin*, Eldredge used the term *"ultra-Darwinians"* to describe biologists who totally distort Darwin's ideas. He laments *"the inherent myopia of ultra-Darwinism,"* and characterizes their approach to evolution as *"a distortedly oversimplified view of the natural world in general, and of evolutionary processes in particular."*[3] Eldredge identifies Richard Dawkins as a prominent leader of the ultra-Darwinian camp.

Personae

In the discussion that follows, only the leading authorities will be quoted – scientists of the caliber of Professors Gould and Eldredge. This is an important point, because many books and articles criticizing evolutionary biologists have recently appeared, written by non-scientists – lawyers, journalists, physicians. *Such books and articles will not be quoted here.* All the sources referred to in this chapter, as well as throughout this book, are the writings of recognized experts in evolutionary biology.

Another important feature of the discussion is that all the scientists mentioned here are *strictly secular*. The science-*vs*-religion debate is *not* at issue here. Rather, the subject under discussion is the objectivity of the statements and claims made by three ultra-Darwinians: Richard Dawkins, Daniel Dennett, and Peter Atkins.

Before turning to the *scientific* statements of the ultra-Darwinians, let us consider their assertions about *religion*. Atkins, Dennett, and Dawkins are all militant atheists, as is shown by the following quotations from their writings: *"Religion is a dreadful disease of society and I think that science liberates people from the world's religions"* (Atkins)[4]; *"The kindly God who loves us, is, like Santa Claus, a myth of childhood, not anything that a sane adult could believe in"* (Dennett)[5]; *"Human vanity cherishes the absurd notion that our species is special"* (Dawkins).[6] Such pronouncements, made in the name of science, illustrate the "objectivity" of ultra-Darwinians and set the tone for our discussion.

Richard Dawkins

Professor Richard Dawkins, holder of a Chair in Public Understanding of Science at the University of Oxford, is the author of several best-sellers on evolutionary biology, including *The Blind Watchmaker*. In the preface of this book, Dawkins tells us of his great concern for truth and honesty: *"I care passionately about what is true and I never say anything that I do not believe to be right"*[7] – inspiring words indeed, if only the book lived up to them.

One would think it to be perfectly natural that what Darwin wrote in 1859 would be altered, even significantly altered, in the course of time, in the light of additional fossil data and new knowledge. Therefore, the introduction of a novel, exciting theory in 1972 into the scientific discipline which Darwin began more than a century ago should be expected, and even welcomed. *But not if one is an ultra-Darwinian!* A characteristic of Darwinian fundamentalism is that all new ideas are to be fought. This is illustrated in *The Blind Watchmaker*, whose "villain," Stephen Gould, had the temerity to propose a new idea in evolutionary biology, known as "punctuated equilibrium" – an idea that does not entirely coincide with what Darwin wrote. As we shall see, the *tactics* used by Dawkins to attack Gould are also characteristic of ultra-Darwinians.

ULTRA-DARWINIAN TACTICS

Dawkins begins his assault by quoting the following statement made by Gould: "*We avoid the excellent question – What good is 5% of an eye? – by arguing that the possessor of such an incipient structure did not use it for sight.*" Dawkins then goes on to ridicule Gould: "*Actually I don't think it is an excellent question. Vision that is 5% as good as yours or mine is very much worth having in comparison with no vision at all. Even 1% vision is better than total blindness. And 6% vision is better than 5%…*"[8]

Note what has happened. Gould's statement about 5% *of an eye* has been transformed by Dawkins into a statement about 5% *vision*, which is then ridiculed. Everyone knows that some vision, however minimal, is better than no vision at all.

But Gould did *not* write about 5% vision. He was discussing 5% of an eye, which clearly provides *no vision whatsoever*. (How high can one fly in 5% of an airplane? How fast can one travel in 5% of a car?) Therefore, 5% of an eye would seem to be completely useless, and Gould had indeed posed an "excellent question."

This example illustrates one of the basic tactics of ultra-Darwinians. Transform your opponent's words into something quite different that can then be easily ridiculed. And this from a man who claims to "*care passionately about what is true … and never says anything that [he] does not believe to be right.*"

PUNCTUATED EQUILIBRIUM

What is the concept of punctuated equilibrium that arouses such antagonism among the ultra-Darwinians? Gould and Eldredge reported, on the basis of a detailed study of the fossil record, that the *gradual* evolution of species *is not observed to occur*.[9] Instead, they discovered that the fossil record typically shows that a species remains unchanged, that is, in "equilibrium," for long periods of time, and then, on rare occasions, this equilibrium is suddenly "punctuated" by an extremely rapid evolutionary change. *Gradualism never appears in the fossil record.* As Gould has written[10]:

> "*The history of most fossil species includes features particularly inconsistent with gradualism: (i) Stasis: Most species exhibit no directional change during their tenure on Earth. They appear in the fossil record looking much the same as when they disappear; morphological change is usually limited and directionless. (ii) Sudden appearance: A species does not arise gradually by the steady transformation of its ancestors; it appears in the fossil record all at once and fully formed.*"

It is quite clear that there are very significant differences between the modern Gould-Eldredge scenario for evolution quoted above and the older, traditional description of Darwin's theory of evolution, as espoused by Dawkins in *The Blind Watchmaker*[11]:

> "*Cumulative selection, by slow and gradual degrees, is the explanation for the existence of life's complex design … It is the contention of the Darwinian world-view that slow, gradual, cumulative natural selection is the ultimate explanation for our existence… Gradualism is the very heart of the evolution theory, giving it the power to dissolve astronomical impossibilities and explain prodigies of apparent miracle.*"

WHY THE CONCEPT OF PUNCTUATED EQUILIBRIUM IS IMPORTANT

As the preceding discussion makes clear, the theory of punctuated equilibrium has confronted the ultra-Darwinians with a new approach to evolution. Following the standard ultra-Darwinian practice of opposing anything that differs from Darwin's original theory, Dawkins devotes an entire chapter of *The Blind Watchmaker* to attacking the theory of punctuated equilibrium. In this chapter, sarcastically entitled "Puncturing Punctuationism," he attempts to trivialize the idea, claiming that the concept of punctuated equilibrium is utterly devoid of any significance. Dawkins tells us again and again that: "*the theory of punctuated equilibrium is but a minor wrinkle on the surface of neo-Darwinian theory"* and *"a minor gloss on Darwinism"* and *"it is really a minor variety of Darwinism."* [12]

Those whose knowledge of punctuated equilibrium comes from Dawkins's book would be quite astonished to learn the views of mainstream evolutionary biologists. *The Cambridge Encyclopedia of Earth Sciences* considers punctuated equilibrium sufficiently important to warrant a detailed discussion, which asserts that: *"the model of punctuated equilibrium has recently become widely accepted."* [13] Similar statements abound in science journals: *"A characteristic of the fossil record is the presence of 'punctuations,' where new species appear on a relatively short geological time scale. Evolution is not a slow process, whereby one species gradually changes into another."* [14] In fact, every modern textbook on biology [15] contains a discussion of punctuated equilibrium.

Professor Steven Stanley of Johns Hopkins University, another leading authority, considered the idea of punctuated equilibrium so significant that he wrote an entire book to explain this new approach to evolutionary biology. His book, appropriately entitled *The New Evolutionary Timetable*, emphasizes the important *new* understanding in the field of evolutionary biology engendered by the concept of punctuated equilibrium. It is especially enlightening to read from Stanley's preface [16]:

> *"What I describe in this book is evidence that evolution is not quite what nearly all of us thought it to be a decade ago. The evidence comes from the fossil record – a record which now reveals that most evolution takes place rapidly ... While this "punctuational" view has displaced the traditional "gradualistic" view in the minds of many evolutionists, there remain dissenters. In this book, I offer opposition to the traditional portrayal. I attempt to give the interested layman access to the punctuational view and its implications. The emergence of the punctuational model of evolution is an exciting time in the history of evolutionary science."*

Note the striking differences between these two views. Whereas Stanley repeatedly stresses the fundamental importance of the discovery of punctuated equilibrium, Dawkins completely dismisses the entire concept (*"a minor wrinkle"*).

RELEVANCE OF PUNCTUATED
EQUILIBRIUM TO NEO-DARWINISM

Of particular significance is how the concept of punctuated equilibrium relates to Darwin's theory of evolution. Dawkins emphasizes in the strongest possible terms that punctuated equilibrium *does not lead to the slightest deviation* from the traditional neo-Darwinian understanding of how evolutionary processes operate. *"What needs to be said now, loud and clear, is the truth: that the theory of punctuated equilibrium lies firmly within the neo-Darwinian synthesis. It will take time to undo the damage wrought by overblown rhetoric."*[17]

How do other evolutionary biologists understand the relationship between neo-Darwinism and punctuated equilibrium? Consider the views of Stanley[18]:

> *"Darwin and the many architects of neo-Darwinism would have been confounded by the fossil evidence ... they would have been shocked ... It was a gradualistic view of evolution that led Darwin and others on their fruitless search ... Believing only in slow, persistent, gradual evolution, they postulated a long, undocumented [incorrect] history of early animal life.*
>
> *The fossil record has now answered with solid evidence, confronting gradualism with an insoluble problem ... Darwin reached in desperation for an ancient mythical kingdom. Other workers sustained this fanciful history into the 1960s to permit gradual evolution to account for the complexity of flowering plants ... Such assignments have now all been deemed erroneous."*

Steven Stanley's description of the relationship between neo-Darwinism and punctuated equilibrium is clearly very different from the "truth" proclaimed by Richard Dawkins. It is with considerable irony that we note that Dawkins's professorship is in the "Public Understanding of Science"!

It is a fundamental belief of the ultra-Darwinians is that natural selection is the *only* explanation for *all* evolutionary processes, and *nothing has changed* in this regard since the day Darwin proposed his theory more than a century ago.

If the reader thinks I am exaggerating, consider the words of Professor Ernst Mayr of Harvard University. When asked whether the concept of punctuated equilibrium requires any alteration in Darwin's theory, Mayr emphatically replied: *"Total rot, a lead balloon, a red herring!"*[19]

We recall the words of Stanley on Darwin and punctuated equilibrium: *"Darwin would have been confounded by the recent fossil evidence... He would have been shocked."*[20] Quite a difference between the views of Mayr and Stanley!

IMPACT THEORY

One of the most exciting discoveries in evolutionary biology was made in 1980 by Nobel laureate Luis Alvarez and his son Walter. They showed that the famous mass extinction that abruptly killed off all the world's dinosaurs, together with most other species, was caused by the impact of a meteor falling from outer space with tremendous speed and then colliding with our planet with devastating results.[21] This seminal finding, known as the impact theory, was the subject of an article in *Physics Today*, which concludes that *"the idea of astronomically caused catastrophes is tremendously important to evolutionary biologists."*[22]

The importance of the impact theory is that the *cause* of the worldwide catastrophe was extraterrestrial, and hence *unrelated* to the local environment. Since the species that perished in the aftermath of the meteoric impact were no less fit than the survivors, the principle of "survival of the fittest" is not relevant to this extinction. This is the central thesis of an article by Professor David Raup, past president of the American Paleontological Union.[23] Raup emphasizes the important distinction between an extinction caused by the inability of a species to adapt to local conditions (Darwin) and an extinction caused by an external event unrelated to the fitness of the species (Alvarez).

In view of the great scientific interest in the impact theory, one would expect the subject to merit a place in a book about evolutionary biology. *But not if the author is an ultra-Darwinian*! The tactic of ignoring important new discoveries finds expression in *The Blind Watchmaker* in that Dawkins does not devote *even one single word* to the impact theory, Alvarez or the meteor. And why? Because the meteoric impact caused an *abrupt* worldwide mass extinction, which is clearly not compatible with Dawkins's claim that "*slow, gradual natural selection is … the very heart of evolution theory*."[24]

This meteoric impact has been described by a Nobel laureate as "*one of the most important single events in the history of our planet*,"[25] characterized by a major scientific journal as "*a tremendously important idea to evolutionary biologists*,"[26] and depicted by a Harvard professor in the following words: "*Consciousness would not have evolved on our planet if this cosmic catastrophe had not claimed the dinosaurs as victims*."[27] But Richard Dawkins *does not even to mention* this event in *The Blind Watchmaker*!

INSULTING OPPONENTS

Some comment should be made about Dawkins's distasteful practice of insulting everyone who disagrees with him – a practice most unbecoming in a scientific debate. For example, Dawkins states that "*Gould has misled himself by his own rhetoric*,"[28] that cladists have "*a remarkably grandiose estimation of the importance of [their] branch of science*,"[29] and that "*the punctuationists sell themselves as revolutionaries*."[30] Dawkins writes of those who does not accept his views of evolution that they "*desperately want not to have to believe*" and they must be disagreeing "*for religious reasons*" or "*for political or ideological reasons*" or "*because it makes good journalistic copy*."[31]

Daniel Dennett

The next evolutionary biologist to be discussed is Daniel Dennett, Distinguished Professor of Arts and Sciences at Tufts University in Medford, Massachusetts. We will focus on his best-seller, *Darwin's Dangerous Idea*.[32] Our interest in Dennett stems from the fact that he too is an ultra-Darwinian, every bit as much as Dawkins. Indeed, their approaches to evolutionary biology are almost identical. It is, therefore, not surprising that on the cover of the paperback edition of Dennett's book, Dawkins proclaims it to be "a surpassingly brilliant book."

CRITIQUE OF DENNETT'S BOOK

Gould's assessment of Dennett's book is quite different. With the skill of the surgeon, Gould wields his critical scalpel to slice Dennett's book to ribbons[33]:

> "This limited and superficial book reads like the caricature of a cari-
> cature – for if Richard Dawkins has trivialized Darwin's richness...
> then Dennett, as Dawkins's publicist, manages to convert an already
> vitiated and improbable account into an even more simplistic and
> uncompromising doctrine... The record of life contains many more
> evolutionary things than are dreamt of in Dennett's philosophy."

Gould characterizes *Darwin's Dangerous Idea* as a book that is riddled with "*fallacy... discussions resting on ridicule and error ... false attribution ... misreading ... false charges ... gratuitous speculation of motives ... high density of errors ... simplistic distortion of Darwin's theory.*"[34] Gould thoroughly documents each and every one of his charges to produce a damning account of this best-seller.

Gould is not the only major scientist who has criticized Dennett's book. Professor Allen Orr of the University of Rochester has published a devastating review of *Darwin's Dangerous Idea* in the leading journal in evolutionary biology. Orr writes[35]:

> "Dennett's book suffers from a number of problems ... marred by
> factual errors... undermining any hope of a balanced presentation
> ... fails to appreciate concerns ... fundamentally misunderstands
> ... is obsessed with defending adaptive story-telling within biology
> ... never confronts legitimate worries... easier for him to ridicule...
> [the book] betrays the fundamental error [and is] confusing about
> how far Darwinism extends ... his chief claim is unconvincing ...
> evidence for each claim is non-existent."

IGNORING NON-DARWINIAN THEORIES

In addition to the extensive criticism recorded above, scientists have leveled another charge against Dennett, one that is particularly enlightening. Dennett simply ignores any idea that is non-Darwinian. There is a new approach to evolution known as the neutral theory of molecular evolution. The details of this theory were given in Chapter 17. It is sufficient to note here that this theory is non-Darwinian. For this reason, Dennett *never even mentions* this extremely important concept.

As Gould comments, *"Dennett's disabling parochialism lies most clearly exposed in his failure to discuss the neutral theory of molecular evolution. Few evolutionary biologists would deny that this theory ranks among the most interesting and powerful adjuncts to evolutionary explanation since Darwin's formulation of natural selection."*[36]

We thus again encounter the standard ultra-Darwinian practice of disregarding any new idea that differs from what Darwin wrote, however important the idea may be.

Peter Atkins

The final scientist to be discussed is Peter Atkins, Professor of Chemistry at the University of Oxford. His many excellent science textbooks are so popular that he has become a millionaire from the royalties.[37] But our interest here is not economic. Professor Atkins has also written a book about the origin and development of the universe. His discussion of evolution shows Atkins to be a committed ultra-Darwinian, no less than Dawkins and Dennett. His book, *The Creation*, written in 1981 and updated in 1992 under the title *Creation Revisited*, has become a best-seller. (Ultra-Darwinians have a remarkable talent for writing best-sellers!)

ATKINS'S CONCLUSION ABOUT THE SUPREME BEING

Atkins's book contains some far-reaching conclusions about religion, the validity of which we shall explore. He presents his manifesto in the preface of his book[38]:

*"I take the view that there is nothing that cannot be understood ...
I want you to live with the idea that everything can be explained
rationally ... My aim is to argue that there is no need to invoke the
idea of a Supreme Being in any of its numerous manifestations."*

Atkins drives home his point in the very first chapter[39]:

*"A great deal of the universe does not need any explanation. Elephants,
for instance. Once molecules have learned to compete and to create
other molecules in their own image, elephants, and things resembling elephants, will in due course be found roaming through the
countryside ... Some of the things resembling elephants will be men
... It is undeniable that [reproducing] molecules, will, somewhere or
other, band together into the form and having functions of men."*

The very essence of Atkins's argument is the assertion that human
beings (or human-like creatures) are the *inevitable* consequence of
evolutionary processes. He claims that it was inevitable that human
beings would eventually appear on this earth. If this were really so,
then Atkins would seem to be justified in writing that *"the necessity
of the Creator will be seen to fade ... That [assumption] leads to the
unnecessary intrusion of a spirit and the invention of a soul."*[40]

THE EXISTENCE OF HUMAN BEINGS

Many scientists who have discussed the existence of human beings
(i.e., creatures possessing high intelligence, consciousness, creative
abilities, etc.) do not share Atkins's optimistic view of our inevitability.
Professor Luis Alvarez of the University of California addresses this
question in his discussion of the meteoric impact that abruptly wiped
out all the world's dinosaurs: *"Had that impact not taken place, the
largest mammals alive today might still resemble the rat-like creatures that
were scurrying around 65 million years ago trying to avoid being devoured
by the dinosaurs."*[41]

In other words, without a completely unexpected and uniquely
rare event of a large meteor falling from outer space with devastating
consequences, Alvarez doubts whether *any* large mammal, including
humans, would *ever* have come into existence.

Alvarez is not the only leading scientist to dismiss the inevitability of human existence. Gould has devoted an entire book to a detailed analysis of this question, writing that *"the pageant of evolution [consists of] a staggeringly improbable series of events, utterly unpredictable and quite unrepeatable ... human beings are an improbable and fragile entity ... it fills us with amazement that human beings ever evolved at all."*[42]

Note the striking difference between Atkins's assertion that it is *undeniable* that the evolution of human beings was *inevitable*, and the exactly opposite opinion expressed by the famous scientists quoted above. If the Atkins's science is incorrect, it follows that his conclusions about religion, based on his incorrect scientific assertions, are also erroneous.

Conclusion

Several books of the ultra-Darwinians have reached the best-seller lists, in spite of the fact that these writers have been denounced and contradicted by their professional colleagues. The modern era of space exploration, seeking life on other planets, genetic engineering, and cloning has also become a period of widespread interest in science, and especially the biological sciences. However, in their thirst for knowledge, the general public tends to read popular science books rather than scholarly articles in journals like *Evolution, Acta Geologica, Science, Europhysics,* and *Physics Today.* As a result, many hundreds of thousands of laymen have been seriously misinformed and misled regarding current scientific understanding of evolutionary biology.

In addition, many ultra-Darwinians have launched vicious attacks on religious belief based on their erroneous "scientific facts." By contrast, Charles Darwin saw no contradiction at all between his theory of evolution and religious belief. Darwin ended his famous book, *On the Origin of Species,* with these stirring words[43]:

> *"There is a grandeur in this view of life, with its several powers, having been originally breathed by the Creator into a few forms ... and from so simple a beginning, endless forms most beautiful and most wonderful have evolved."*

NOTES

1. S.J. Gould, 12 June 1997, in *The New York Review*, pp. 34–37.
2. S.J. Gould, 1984, in *Conceptual Issues in Evolutionary Biology*, ed. E. Sober (Massachusetts Institute of Technology Press: Cambridge, MA), p. 260.
3. N. Eldredge, 1995, *Reinventing Darwin* (Wiley: New York), pp. ix–xi, 4.
4. P. Atkins, 27 November 1998, in *The Times – Higher Education Supplement*, p. 2.
5. D.C. Dennett, May/June 1995, *The Sciences*, p. 40.
6. R. Dawkins, 1986, *The Blind Watchmaker* (W.W. Norton: New York), p. 50.
7. Dawkins, p. x.
8. Dawkins, p. 81.
9. N. Eldredge and S.J. Gould, 1972, in *Models of Paleobiology*, ed. T.J.M. Schopf (Freeman, Cooper: San Francisco), pp. 82–115.
10. S.J. Gould, 1980, *The Panda's Thumb* (W.W. Norton: New York), p. 151.
11. Dawkins, pp. 317–318.
12. Dawkins, pp. 250, 251, 287.
13. D.G. Smith, ed., 1981, *The Cambridge Encyclopedia of Earth Sciences* (Cambridge University Press), p. 381.
14. P. Alstrom, 1999, *Europhysics News*, vol. 30, p. 22.
15. See, for example, the widely used university textbook, E.P. Solomon, L.R. Berg, D.W. Martin and C. Villee, 1996, *Biology*, 4th ed. (Harcourt Brace College Publishers: New York), pp. 442–443.
16. S.M. Stanley, 1981, *The New Evolutionary Timetable* (Basic Books: New York), pp. xv–xvi.
17. Dawkins, p. 251.
18. Stanley, pp. 89, 90, 114.
19. E. Mayr, August 1994, interviewed by *Scientific American*, pp. 14–15.
20. Stanley, p. 114.
21. L.W. Alvarez, W. Alvarez, *et al.*, 1980, *Science*, vol. 208, pp. 1095–1108.
22. H.L. Shipman, January 1985, *Physics Today*, p. S11.
23. D.M. Raup, 1981, *Acta Geologica Hispanica*, vol. 15, pp. 25–33.
24. Dawkins, p. 318.
25. L.W. Alvarez, July 1987, *Physics Today*, p. 33.
26. *Physics Today*, January 1985, p. 11.
27. S.J. Gould, 1989, *Wonderful Life* (W.W. Norton: New York), p. 318.
28. Dawkins, p. 244.
29. Dawkins, p. 283.
30. Dawkins, p. 224.
31. Dawkins, pp. 250, 251.

32. D.C. Dennett, 1995, *Darwin's Dangerous Idea* (Simon and Schuster: New York).
33. S.J. Gould, 12 June 1997, in *The New York Review*, p. 36.
34. S.J. Gould, 26 June 1997, in *The New York Review*, pp. 48, 49, 52.
35. H.A. Orr, 1996, *Evolution*, vol. 50, pp. 467–472.
36. Gould, p. 36
37. "Formulas for riches and fame," 27 November 1998, *THES – Textbook Guide*, p. 2.
38. P.W. Atkins, 1981, *The Creation* (W.H. Freeman: Oxford), p. vii.
39. Atkins, p. 3.
40. Atkins, pp. 35, 95.
41. L.W. Alvarez, July 1987, *Physics Today*, p. 33.
42. S.J. Gould, 1989, *Wonderful Life* (W.W. Norton: New York), pp. 14, 289, 319.
43. C. Darwin, 1859, *Origin of Species* (reprint edition, 1958, Mentor Books: New York), p. 450.

19

Life on Mars?

Headlines

The headline of the *New York Times* screamed: "NEW HINT OF LIFE IN SPACE: Meteorites Yield Fossilized, One-Cell Organisms Unlike Any Known on the Earth." *Newsweek* asserted dramatically: "Something Out There!" Respected scientists told crowds of reporters that their research work, published in a prestigious journal, revealed complex hydrocarbons and what appeared to be fossilized bacteria buried deep within a meteorite. They claimed to have found *"the first physical evidence for the existence of forms of life beyond our planet."*

The events described above occurred in 1961 and the meteorite in question had fallen in Orgueil, France, more than a century earlier. However, the "fossils" ultimately proved to be ragweed pollen and the "organic chemicals" turned out to be furnace ash!

How did such blunders occur? One would have thought that as soon the meteoritic substances were examined by leading authorities, the truth would *immediately* become evident. How could any scientific expert fail to distinguish between "fossilized bacteria" and ragweed pollen or between "prehistoric complex hydrocarbons" and furnace ash? But that is *exactly* what happened! Indeed, *many years* were to pass before the embarrassing truth finally became recognized. *As late as 1971*, a well-known biology textbook, written by a Harvard University professor, informed us that *"Evidence for life in other parts of the cosmos came from the discovery in 1961 of what were identified as fossils of microscopic organisms, somewhat like algae, in meteorites."* [1]

231

History Repeats Itself

Three decades later, history repeated itself with the dramatic announcement on 7 August 1996 by NASA Administrator Daniel Gordin (NASA is the U.S. Space Agency) asserting that *"a meteorite, consisting of a chunk of Mars rock, bears evidence of ancient life."*[2] The NASA research team, headed by geologist David McKay, claimed that *"the peculiar features found in meteorite ALH84001 are best explained by the existence of primitive life on early Mars."*[3]

Just what had been discovered? Under discussion is a meteorite – essentially a rock about the size of a grapefruit and weighing 1.9 kilograms – found in the snows of Antarctica. For technical reasons that need not concern us here, this meteorite (denoted ALH84001) is believed to have originated on Mars. The excitement centered on the possibility that living creatures had once inhabited the meteorite. No signs of life were actually found in this meteorite, but a number of different types of minerals were present in configurations that are produced by bacteria, the smallest and simplest living cells. On this basis, the article written by NASA researcher McKay and his colleagues exclaimed: *"When these phenomena are considered collectively, particularly in view of their spatial association, we conclude that they are evidence for primitive life on early Mars."*[4]

The bubble burst before the end of the year. The December 1996 issue of *Scientific American* carried the following news item:

> *"Believers had a big thrill last summer when NASA announced that they had uncovered signs of Martian life in a meteorite. The evidence came in the form of tiny, sausage-shaped imprints, which the scientists said were most likely left by "nanobacteria." Now, however, researchers at the Massachusetts Institute of Technology have demonstrated that purely inorganic happenings can make identical marks."*

A British science journal was even more dramatic in presenting the evidence against life on Mars. Its news item, sarcastically entitled "Death Knell for Martian Life – New Studies Indicate That This 'Fossil'

Was Never Alive," begins as follows: *"As 1996 draws to a close, those heady days of summer seem like a dream. In August, scientists led by NASA's David McKay stunned the world by producing evidence of past life on Mars. But now, two new analyses put the final nail in the coffin of that claim."*[5]

Objectivity and Budgets

How did it all happen? How could the embarrassments of 1961 be repeated so soon? Perhaps some insight can be gained by examining some of the immediate effects of the claims by NASA scientists of having found evidence for life on Mars.

The journal *Science* reported that the NASA announcement generated *"an almost unheard-of agreement between House Speaker Newt Gingrich and Vice-President Albert Gore for additional government spending ... President Bill Clinton himself announced that Gore will organize a White House meeting to map out a bipartisan course to focus the U.S. space program on the issues raised by the new findings."*[6]

This news was heaven-sent for NASA. U.S. space science had been laboring under serious budgetary constraints since the 10% cut in funding contained in President Clinton's 1997 budget request. Even worse, NASA budget cuts were scheduled for the next five years. The pessimistic words of the NASA space science advisory committee set the tone: *"We see the handwriting on the wall. The outlook is very bleak."*[7]

Everything suddenly changed with the dramatic findings about life on Mars, *"which are already breathing new life into solar system exploration. Representative Jerry Lewis, chairman of the House of Representatives panel that oversees NASA funding, stated that he now supports increasing the agency's budget to accommodate more aggressive exploration of Mars."*[8]

Similarly, John Logsdon, of the Space Policy Institute at George Washington University, pointed out that following the NASA announcement of their discovery of life on Mars, *"the extreme cuts to NASA's budget floated in budget projections earlier this year now seem unlikely."*[9]

234 · FOSSILS AND FAITH

Since the 1986 *Challenger* disaster (in which seven astronauts died in an explosion) and other failures, NASA had come under increasing criticism regarding the running of its space programme. A dramatic discovery, such as life on Mars, would do much to bolster its public image. Therefore, there are valid reasons for questioning the scientific objectivity of NASA's wildly optimistic claims regarding the evidence for life on Mars.

NOTES

1. C.A. Villee, 1971, *Biological Principles and Processes* (Saunders: Philadelphia), p. 320.
2. News, *Science*, 16 August 1996, vol. 273, p. 865.
3. News and Analysis, October 1996, *Scientific American*, p. 12.
4. D.S. McKay *et al.*, 16 August 1996, *Science*, vol. 273, pp. 922–930.
5. This Week, 21 December 1996, *New Scientist*, vol. 150, p. 4.
6. News, *Science*, 16 August 1996, vol. 273, p. 865.
7. News, *Science*, 22 March 1996, vol. 271, p. 1660.
8. News, *Science*, 16 August 1996, vol. 273, p. 865.
9. News, *Nature*, 7 November 1996, vol. 384, p. 4.

Biblical Commentators and Philosophers

Biographical notes about the biblical commentators and philosophers mentioned in the text

Bachya ibn Paquda (second half of 11th century)
> Rabbi Bachya ben Joseph of Spain.
> Philosopher and poet.

Gaon of Vilna (1720–1797)
> Rabbi Elijah ben Solomon Zalman of Vilna, Lithuania.
> Greatest talmudic scholar of the last 500 years.
> Wrote important commentaries on works of kabbalah.

Maimonides (1135–1205)
> Rabbi Moses ben Maimon of Spain, Egypt, and North Africa.
> Greatest of the Jewish philosophers and law codifiers.

Malbim (1809–1879)
> Rabbi Meir Loeb ben Yechiel Michael (acronym – Malbim)
> Served as rabbi in several important Jewish communities in Eastern Europe, including Poland and Romania.
> His commentary on the Bible, especially the Torah, was designed to reply to the biblical interpretations proposed by Reform Jews.

Onkeles (second century)

Lived in Roman Palestine, witnessed the destruction of Second Temple.

Wrote the definitive translation of the Bible into Aramaic according the tradition of the talmudic sages Rabbi Eliezer and Rabbi Yehoshua.

Radak (1160–1235)

Rabbi David Kimche of Provence, Southern France.

Among the greatest of the biblical commentators and grammarians.

His commentary stresses the literal translation and grammatical forms.

Ramban (1194–1270)

Rabbi Moses ben Nachman of Northern Spain.

Physician, talmudist, and biblical commentator.

Community leader who issued many rulings of Jewish law.

Rashi (1040–1105)

Rabbi Shlomo ben Isaac of Northern France.

Most famous of the biblical and talmudic commentators.

Had many outstanding students, including his grandsons Rabbenu Tam and Rashbam.

Sa'adiah Gaon (882–942)

Rabbi Sa'adiah ben Joseph of Egypt and Babylonia.

Greatest of the later Babylonian scholars.

Biblical commentator and philosopher.

Community leader who fought the spread of Kararite influences in Babylonia.

Sforno (c. 1470–1550)

Rabbi Ovadiah ben Jacob of Italy.

Physician, scholar, and biblical commentator.

His commentary places great emphasis on issues of faith and morality.

Soloveitchik, Rabbi Joseph B. (1903–1993)

Lived in Poland, Belorussia, and the United States (since 1932).

Talmudic scholar and philosopher.

Community leader and spiritual mentor to a generation of American rabbis.

Yehuda Halevi (c. 1075–1141)

Lived in various cities in Spain.

Philosopher, poet, and physician.

Index of Scientists

Allegre, Claude, 20
Alvarez, Luis, 29–31, 203, 209–12,
226–27
Alvarez, Walter, 28, 203, 209
Anderson, Philip, 204, 207, 212
Arrow, Kenneth, 204
Atkins, Peter, 217, 225–27
Azbel, Mark, 135–36

Bailin, David, 4
Bak, Per, 205, 207, 212
Bethe, Hans, 24
Bock, Walter, 189

Cairns, John, 190–91
Callaway, David, 4
Childe, Gordon, 161
Coppens, Yves, 181
Crick, Francis, 28

Dawkins, Richard, 192–94, 202–3,
217–23
de Haan, Laurens, 147
Dennett, Daniel, 200–2, 217, 223–25
Depew, David, 193
Diamond, Jared, 157–58
Dirac, Paul, 6
Dunnet, George, 136–37

Eldredge, Niles, 168–69, 180, 216
Endler, John, 195

Falk, Raphael, 32–34, 211
Feynman, Richard, 33–34
Finch, Caleb, 135

Galinsky, Norman, 192
Gell-Mann, Murray, 204
Gordon, Daniel, 232
Gould, Stephen Jay, 9, 30–32, 169,
172–74, 192–94, 203, 209–11,
215–19, 223–27
Greene, Brian, 6
Guth, Alan, 6

Hall, Barry, 191
Hawking, Stephen, 6
Hayflick, Leonard, 136
Hoyle, Fred, 7

Jablonski, David, 30
Jazwinski, Michal, 134, 136
Jensen, Henrik, 206
Johanson, Donald, 172
Johnson, Tom, 136

Kadanoff, Leo, 207, 212
Kauffman, Stuart, 201, 205–6, 212
Kimura, Motoo, 202, 207–8, 212
Klein, Harold, 28
Kruskal, William, 112

Laskar, Jacques, 130
Leakey, Meave, 181

Mallet, James, 189
Manton, Kenneth, 149
Mayr, Ernst, 197, 203–4, 222
McKay, David, 232–33
Mitton, Jeffrey, 195

Orr, Allen, 224

Penzias, Arno, 7
Perls, Thomas, 147
Pilbeam, David, 176–77, 181, 183

Raup, David, 9, 30, 210–12, 222
Raven, Peter, 189
Renfrew, Colin, 158–59
Rose, Michael, 136
Ruelle, David, 127

Savage-Rumbaugh, Sue, 78
Shaffer, Bradley, 195–96
Silk, Joseph, 6
Simon, Barry, 14, 62
Smith, Richard, 147

Stanley, Steven, 166, 212, 220–22
Sternberg, Shlomo, 62
Suzman, Richard, 148

Tattersall, Ian, 41–43
Templeton, Alan, 184
Trinkaus, Erik, 42, 167–69, 184–85

Walker, Alan, 181
Weinberg, Steven, 8
Wheeler, John, 7
Williams, George, 140
Wilson, Robert, 7
Witztum, Doron, 62

Young, Thomas, 156
Yule, George, 30

Subject Index

Abraham and Sarah, 133, 141–42
Adam and Eve, 40, 48, 73, 138–39
Africa, 152, 176, 181–84
Afro-Asiatic languages, 152
aging and longevity, 133–49
Agricultural Revolution, see
    "Neolithic Revolution"
Akkadian language, 161
amidah prayer, 107–8, 116
anthropic principle, 23–37
Aquinas, Thomas, 53, 60
argument from design, 57–59
Aristotle, 54–55, 88
astronomy, 5, 13, 27, 53, 68–72, 84–85
atmosphere, 26–27, 121–24, 128–31
atoms and molecules, 7–8, 86–87, 90,
    92–93
Australopithecus, 176, 180–81

Babal, Tower of, 151, 160
Bachya ibn Paquda, 54
Bacon, Francis, 65, 72
bacteria, 28, 70, 190–91, 231–32
Bible codes, 60–64
big bang theory, 5–7, 14
Boule, Marcellin, 167–69, 176
brain size, 42, 44, 47
Bryan, William Jennings, 173–75
"butterfly effect", 128–29

calendar, biblical, 13–20, 48–49,
    69–70, 79–81
Calment, Jeanne, 146, 148

cave paintings, 43
chaos, 127–31
chimpanzee, 74–78
clockwork universe, 85–87, 91
COBE satellite, 6
color, 7
complexity theory, 201, 204–7
computer, 123–27
conscience, 50
Copernicus, Nicolas, 71
cosmology, 5–8, 14, 69, 73
creation of universe, 5–8
    time-scale, 13–20
creationists, 67–74, 81, 165
Cro-Magnon Man, 41, 176

Darrow, Clarence, 173
Darwin, Charles, 72, 166, 173, 212
    Darwinian fundamentalism, 215–27
    Darwin's theory of evolution,
        187–96
    non-Darwinian theories, 199–212
Dawson, Charles, 169–70
"day of creation", 13–20, 69–70, 79–81
determinism, 87–93
deuteron, 25–26
Deuteronomy, Book of, 16, 50, 63–64,
    109, 126, 131
dinosaurs, 28–31, 208–11, 222–23, 226
directed mutation, 190–91
divine providence, 101, 107–15, 125–26
DNA, 27–28, 40, 74–75, 135, 182–84,
    190

Drosnin, Michael, 62–64

Earth, 13–14, 26–27
Egypt, 100–1, 104, 126
Einstein, 49, 194, 200–1
electron, 4, 92
Elijah, 104
Elisha, 102–3
epicycle, 71–72
Esther, Book of, 99–100
existence of God, proofs for, 53–65
Exodus, Book of, 16, 18, 100, 104
Exodus from Egypt, 99–101, 104, 133
extreme value theory, 147, 150

faith and belief, 3–10, 64–65, 105
Feinstein, Rabbi Moshe, 110–15
FLOPS (floating-point operations per second), 122, 127
fossils, 13, 165–85, 218–22, 230, 231–33
free will, 83–97
future, 87–96, 120–31

galaxies, 6
Galileo, 68
Galton, Francis, 111
Gaon of Vilna, 61–62
genes, 28, 135–36, 139–42, 183–84, 187, 190, 207, 210
Genesis, Book of, 3, 5–10, 13–21, 32, 39–41, 46–50, 73, 77–80, 133, 138–42, 145–46, 151–53, 160
"Genesis man", 40–41, 47–49
geocentric solar system, 68–73
"Goldilocks problem of climatology", 27
gradual evolution, 180, 199, 205, 218–21
gravity, 14, 25, 84–87, 89, 121

Hamito-Semitic languages, 152
harmony between science and the Bible, 5–10, 14–19, 23–24, 36–37, 41, 47–49, 65, 78–81, 131, 133–60
Hayflick limit, 135
Heidelberg Man, 176, 182

helium, 24
Hesperopithecus, 172–76
hominid, 165–85
Homo, 40, 180–82
Homo sapiens, see "Modern Man"
Hopfield, John, 98
Hubble, Edwin, 6
human beings, see "mankind"
hydrogen, 24

impact theory, 29–31, 203, 208–12, 222–23
Indo-European languages, 155–61
    proto-Indo-European (PIE), 157–59, 161
inertia, law of, 55
Inquisition, 68
intellectual curiosity, 49–50

Japhethide languages, 151–60
Java Man, 176
Job, Book of, 16, 174–75
Jones, William, 155
Joshua, Book of, 69

kabbalah, 61
Kafka novel, 185
Keith, Sir Arthur, 170, 176
Kepler, Johannes, 55, 84
Kierkegaard, Soren, 65
Kings, Book of, 102–4
Kuhn, Thomas, 212

lactose, 190–91
languages, 40, 49, 74, 78, 151–60
Laplace, Pierre Simon, 56, 85–87
Leviticus, Book of, 16
life, existence of, 24–27
    on other planets, 231–34
    origin of, 27–28
life span, 133–49
light-ball, primeval, 7
longevity, see "aging"
"luck", 9, 23, 30–36, 62, 226–27

Maimonides, 53–54, 65, 101, 107, 112–13

approach to understanding Torah, 15–17, 79
Malbim, 80
mankind, 9–10, 16–32, 36–50, 70–71, 226–27
Mars, 24, 231–34
mass extinction, 29–32, 206, 208–11, 222–23, 226
Maxwell, James Clerk, 86, 194
Messiah, 17
meteor, 29–32, 209–11, 222–23, 226, 231–32
meteorology, 120–31
Methuselah, 133, 139–40
microwave background radiation, 6
miracles, 99–105, 125, 141
Modern Man, 39–48, 166–67, 170–72, 177, 182–84
molecular biology, 27, 74–75
"molecular clock", 74–75, 183
molecules, see "atoms"
Moses, 138–42
Multiregional theory, 183–84
Munk, Rabbi Eli, 18
mutation, 190–91

Nachmanides, see "Ramban"
Nazis, 24, 161
Neandertal Man, 41–44, 166–69, 176, 182, 184
Neolithic Revolution, 44–49
neural networks, 93, 98
neutral theory of evolution, 202, 207–8, 225
neutron, 4, 25
Newton, Isaac, 14, 49, 55–57, 68, 84–85, 87, 91, 121
Noah, 138–42, 151–53, 159
Nobel Prize, 6–8, 24, 28, 32, 89, 203–4, 222–23
nuclear force, 25–26, 98
"oldest old", 145–49
omnipotence of G-d, 95, 104

omniscience of G-d, 93–96
Onkeles, 40
Osborn, Henry Fairfield, 173–77
Out of Africa theory, 183–84
oxygen, 20, 120

paleoanthropology, 168, 179, 185
Paleolithic Age, 45
paleontology, 165–71, 175–76, 181, 184, 203
Paley, William, 57
Peking Man, 176
Permian Period, 19
Piltdown Man, 169–72, 176
planets, 55–57, 71–72, 84–85, 130
plants, 19–20,
plausibility arguments, 3–5
Popper, Karl, 11
prayer, 107–15, 119, 124–25, 131
prehistoric man, 165–85
prime mover argument, 54–57
probabilities, 32–36, 90–92
proton, 4, 24–26
punctuated equilibrium, 203, 218–22
Purim, 99–100

quantum theory, 90–93
quark, 4

Rabin, Yitzchak, 63–64
Radak, 74
radioactive dating, 13
rainbow, 68
Ramban, 40, 47, 74, 108
randomness, 190–91, 206, 211
Rashi, 40, 70, 74, 143
relativity, theory of, 14

Sa'adiah Gaon, 40, 54, 74
Sabbath, 18, 21
Sanskrit, 155, 157
Schroedinger, Erwin, 89, 194
Scopes trial, 173, 175
Sforno, 40, 48, 74, 78–79
Shem, 151–52

Smith, Sir Grafton Elliot, 170–71, 176
snowflakes, 58
soccer (football), 91–92
solar energy, 24–26
solar system, see "planets"
Soloveitchik, Rabbi Joseph B., 9, 48,
    64–65, 77
soul, 78
space, 7
speciation, 195–96
species, 176–85, 188–89, 195–96
  "species problem", 188–89
spirituality of mankind, 39, 47–50,
    72–81, 90, 108–9, 115
stasis of species, 205–6, 219
sun, 17, 20, 24–26, 69, 71, 79, 84–85,
    124–25

Talmud, 17, 20, 37, 54, 101, 112–14, 119,
    126

Ten Commandments, 18
Ten Plagues, 104
time, 7–8, 14, 95
time scale, 13–20, 40, 48–49

"ultra-Darwinians", 216–27
uncertainty principle, 91
universe, age of, 13–20, 69–70, 73, 79
    expansion of, 6
    origin of, 5–8, 16–17
    stability of, 85

Venus, 26
vital force, 88–89

"watchmaker argument", see "argu-
    ment from design"
water, 26–27, 119–24
weather, 119–31
Woodward, Sir Arthur Smith, 170, 176
Yehuda Halevi, 54